The
Bon Appétit

Dinner Party
Cookbook

The Bon Appétit

Dinner Party Cookbook

THE KNAPP PRESS
Publishers
Los Angeles

Copyright © 1983 by Knapp Communications Corporation

Published by The Knapp Press
5900 Wilshire Boulevard, Los Angeles, California 90036

Library of Congress Cataloging in Publication Data
Main entry under title:
Bon appétit dinner party cookbook.
Includes index.
1. Dinners and dining.   2. Menus.   I. Bon appétit.
II. Title: Dinner party cookbook.
TX737.B65   1983   641.5'4   83-255
ISBN 0-89535-118-8

Printed and bound in the United States of America

10   9   8   7   6   5   4   3   2

Contents

Introduction by Jinx and Jefferson Morgan   vii
The Right Wine by Anthony Dias Blue   x

CASUAL SUPPERS
A Family Affair   2
Informal Buffet   8
Make-Ahead Seafood Dinner   14
Italian Flair   20
French Country Feast   26
Festive Springtime Fare   32

ELEGANT DINNERS
Easy Elegance   40
Make-Ahead French Feast   46
A Touch of Sophistication   54
For Special Occasions   62
Stylish Celebration   70

LIGHT MEALS
Shellfish Festival   80

Cool and Casual   90
Easy Buffet for Friends   96
Dieters' Dinner Party   106
Slim Cuisine with Style   112

REGIONAL AMERICAN MENUS
Colonial Feast Updated   122
Classic Southern Supper   130
Pacific Northwestern Party   138
Rocky Mountain Buffet   146
In the Tex-Mex Style   152

INTERNATIONAL MENUS
Easy Chinese Cuisine   164
A Taste of Japan   172
Buffet from Northern India   180
La Cucina Nuova from Italy   190
Provençal Buffet   198

SEASONAL CELEBRATIONS
A Gala New Year's Eve   208
A Greek Islands Easter   218
Classic Summer Picnic   228
Garden-Fresh Summer Menu   234
The Great All-American Thanksgiving   242
Hearty Holiday Feast   252
Festive Winter Fare   258

Mix and Match Chart   266
Index   270

Introduction

⬛

SOME PEOPLE SEEM TO BE born entertainers. They can pull together an impromptu party at the drop of an invitation. We mere mortals sometimes find hosting a dinner party is an enterprise fraught with landmines: menus that don't quite mesh, an overburdened oven, rebellious soufflés and a terminal case of frazzled nerves.

While a bent for handling hospitality with casual ease is a gift of nature, like curly hair or the ability to run a four minute mile, even those less blessed can become first class party givers by following the menus and advice in this book. With tried and true recipes from the pages of *Bon Appétit* magazine, provocative menus, shopping lists, party plans, and the guidance of experts, the most inexperienced and timid cook can, with confidence, pronounce those six fateful words: "How about dinner at our house?"

Veteran party givers all agree that careful planning can take the kinks out of even the most elaborate event and allow the host and hostess to enjoy the occasion. Narsai David, California restaurateur and caterer who has at times coped with the care and feeding of 3,000 people at a single event, sums up his party plotting this way: "Organizing a large party is very much like planning a miniature military exercise."

Although David is most often involved with large-scale festivities, his advice is also applicable to more modest affairs. Once you've pinned down the guest list and issued the invitations, he suggests the next step is to orchestrate the selection and preparation of the menu.

"I like to design menus to take advantage of what's in season. And it's a good idea to plan dishes that complement each other in terms of the amount of work they require. Don't make every dish complicated or demanding or you'll get frustrated," David advises. "There's virtue in simplicity. And be sure you don't plan a lot of dishes that need last-minute cooking. Guests feel uncomfortable if the host or hostess spends the whole evening in the kitchen."

Planning is also the secret of the successful parties given by an accomplished hostess of our acquaintance. Her desk contains a box of three-by-five cards that show at a glance the blueprint of every party she's given including menu, dates, flowers, wines, and names of guests.

"It helps me avoid becoming bogged down in details," she explains. "If you plan what can be done ahead of time, then you won't be left with mountains to do at the last minute. It means sorting it out on paper. Sometimes I spend a long time sitting at my desk making lists. But then when I'm ready I know exactly what to do and I don't waste any time."

Knowing your own style is an important part of planning a party. If you live in a baronial mansion with classic silver, elegant china, and hot and cold running footmen, then chili probably would be out of place on your menu. On the other hand, if you're entertaining in a casual beach cottage or in a minute city apartment, then serving a five course dinner with fingerbowls might be overreaching.

We used to attempt rather formal dinners for four to six guests which meant that one or the other of us spent the bulk of the evening scampering into the kitchen to attend to last-minute chores. Then we realized we were forever shooing our guests out of the kitchen before dinner. "Why don't you go join the party?" we'd suggest through tightly drawn lips.

Then one day the realization dawned. In our house, the kitchen *was* the party. Now the guests sip and talk while we finish up preparations in a leisurely way and no one feels left out. It is not a style of entertaining that would suit everyone, but for us it's now become as comfortable as an old sneaker and we can't imagine returning to our former more traditional party plans.

Once you've decided on the type of party that best fits your life, then the menu is the next thing on the agenda. For some cooks, one special dish will be the centerpiece around which the rest of the menu revolves. For others, the season will dictate the design of the party. A collection of pretty plates or bowls or a lovely tureen you want to show off might also influence your final decision. Planning harmonious, interesting menus is an inexact science at best, but there are some useful guidelines to keep in mind.

First you must consider the taste and eccentricities of your guests. If you are serving people you don't know well, it's always a good idea to take a cue from wily politicians and cling to the middle of the road. As your friendship progresses you may find your guests are as adventurous as you are, in which case, the next time you invite them to dine you can pull out all the stops. Allergies and aversions should also be taken into account. We have a friend who cannot bear to be in the same room with broccoli. We don't know why, since broccoli has always seemed an innocent enough vegetable to us. But when he's at our table, he knows he'll never find the offending vegetable lurking in some sneaky disguise and we suspect he's a much happier man—and a contented guest—for it.

Composing a perfect menu is really a matter of balance: simple dishes are necessary to complement the more complex, colors should weave lovely patterns of light and dark, bright and pale, and sharp or strong flavors should be relieved by something gently persuasive.

Equally important, take into account the time each dish takes to prepare and how far ahead it can be made. Some cooks like to make a chart indicating when each item should be made or what steps can be completed in advance. Think each dish through and simplify your life by completing as many steps as you can before the big day. If you're making a cake, perhaps the layers can be made ahead, wrapped and frozen. A cold vegetable salad? Cook and chill the vegetables the day before. Often sauces can be completed in advance and refrigerated or frozen. Desserts, breads, fillings, and parts of many dishes often can be safely created at your leisure, eliminating much of the potential for last-minute panic.

A dress rehearsal of any particularly challenging dish you are eager to make for guests is not always necessary but will assure success and boost your self-confidence on the night of the actual occasion. A trial run also will allow you to adjust the recipe to your own taste and will give you a firm assessment of the time and equipment it demands.

Except for the all-out, no-holds-barred occasions that occur a few times in everyone's life, for most people the budget is another factor in planning a party. Being slightly overextended in the exchequer need not, however, dampen the warmth and graciousness of your welcome. The idea here is to tailor your menu along trim lines, but to do it with a spirit of generosity. It's much better, we think, to have lots of something inexpensive than to have a mingy amount of an extravagant luxury. Bring on heaps of beautiful golden carrot salad in a tangy vinaigrette rather than two thin spears of out-of-season asparagus. Ply your guests with a river of a sound, carefully chosen, priceworthy wine instead of a few sips of some bottle that once resided in the cobweb-filled basement of an archduke.

With the food question well in hand, you can begin creating the setting for your party. Don't be afraid to follow your own instincts to break away from the conventional. A centerpiece doesn't always have to be flowers. It can be a handwoven basket filled with an armload of fresh bread, a collection of beautifully polished stones, a blaze of candles in a variety of candlesticks, a cornucopia of dewy vegetables or whatever appeals to your own personal taste. A centerpiece can be, in fact, just about anything that tickles your fancy, looks good to you and enhances conversation (towering vases of gladioli looming in everyone's line of sight need not apply). You can stick to a classical theme and match everything perfectly or show your independence by mixing plates, platters, silver, and glasses to suit your whim.

The way food looks is part of our sensual enjoyment of it. Garnishing touches like parsley, watercress, green onion flowers, fruit slices, lemon wedges, and other vivid punctuation marks will help pique appetites. Leaves or flowers from the garden can be colorful additions to a platter that needs perking up.

Organizing food, wine, and decor is a simple matter compared to orchestrating the social dynamics of your party. Some hosts and hostesses simply let the chips fall where they may and hope that the people who come to their parties will sort themselves into compatible groups. On the other hand, some hostesses take as much care with their seating plans as they do with the food. "I've read about hostesses who like to let people sit anywhere they want at the table," says one. "I don't. I take great trouble to try to balance the table between talkers and nontalkers, friends and newcomers. I even sketch it all out on paper to see how it looks."

This comment brings us to a vital point. It's important to remember that your guests should be the focal point of any event. Too many people these days, it seems, are so intent on being the first on their block to serve warm goat cheese salad or impress their neighbors with a wine discovery, that they lose track of the main reason for entertaining. We think the spirited gathering of friends over a pot of indifferent spaghetti and a jug of red wine the pedigree of which might be better left unexplored, says more about the gift of hospitality than a multi-course dinner of culinary perfection at which the hostess and host rarely make an appearance, so overwhelmed are they by the magnitude of the undertaking.

In this book you will find a happy compromise. In addition to a stunning array of imaginative menus and recipes to suit a variety of occasions, there are strategic suggestions to smooth the way: shopping lists, and timetables for the meal's preparation, as well as some astute wine proposals to accompany each menu. You'll find chapters dealing with everything from casual suppers where you won't be lockstepped into schedules to sumptuous seasonal celebrations, with elegant dinners, light meals, regional American and international menus in between.

After all the preparations are complete, when seductive smells are wafting from the kitchen and the wine is chilling, when the doorbell rings and you know the time has finally come, the single most important thing to remember, we think, is to have a wonderful time at your own party. For if you do, so will your guests. And with the following menus and recipes to act as your guides, a good time will be had by all.

—Jinx and Jefferson Morgan

The Right Wine

SELECTING THE CORRECT WINE to serve at a dinner party can sometimes become the occasion for lengthy debate and anxious examination of label after label on the bottles ranked forbiddingly on the shelves of your local wineshop or grocery store. Fortunately, this needn't be the case. One of the most useful discoveries that is made by the practiced host and hostess is that there are lots of "right" choices and very few "wrong" choices.

It used to be that the watchword for choosing wine was: "White with white meat; red with red meat." Easy. Well, almost. What about chicken? A white wine, of course. But what about chicken in a red wine sauce? What about turkey? And what about a meatless meal?

Each situation has to be dealt with on its own, and many factors have to be taken into consideration. Besides the food itself you must also think of such things as the time of day, the setting, the company and the weather.

Let me cite an example. Let's say you decide to try out a nice recipe for chicken sautéed with tomatoes and finished with mustard. You experiment by making it for your family as a Sunday lunch, served outside on the patio. For this situation you choose a crisp white wine—an off-dry Johannisberg Riesling or a fresh, light Sauvignon Blanc.

You like the dish so much that you decide to have it for company. On a weekday night you have your best friends over for a casual dinner. You make the chicken dish, but this time you serve fettuccine first. With the pasta you pour a snappy, chilled Soave, a white wine; instead of using another white wine, you match the chicken with a lightly chilled Beaujolais, a red wine.

Later that year, in the winter, you make the dish again—this time for a formal dinner party. You serve a fine Chardonnay with the shrimp first course and your favorite Cabernet Sauvignon with the chicken dish.

On three separate occasions you have served the same dish and each time the wine accompaniment has been different. And in each situation more than just the dish was considered. The simple al fresco luncheon called for an undemanding, simple white wine; the casual dinner required an uncomplicated wine that, nevertheless, had to follow, and be a bit more substantial than, a medium-bodied white wine—thus the choice of a light red wine; and on a cold evening, following a heavy white wine, the choice of a somewhat weighty red was quite appropriate.

Of course, there are certain basic, commonsense concepts that you should keep in mind when choosing wine to go with food. The key is balance. The wine shouldn't blow the food off the table and the food shouldn't reduce the wine to the role of merely cleansing the palate between bites or courses.

I'm not necessarily saying that a weighty dish requires a weighty wine. In fact, often a wine with contrasting characteristics is more appropriate with certain foods, especially those on the outer extremes of fattiness or heaviness.

There are times, however, when the wine must come up to the food or be lost in the shuffle. If you are serving fish in a creamy sauce, a full-bodied white wine, such as a big Chardonnay, will provide the weight necessary to stand up to the rich flavors of the food. If you are serving game or a roast of beef or lamb you will need a muscular Cabernet Sauvignon or a Zinfandel to balance the assertive flavors of the meat.

If you are planning to use several wines with a meal, the lightest wine should come first, which usually means white wines before red. This corresponds to the sequence of most meals—from light to heavy. Also, it is a good idea to serve simple, fresh young wines early in the meal, and then follow them with the more complex, older wines. Sweet wines should wait until dessert (there are even exceptions to this idea; the French love to serve sweet Sauternes with foie gras as an appetizer).

Actually, there are some foods that don't go well with any wine. Soups are not particularly compatible with wine (unless they contain sherry, then you can serve sherry) nor does wine blend well with salad dressings made with vinegar. Very spicy foods can be a problem. Indian, Mexican, Indonesian and some Chinese food can make it difficult to taste the subtleties of wine. Often beer is preferable in such cases.

In addition, there are certain ingredients that are not friendly to wine. For instance, artichokes have an odd effect on the tastebuds that can throw the wine palate way off. It is also very difficult to find a wine that matches well with a chocolate dessert.

Most other foods not only blend well with wine but are actually enhanced by a wine accompaniment. The marriage of wine and food is certainly one of those blissful combinations about which one can often say, "The total is greater than the sum of the parts." I can think of many occasions when I have happened upon a wine/food combination which resulted in either the wine, the food, or both being elevated to a much higher plane than was ever achieved when the elements were on their own. Wine can stimulate the palate, beyond its normal acuity, to appreciate the subtleties of a dish and, in the same way, certain foods can bring out hidden nuances in a particular wine.

It is often a good idea to serve regional wines with regional foods. If you are preparing a French dinner, plan to pour French wines. Use Italian wines with Italian food, and so on. If your recipe calls for a certain type of wine to be used in cooking, it is also a good idea to serve that same type of wine with the dish. Such a match-up will be quite harmonious.

The guiding impulse to selecting the best wine and food combinations should be a well-developed sense of proportion. What should rule the choice is not color or variety or price, but appropriateness and balance.

Experience is an excellent teacher. Think back over past combinations that struck you as particularly apt. Use these harmonious food and wine alliances as touchstones for future choices. Experiment. Be courageous, be outrageous, and make every new match-up a learning experience. Above all, don't be intimidated. Have fun with this magical union. Food and wine are two of life's greatest pleasures. When combined in a harmonious way they can be pure poetry.

—Anthony Dias Blue

Casual Suppers

GREAT FOOD IS ONLY one of the keys to successful entertaining. Equally important is matching the menu to the occasion and the guests. And when the occasion is a simple get-together and the guests are a few good friends, a relaxed atmosphere and lively conversation are ingredients every bit as essential as salt and pepper.

The six menus in this chapter are perfect for informal dining. All are original and intriguing enough to turn an evening with family and friends into something a little special, but each is designed to be very easy on the host or hostess—there is a minimum of specialty ingredients, elaborate presentation or complex preparation. After all, nothing can spoil a casual ambience more quickly than a cook who looks as if he or she has just finished running a marathon. With some intelligent planning, these supper ideas will make entertaining both possible and pleasurable any night of the week—no matter how hectic your schedule.

Each menu follows a simple formula: an appetizer or two, a substantial main course with a couple of side dishes, perhaps a salad or a bread, and an easy-to-make dessert. The delicious entrées range from wine-sauced marinated lamb (page 6), Game Hens with Spinach-Sage Stuffing (page 12) and fresh-tasting veal with parsley pesto and orzo (page 23) to colorful grilled salmon with a piquant tarragon mayonnaise (page 36). With the desserts, the aim is to satisfy rather than overwhelm; they include refreshing Almond Tulips with Fresh Banana Ice (page 36), easy and elegant Vermouth-Glazed Pears (page 31), and a rich but not-too-sweet Chocolate Apricot Roll (page 24). And by following the strategies that precede each menu, your job is even easier.

These casual suppers share a common philosophy: With close friends, less is often more—and simplicity combined with style can create an absolutely perfect evening.

A Family Affair

THE MENU

Potage Puree Crecy

*Marinated Boned Lamb
with Zinfandel Sauce*

Joyce's Basque Beans

Quick Zucchini

Coeur à la Crème

Serves 6

*Left to right: Quick Zucchini, Joyce's Basque Beans and
Marinated Boned Lamb with zesty Zinfandel Sauce.*

THE STRATEGY

An easy supper that blends elegance with some rustic French-inspired touches. Begin with a smooth puree of vegetables enhanced with milk and half and half. An herbed wine-sauced lamb, hearty bean salad and simple zucchini dish provide the main course. For dessert, offer rich Coeur à la Crème with a bright berry sauce.

Shopping List

1½ cups chicken stock
  3 racks of lamb or lamb rib eyes (have butcher bone for you)
  2 cups fresh strawberries plus additional strawberries for garnish
  2 cups whole raspberries
  1 pound small white beans
  3 large zucchini
  4 garlic cloves
1½ pounds carrots
  1 large onion
  1 small red onion (½ cup chopped)
  ¾ pound russet potatoes
     Fresh chives for garnish
     Parsley (½ cup leaves, ¼ cup chopped plus additional parsley for garnish)
     Fresh lemon juice
1½ cups milk
  1 cup half and half
  2 eggs
  ¾ stick butter
  1 8-ounce package cream cheese
  ½ cup cottage cheese
  2 cups whipping cream
     Parmesan cheese
     French bread for crouton garnish
     Baking soda
     Powdered sugar
     Sugar
     Salt
     White pepper
     Vanilla extract plus ½ vanilla bean
     Soy sauce
     Olive oil
     Sesame oil
     Salad oil
     Red wine vinegar
     Black pepper
     Thyme

     Rosemary
     Dry mustard
     Mace
     Oregano
  1 cup seedless black raspberry jam or 1 cup red currant jelly
     Zinfandel wine
     Framboise (raspberry brandy) or dark rum

Special Equipment

4-cup heart-shaped mold (optional but preferable; any similar-sized decorative mold can be substituted)
Cheesecloth

Tips

Twelve 3-inch heart-shaped molds can be substituted for single large mold for Coeur à la Crème. All recipes can be easily doubled (use two separate molds for dessert). The following recipes can be halved: Potage Puree Crecy and Quick Zucchini.

Countdown

1 week ahead
Prepare Potage Puree Crecy. Let cool completely and freeze.

3 days ahead
Prepare Coeur à la Crème and pack into mold. Refrigerate.

2 days ahead
Soak beans for Joyce's Basque Beans overnight in water to cover.

1 day ahead
Finish Joyce's Basque Beans and refrigerate.
Blend sauce for dessert and refrigerate.
Remove potage puree from freezer and let thaw in refrigerator overnight.

About 1½ hours before serving
Mix marinade and add lamb; let stand for 1 hour at room temperature, turning several times.

Parboil zucchini; halve lengthwise and set aside on
  paper towels.
Remove dessert sauce from refrigerator and let
  stand at room temperature until ready to
  serve, stirring occasionally.
Fry croutons for soup garnish and set aside at
  room temperature.

About 25 minutes before serving
Place lamb in shallow pan and roast, basting frequently with marinade.

About 10 minutes before serving
Mix sauce for lamb.
Rewarm potage puree over very low heat, stirring
  occasionally.

Transfer zucchini to baking sheet; finish with remaining ingredients; preheat broiler.

Just before serving
Finish zucchini in broiler.
Unmold Coeur à la Crème and return to refrigera-
  tor; do not decorate until ready to serve.

Wine Suggestions

Serve the same Zinfandel used in cooking the lamb—
a hearty, rich wine with a delightful hint of berries
in its bouquet.

THE RECIPES

Potage Puree Crecy

6 to 8 servings

¼ cup (½ stick) butter
1½ pounds carrots, thinly sliced
 1 large onion (about ½ pound), thinly sliced
¾ pound russet potatoes, unpeeled and thinly
   sliced
1½ cups chicken stock
   Pinch of sugar

1½ cups milk, scalded
 1 cup half and half
 2 egg yolks, beaten
   Salt and freshly ground white pepper
   Minced fresh chives and parsley (garnish)
   Fried croutons (garnish)

Melt butter in heavy 3-quart saucepan over medium
heat. Add carrot, onion and potatoes and sauté until
onion is golden brown. Stir in stock and sugar, reduce
heat and simmer until vegetables are very soft (test
by mashing with back of spoon). Transfer to food
processor or blender in batches and puree.

Return to saucepan and place over low heat.
Gradually stir in milk, blending well. Combine half
and half with yolks and blend into puree. Bring to
simmer, stirring frequently. Season to taste. Serve hot,
garnished with chives, parsley, croutons.

*Potage can be frozen. Defrost in refrigerator
overnight before reheating over low heat.*

*Scalded milk is slowly whisked into the puree of
vegetables for Potage Puree Crecy.*

Marinated Boned Lamb with Zinfandel Sauce

6 servings

Marinade
½ cup soy sauce
½ cup olive oil
½ cup sesame oil
½ cup parsley leaves
2 garlic cloves, mashed
1 tablespoon thyme
1 teaspoon rosemary
1 teaspoon dry mustard
½ teaspoon mace
½ teaspoon oregano

3 racks of lamb or lamb rib eyes, boned

1 cup Zinfandel wine
    Parsley sprigs (garnish)

Combine marinade ingredients in food processor or blender and mix. Transfer ½ cup to small saucepan.

Place lamb in shallow dish and pour remaining marinade evenly over meat. Cover and let stand 1 hour at room temperature, turning several times.

Preheat oven to 450°F. Transfer lamb to rack in shallow roasting pan and bake 20 to 25 minutes, basting frequently.

About 10 minutes before serving, combine wine with reserved ½ cup marinade and simmer, stirring occasionally. Place lamb on heated serving platter and garnish with parsley. Pour sauce into sauceboat and pass separately.

Joyce's Basque Beans

6 servings

1 pound small white beans
½ cup chopped red onion
¼ cup chopped fresh parsley
2 garlic cloves, minced
½ teaspoon salt
¾ cup red wine vinegar
⅓ cup salad oil
1 teaspoon salt
¼ teaspoon freshly ground pepper
    Dash of oregano

Soak beans several hours or overnight in enough cold water to cover. Drain well. Cover again with water and bring to boil. Reduce heat and simmer until tender, about 50 to 60 minutes, stirring occasionally. Drain thoroughly in colander, rinse under cold running water and drain again. Transfer to mixing bowl. Add onion, parsley, garlic and ½ teaspoon salt and mix gently but thoroughly, being careful not to crush beans. Combine remaining ingredients and blend well. Pour over beans and toss gently to coat evenly. Cover and refrigerate 6 to 8 hours or overnight.

Quick Zucchini

6 servings

3 large zucchini
1½ tablespoons butter
3 tablespoons freshly grated Parmesan cheese
    Salt and freshly ground pepper

Preheat broiler. Parboil zucchini until crisp-tender, about 4 minutes. Transfer to baking sheet and halve lengthwise. Dot with butter and sprinkle with cheese, salt and pepper. Place under broiler until lightly golden and bubbly.

Coeur à la Crème

8 servings

1 quart (4 cups) ice water
1 tablespoon fresh lemon juice
    Pinch of baking soda
    Double thickness of cheesecloth

1 8-ounce package cream cheese, room temperature
½ cup cottage cheese
½ cup powdered sugar, sifted
1½ teaspoons vanilla
½ vanilla bean, seeds only
2 cups whipping cream

    Halved fresh strawberries (garnish)
    Fresh Strawberry or Fresh Raspberry Sauce
    (see following recipes)

Combine water, lemon juice and baking soda in 2-quart mixing bowl. Cut square of cheesecloth large enough to line 4-cup heart-shaped mold leaving 2-inch overhang. Soak cheesecloth in water mixture while preparing crème.

Beat cream cheese in large bowl of electric mixer

Spoon crème into mold.   *Lift off cheesecloth.*   *Decorate with strawberries.*

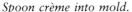

until soft and fluffy. Add cottage cheese and blend well. Add sugar, vanilla and vanilla *seeds* and beat until smooth. In separate bowl, whip cream until stiff. Gently fold into cream cheese mixture.

Wring cheesecloth well and line mold, leaving overhang. Spoon crème evenly into mold, smoothing gently. Fold cheesecloth over top and tap mold lightly to allow mixture to settle. Place on baking sheet and chill until firm, at least 2 hours, preferably overnight.

To serve, carefully lift cloth from top of crème. Invert mold onto platter and unwrap carefully; smooth top with spatula if necessary. Decorate with halved fresh strawberries and serve with Fresh Strawberry or Fresh Raspberry Sauce.

Coeur à la Crème can be prepared 3 days ahead and stored in refrigerator. Unmold and decorate just before serving.

Twelve 3-inch heart-shaped molds may be substituted for single large mold.

Fresh Strawberry Sauce

Makes about 3 cups

  2 cups strawberries
  1 cup seedless black raspberry jam
  ¼ cup framboise

Combine all ingredients in food processor or blender and mix well. Serve chilled or at room temperature.

Fresh Raspberry Sauce

Makes about 3 cups

  1 cup red currant jelly
  ¼ cup dark rum
  2 cups whole raspberries

Melt jelly in small saucepan over very low heat. Remove from heat and stir in rum. Add raspberries and mix gently, being careful not to crush.

Informal Buffet

THE MENU

Smoked Trout Salad with
Chuck's Special Dressing

Carpaccio with
Watercress Sauce

Game Hens with
Spinach-Sage Stuffing

Matchstick Pommes Frites

Broccoli Timbales

Ginger-Orange Carrots

Hazelnut Oeufs à la Neige

Serves 6

Carpaccio with Watercress Sauce whets the appetite for
the buffet's main attraction—Game Hens with Spinach-Sage Stuffing
surrounded by Matchstick Pommes Frites.

THE STRATEGY

Here is an easy and elegant menu served buffet style. A delicious smoked trout salad leads off, followed by a quick-to-prepare carpaccio served with a zesty watercress sauce. Vegetable- and herb-stuffed game hens, crisp potatoes, broccoli timbales and glazed carrots round out the main course. Light and fluffy hazelnut puffs provide the perfect finish.

Shopping List

  2 pounds fresh trout
  1 ½- to ¾-pound beef fillet
  6 game hens
  5 lemons
  2 garlic cloves
  1 large bunch watercress
  3 bunches fresh spinach
  ¼ cup finely chopped leek
  4 fresh tarragon sprigs (optional; 4 teaspoons dried can be substituted)
  1 pound green beans
  1 bunch radishes
  2 large tomatoes
  1 pound fresh broccoli
 24 baby carrots (or 12 medium carrots)
 1¼ cups orange juice
 12 sage leaves
 10 medium White Rose potatoes
    Fresh lemon juice
    Watercress sprigs for garnish
    Cilantro, also known as coriander or Chinese parsley, for garnish
  2 sticks butter
 1½ cups milk
 13 eggs
 2½ cups whipping cream
  ⅓ cup hazelnuts
 1½ cups sugar
    Peanut oil
    Safflower oil
    Olive oil
    White wine vinegar (preferably French)
    Cream of tartar
    Dijon mustard
    Salt
    White pepper
    Black pepper
    Ground red pepper
    Pink peppercorns (optional)

Whole nutmeg
Dried thyme
Fresh or ground ginger
Cognac
Vermouth
Hazelnut liqueur

Special Equipment

Hickory chips
Electric smoker (optional)

Tips

Regular medium-size carrots can be substituted for baby carrots. Heavy skillet can be used to smoke trout (see recipe).
Trout can be poached in fish fumet or court bouillon instead of smoked.
All recipes can be easily doubled to serve a larger group.
The following recipes can be halved: Smoked Trout Salad, Game Hens with Spinach-Sage Stuffing, Matchstick Pommes Frites and Ginger-Orange Carrots.

Countdown

2 weeks ahead
Prepare smoked trout for salad and refrigerate.

1 day ahead
Mix Chuck's Special Dressing and refrigerate.
Prepare custard sauce for dessert and refrigerate.
Blanch broccoli florets for timbales and refrigerate. Bring to room temperature before using.

Morning of dinner
Poach hazelnut puffs for dessert and refrigerate.
Mix watercress sauce for carpaccio and refrigerate.
Cook beans for salad, then prepare salad platter with trout and remaining vegetables. Cover loosely and refrigerate.

About 1 hour before serving
Make stuffing for game hens; fill birds and roast.

About 45 minutes before serving
Flash freeze beef for carpaccio.

Blend cream mixture for timbales; fill molds and bake.

Peel and cut matchstick potatoes; set aside in acidulated water until ready to fry.

Let Chuck's Special Dressing stand at room temperature.

Let Watercress Sauce stand at room temperature.

About 15 minutes before serving

Let Smoked Trout Salad stand at room temperature until ready to serve.

Cook Ginger-Orange Carrots.

Fry matchstick potatoes; drain on paper towels.
  Transfer to large platter.

Just before serving

Slice beef for carpaccio and assemble platter.

Unmold timbales onto serving platter and surround with carrots.

Arrange game hens over potatoes.

Wine Suggestions

Offer a selection of wines: a brut Champagne or sparkling wine, a crisp, young Chardonnay from California or Mâcon and a fruity Beaujolais such as those made by Georges Duboeuf.

THE RECIPES

Smoked Trout Salad with Chuck's Special Dressing

6 servings

  2 **cups hickory chips**
  2 **pounds fresh trout (about 4 small), cleaned but not boned**

  1 **pound green beans**

    Escarole leaves
  1 **bunch radishes, shredded**
  2 **large tomatoes, peeled, seeded and chopped**
    Chuck's Special Dressing (see following recipe)

Soak hickory chips in water 20 minutes. Arrange in bottom of electric smoker.* Place tray half filled with water over chips. Set trout on grill, cover and smoke 1 hour; do not remove lid while cooking. (*Procedure may vary with manufacturer's instructions. Smoked trout can be refrigerated up to 2 weeks.*)

Transfer trout to work surface. Remove skin, bone carefully and cut fish into narrow strips. Wrap fish tightly in foil and refrigerate until ready to use.

French-cut beans. Blanch in boiling salted water until crisp-tender, about 2 minutes. Plunge into cold water to stop cooking process. Drain beans well; gently pat dry with paper towels.

Cover serving platter with escarole leaves. Place beans down center of platter. Arrange trout in lengthwise strips over beans. Place narrow strip of radishes on each side of beans. Arrange tomatoes at top and bottom of platter. Refrigerate at least 1 hour. (If salad has been chilled over 3 hours, let stand at room temperature 15 minutes before serving.) Serve immediately with Chuck's Special Dressing.

*If commercial smoker is not available, soak 2 cups hickory chips in water 20 minutes. Meanwhile, line very heavy skillet or lidded casserole with heavy-duty aluminum foil, bringing enough foil up above rim so it will completely cover lid and form tight seal. Arrange hickory chips in single layer in bottom of skillet. Sprinkle 1 tablespoon sugar over chips. Set rack about 2 to 3 inches above chips. Generously butter rack. Arrange trout on rack and cover skillet with lid. Bring foil up over lid, folding and pleating to make tight seal. Smoke fish over high heat 20 minutes; do not overcook.

For variation, poach trout in fish fumet or court bouillon; do not overcook.

Chuck's Special Dressing

Makes about 1 cup

  ½ **cup olive oil**
  ¼ **cup fresh lemon juice**
  3 **tablespoons white wine vinegar (preferably French)***
  1 **egg yolk**
  ¼ **teaspoon dried thyme, crumbled**
    Salt and freshly ground pepper

Mix oil, lemon juice, vinegar, egg yolk and thyme in small bowl. Season with salt and pepper. Cover tightly and refrigerate until ready to use.

*For a milder dressing, reduce vinegar to 1½ tablespoons.

Carpaccio with Watercress Sauce

6 servings

1 ½- to ¾-pound beef fillet
2 lemons, halved and thinly sliced (garnish)
   Watercress sprigs (garnish)
   Watercress Sauce (see following recipe)

Flash freeze fillet until slightly firm, about 30 to 45 minutes. Slice meat paper thin and arrange on serving platter. Garnish with lemon slices and watercress sprigs. Pass sauce separately.

Watercress Sauce

Makes about 1 cup.

1 large bunch watercress, stems included

1 egg yolk
1 teaspoon Dijon mustard
1 garlic clove, minced
   Juice of 1 small lemon
   Pinch of salt
¾ cup plus 1 tablespoon olive oil

½ cup whipping cream
1 tablespoon Cognac
   Salt and ground red pepper
   Cracked pink peppercorns
   (baies roses)* (optional)

Finely puree watercress in processor or blender and set aside.

Combine egg yolk, mustard, garlic, half of lemon juice and salt in medium bowl and blend well. Let stand 5 minutes. Add oil 1 tablespoon at a time, mixing constantly until each addition is well incorporated. Add remaining lemon juice to taste and blend well (mixture will thin).

Beat cream in small bowl until thick. Add Cognac. Whisk cream mixture and watercress puree into egg mixture. Season to taste with salt and ground red pepper. Refrigerate until ready to use. Garnish with pink peppercorns.

For a less peppery sauce, omit stems.

*Available in specialty food markets.

Game Hens with Spinach-Sage Stuffing

6 servings

3 bunches fresh spinach (about 2½ pounds), stems removed

¼ cup finely chopped leek
4 fresh tarragon sprigs or 4 teaspoons dried, crumbled
1 small garlic clove
1 cup (2 sticks) butter
   Salt and freshly ground white pepper

6 game hens
3 lemons, quartered (peel removed in fine julienne)
12 sage leaves
½ cup vermouth
   Salt and freshly ground white pepper
   Matchstick Pommes Frites (see following recipe)

Wash fresh spinach thoroughly. Shake to remove excess water. Transfer to 5- to 6-quart saucepan or Dutch oven and cook over low heat until wilted, stirring occasionally, 4 to 5 minutes. Drain well.

Combine leek, tarragon and garlic in processor and puree. Add butter and spinach and puree again. Season with salt and white pepper to taste.

Preheat oven to 450°F. Stuff each hen with 2 lemon quarters and 2 sage leaves. Starting at neck cavity, carefully separate skin from breast using fingers, being careful not to tear skin. Spoon spinach mixture between skin and meat, pressing gently to distribute evenly. Arrange game hens, breast side up, in shallow large pan. Pour in vermouth. Sprinkle lemon julienne over top. Sprinkle with salt and pepper to taste. Roast 10 minutes. Baste hens with pan juices. Reduce oven temperature to 350°F. Continue roasting, basting frequently, until skin is crisp, juices run yellow when bird is pricked with fork and meat thermometer inserted in thickest part of meat without touching bone registers 180°F, about 20 to 30 minutes. Arrange hens on bed of Matchstick Pommes Frites. Spoon pan juices over birds. Serve hot.

Matchstick Pommes Frites

6 servings

   Peanut oil and safflower oil for deep frying
10 medium White Rose potatoes, peeled and cut into 2- to 3-inch-long matchsticks
   Salt

Pour equal amounts of peanut and safflower oil into deep fryer and heat to 400°F. Pat potatoes dry with paper towels. Add potatoes to oil in 3 batches and fry each until crisp and golden brown. Remove from oil using slotted spoon. Drain on paper towels. Sprinkle with salt and serve immediately.

Broccoli Timbales

6 servings

    1 pound fresh broccoli, trimmed to 3 inches
       below florets
    5 eggs
    1 cup whipping cream
  ½ teaspoon salt
  ¼ teaspoon freshly ground white pepper
       Pinch of freshly grated nutmeg
       Pinch of ground red pepper
       Ginger-Orange Carrots (see following recipe)
       Fresh cilantro (garnish)

Preheat oven to 350°F. Generously oil six ½-cup timbale molds or custard cups. Bring 1½ quarts salted water to boil in large saucepan over high heat. Add broccoli florets and blanch to retain color and crispness, about 1 minute. Drain. Combine all remaining ingredients except carrots and garnish in large bowl and mix well. Arrange florets in molds, stem side up, trimming stems to top of mold. Pour egg mixture evenly into molds. Set molds in shallow roasting pan. Fill pan with enough boiling water to come halfway up sides of molds. Bake until knife inserted in centers comes out clean, about 40 minutes. Invert molds onto large platter. Intersperse Ginger-Orange Carrots between timbales. Garnish with cilantro. Serve hot.

Ginger-Orange Carrots

6 servings

   24 baby carrots (or 12 medium carrots halved)
 1¼ cups orange juice
    1 tablespoon chopped fresh ginger or ½
       teaspoon ground ginger

Combine carrots, orange juice and ginger in medium saucepan. Simmer over medium-low heat until tender, about 15 minutes. Arrange on serving platter with Broccoli Timbales.

Hazelnut Oeufs à la Neige

6 servings

    2 quarts water
    6 egg whites, room temperature
       Pinch *each* cream of tartar and salt
  ¾ cup (12 tablespoons) sugar

    1 cup whipping cream
    1 cup milk
    6 egg yolks, room temperature
  ⅔ cup sugar
  ⅓ cup hazelnut liqueur
  ⅓ cup toasted hazelnuts, husked and ground

Bring water to simmer in large saucepan or deep skillet over medium heat. Beat egg whites, cream of tartar and salt at medium speed in large bowl of electric mixer until soft peaks form. Beat in ¾ cup sugar 1 tablespoon at a time until very stiff.* Carefully spoon 6 mounds from *half* of egg white mixture into simmering water. Poach meringues, uncovered, 7 minutes on one side, then turn over with slotted spoon and poach 3 more minutes. Remove with slotted spoon and drain on paper towel. Repeat with remaining egg whites, forming a total of 12 puffs. Refrigerate at least 30 minutes.

Scald cream and milk in heavy large saucepan. Combine egg yolks and sugar in large mixing bowl and beat at medium-high speed until thick and lemon colored. *Gradually* beat in cream and milk. Transfer mixture to large saucepan over medium-low heat. Add liqueur and hazelnuts and cook, whisking constantly, until mixture thickens enough for finger to leave path when drawn across spoon.

Transfer custard to large bowl. Cool at room temperature. Lay plastic wrap on surface of custard (to prevent skin from forming). Refrigerate 30 minutes or until ready to serve.

Spoon custard into individual dessert dishes. Arrange 2 puffs over top.

*If heavy-duty mixer is used, beat egg whites, cream of tartar and salt until stiff and dry, then gradually fold sugar into whites, blending gently but thoroughly.

Make-Ahead Seafood Dinner

THE MENU

Liver Pâté

Vintner's Salad

Processor French Bread

Cioppino

Biscuit Tortoni

Serves 8

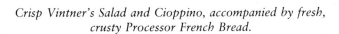

*Crisp Vintner's Salad and Cioppino, accompanied by fresh,
crusty Processor French Bread.*

THE STRATEGY

Casual entertaining has never been easier. This delicious meal spotlights a superb do-ahead Cioppino, accompanied by a crisp salad garnished with walnuts and French bread mixed in an instant in the food processor. Everything can be made in advance. Let your guests enjoy a smooth liver pâté with cocktails and wine while you finish up the Cioppino in just ten minutes. Biscuit Tortoni is a refreshing finale.

Shopping List

    3 pounds fresh cod, sole or rockfish fillets
2½ pounds prawns
    4 pounds cherrystone clams
  ½ pound liver sausage
    3 to 4 fresh or frozen crabs (preferably Dungeness)
  ½ pound mushrooms
    2 heads Bibb lettuce
    1 head romaine lettuce (only half will be used)
    1 bunch watercress
    2 large onions
    2 large green bell peppers
    4 to 6 celery stalks
    5 large garlic cloves
    4 large tomatoes
    Parsley
2½ cups whipping cream
    1 8-ounce package cream cheese
  ½ stick butter
  ½ cup grated Gruyère cheese
    1 cup crushed macaroons
    Crackers or dark bread
    French bread
  ¼ cup sliced almonds
  ½ cup walnut halves or chopped walnuts
    2 packages active dry yeast (only 1½ will be used)
3½ cups bleached or unbleached all purpose flour plus additional flour for board
    4 bay leaves
    4 dried red chilies
    Sugar
    Powdered sugar
    Salt
    Black pepper
    Italian seasoning

    Hot pepper sauce
    Dijon mustard
    Olive oil, ¾ cup of which should be imported
    Red wine vinegar
    Vanilla
    1 46-ounce can mixed vegetable juice cocktail
    1 8-ounce bottle clam juice
    1 6-ounce can tomato paste
1½ cups dry white wine
1½ cups red wine plus 2 tablespoons red wine for salad dressing
    Dark rum

Special Equipment

Baquette pans (optional but preferable; loaves can also be shaped and baked on baking sheet)

Tips

All recipes can be doubled (pack pâté into separate crocks and freeze Biscuit Tortoni in two bowls).

Countdown

1 month ahead
Prepare Liver Pâté and freeze.
Mix and bake Processor French Bread. Let cool completely, wrap tightly and freeze.

1 day ahead
Remove French bread from freezer and let thaw in refrigerator overnight.
Remove pâté from freezer and let thaw in refrigerator overnight.
Mix dressing for salad and refrigerate.
Prepare broth base for Cioppino. Let cool completely and refrigerate overnight.

Morning of dinner
Ready greens for salad and refrigerate.

About 3 hours before serving
Let salad dressing stand at room temperature.
Combine salad greens, nuts and cheese in large bowl. Return to refrigerator.

Prepare Biscuit Tortoni to point of whipping cream. Refrigerate.

Let broth base for Cioppino stand at room temperature.

About 2 hours before serving
Finish Biscuit Tortoni and freeze.

About 15 minutes before serving
Rewarm French bread in low oven if desired.
Bring broth for Cioppino to simmer.

About 10 minutes before serving
Finish Cioppino.

Just before serving
Toss salad with dressing.

Wine Suggestions

This meal will be nicely complemented by a full-bodied California Chardonnay, a true Chablis from France or a nice Italian Soave. A frisky Asti Spumante would make a delightful finish.

Fresh from the sea—the makings for Cioppino: Dungeness crab, prawns, clams and white fish.

THE RECIPES

Liver Pâté

Makes about 4 cups

¼ cup (½ stick) butter
½ pound mushrooms, chopped
½ teaspoon salt
½ teaspoon freshly ground pepper

½ pound liver sausage, room temperature
1 8-ounce package cream cheese, room temperature
   Crackers or dark bread

Melt butter in medium skillet over medium heat. Add mushrooms, salt and pepper and sauté until mushrooms are softened.

Combine mushrooms with sausage and cream cheese in blender or food processor and mix thoroughly. (If using blender, process in several batches.) Pack into crock, mold or other serving container, cover and refrigerate several hours to allow flavors to blend. Serve with crackers or bread.

Pâté can be frozen up to 1 month or kept in refrigerator up to 1 week.

Vintner's Salad

8 servings

2 heads Bibb lettuce
½ head romaine
1 bunch watercress
½ cup walnut halves or chopped walnuts
½ cup grated Gruyère cheese
½ cup olive oil
2 tablespoons red wine
1 tablespoon plus 1 teaspoon red wine vinegar
1 tablespoon Dijon mustard
1 teaspoon salt
¾ teaspoon freshly ground pepper

Wash greens, dry thoroughly and chill. Combine with walnuts and Gruyère in large salad bowl. Thoroughly blend remaining ingredients in small bowl or jar with tight-fitting lid. Just before serving, pour over salad and toss gently.

Processor French Bread

Makes 2 loaves

½ cup warm water (105°F)
1½ packages active dry yeast
1 teaspoon sugar

3½ cups all purpose unbleached flour
2 teaspoons salt
1 teaspoon sugar
1 cup warm water (105°F)

Flour

Generously grease baguette pans.

Combine ½ cup warm water with yeast and 1 teaspoon sugar in small bowl and let stand until yeast is dissolved and mixture is foamy, about 5 minutes.

Combine flour, salt, remaining sugar and yeast mixture in work bowl of food processor. With machine running, slowly begin adding 1 cup warm water. *A soft ball should form in several seconds; if not, add a little more warm water.* Let machine run 15 to 20 seconds, adding more flour if dough seems too soft.

Transfer dough to lightly floured board and knead with a little additional flour for several turns. Divide dough in half and shape into two cylinders 8 to 10 inches long. Transfer to prepared pans and cut 3 or 4 diagonal slashes in top of each loaf with tip of knife or single-edged razor blade. Cover and let rise in warm place until doubled, about 45 minutes to 1 hour.

After about 30 minutes, place racks in middle and lower quarters of oven and begin preheating to 450°F. Center shallow pan of water on lower rack. When dough has doubled, place on middle rack directly above water and bake 10 minutes. Reduce heat to 400°F and continue baking an additional 15 minutes, or until loaves are golden brown and have a hollow sound when tapped with finger.

Cioppino

8 to 12 servings

- ¾ cup imported olive oil
- 2 large onions, chopped
- 2 large green peppers, seeded and chopped
- 4 to 6 celery stalks, chopped (including some leaves)
- 5 large garlic cloves, crushed
- 1 cup minced fresh parsley
- 1 46-ounce can mixed vegetable juice cocktail
- 1½ cups dry white wine
- 1½ cups red wine
- 1 8-ounce bottle clam juice
- 1 6-ounce can tomato paste
- 4 large tomatoes, peeled, seeded and chopped
- 1 tablespoon plus 2 teaspoons Italian seasoning
- 4 bay leaves
- 4 dried red chilies, chopped
- 2 teaspoons sugar
  Hot pepper sauce
  Salt and freshly ground pepper

- 3 pounds fresh white fish fillets (cod, sole or rockfish), cut into 1½-inch chunks
- 2½ pounds prawns, cleaned and deveined
- 4 pounds cherrystone clams, scrubbed
- 3 to 4 fresh or frozen crabs (preferably Dungeness), cracked
  French bread

Heat olive oil in Dutch oven or stockpot over medium-high heat until hot. Add onion, green pepper, celery, garlic and ¾ cup minced parsley and cook until vegetables are limp. Add vegetable juice, wines, clam juice, tomato paste, tomatoes, Italian seasoning, bay leaves, chilies, sugar, hot pepper sauce, salt and pepper and blend well. Bring to just below boiling point, then reduce heat and simmer for about 30 minutes, stirring frequently.

Add white fish and simmer 5 minutes. Add prawns and continue simmering just until pink, about 3 minutes. Add clams and crabs and cook until clams open, about 2 minutes longer. Ladle into soup bowls and garnish each with remaining ¼ cup parsley. Serve with French bread.

Cioppino is best if broth base is prepared ahead and refrigerated overnight to blend flavors.

Biscuit Tortoni

8 to 10 servings

- 1 cup crushed dry macaroons
- 2½ cups whipping cream, well chilled
- ½ cup powdered sugar
  Pinch of salt

- ¼ cup dark rum
- 1½ teaspoons vanilla
- ¼ cup sliced almonds, toasted

Combine crumbs, 1¼ cups cream, and sugar and salt in medium bowl and blend well with spoon. Cover and refrigerate 30 to 45 minutes, until macaroons are soft.

Whip remaining cream until soft peaks form. Fold into macaroon mixture with rum and vanilla. Spoon into small dessert dishes or wine glasses. Sprinkle with almonds, cover and freeze about 2 hours before serving.

Biscuit Tortoni is the smooth and refreshing finale.

Italian Flair

THE MENU

Caviar Mousse

Veal with Pesto and Orzo

Arugula Salad with Creamy Dijon Dressing

Chocolate Apricot Roll

Serves 8

Caviar Mousse served with thin cucumber slices, fresh Arugula Salad, Veal with Pesto and Orzo in a tomato-wine sauce, and for dessert, Chocolate Apricot Roll topped with cream rosettes.

THE STRATEGY

An easy-to-prepare dinner with Italian flair. The sophisticated menu begins with a smooth Caviar Mousse. Pesto-stuffed veal accompanied by rice-shaped orzo pasta and a salad of arugula, watercress and Belgian endive with a zesty mustard dressing is a delicious main course. Chocolate Apricot Roll is a spectacular dessert that can be prepared a full week ahead of serving and frozen.

Shopping List

    4 ounces red lumpfish caviar
    1 4½-pound breast of veal (3-to 4-pounds
       boned)
    2 strips fresh pork fat or bacon
    1 cup chicken stock (total)
    3 large garlic cloves plus ½ teaspoon minced
    2 medium onions plus 1 small Spanish onion (2
       tablespoons finely minced)
    2 carrots
    4 Italian plum tomatoes
    1 large bunch arugula (escarole can be
       substituted)
    1 large bunch watercress
    4 heads Belgian endive (Boston lettuce can be
       substituted)
    ½ pound dried apricots
    1 cucumber
       Parsley
       Fresh lemon juice
       Lemon (for peel)
    1 cup sour cream
    9 eggs
    ¼ stick butter
    ½ cup whipping cream plus additional for
       garnish
       Parmesan cheese
    1 pound orzo (rice-shaped pasta)
       Rye melba toast
    ½ cup walnuts
    8 ounces sweet chocolate
  1¼ cups sugar
       Powdered sugar
       Unsweetened cocoa powder
       Vanilla
       Salt
       Black pepper
       Dried basil
       Olive oil

Parsley pesto is spread on the boned side of the veal.

       White wine vinegar
       Dijon mustard
       Hot pepper sauce
       Coffee
       Unflavored gelatin
       Dry white wine
       Brandy, orange liqueur or apricot liqueur

Tips

Parsley pesto recipe can be doubled and used with
    hot pasta.
Creamy Dijon Dressing recipe can be doubled.

Countdown

1 week ahead
Prepare Chocolate Apricot Roll to point noted in
    recipe. Wrap tightly and freeze.

1 day ahead
Mix Creamy Dijon Dressing and refrigerate.
Blend parsley pesto for veal and refrigerate.
Prepare Caviar Mousse and refrigerate.
Remove Chocolate Apricot Roll from freezer and
    let thaw in refrigerator overnight.

Morning of dinner
Ready arugula, watercress and endive. Combine in
    large bowl and refrigerate.
Remove pesto from refrigerator and let stand at
    room temperature.

About 2½ hours before serving
Begin preparation of veal.
Cook orzo until *al dente*; drain well and set aside
    at room temperature, fluffing with fork
    occasionally.

About 15 minutes before serving
Remove Caviar Mousse from refrigerator and let
    stand at room temperature.

Just before serving
Finish sauce for veal.
Unmold mousse onto platter if desired.
Assemble salad.
Garnish cake.

Wine Suggestions

Serve a dry sparkling wine with the Caviar Mousse, such as Piper Sonoma or Domaine Chandon Brut; with the veal serve a young Chianti, a Valpolicella or a California Gamay Beaujolais.

THE RECIPES

Caviar Mousse

8 to 12 appetizer servings

    4 ounces red lumpfish caviar
    3 tablespoons chopped fresh parsley
    2 tablespoons finely minced Spanish onion
    1 cup sour cream
    ¼ teaspoon freshly ground pepper
    1½ teaspoons unflavored gelatin
    2 tablespoons water
    ½ cup whipping cream, whipped
      Cucumber slices
      Rye melba toast

Set aside 2 tablespoons caviar, 1 tablespoon parsley and 1 tablespoon onion for garnish; cover and refrigerate. Combine remaining caviar, parsley and onion with sour cream and pepper in medium-size nonmetallic bowl and blend well. Sprinkle gelatin over water in small saucepan. Stir over low heat until gelatin dissolves completely. Remove from heat and stir into caviar mixture. Fold in whipped cream. Turn into 2-cup nonmetallic crock or mold. Cover and refrigerate until set. Let stand at room temperature 15 minutes before serving. Spoon mousse from crock or unmold onto nonmetallic platter. Surround with cucumber slices and melba toast. Garnish top with reserved caviar, parsley and onion.

Veal with Pesto and Orzo (Vitello al Pesto con Orzo)

8 servings

Parsley Pesto
    ½ cup walnuts
    ½ cup (packed) parsley sprigs
    ¼ cup freshly grated Parmesan cheese
    ¼ cup olive oil
    1 teaspoon dried basil, crumbled
    1 teaspoon fresh lemon juice
    3 large garlic cloves
      Freshly ground pepper

    1 4½-pound breast of veal (3- to 4- pounds
      boned)
      Olive oil
      Salt and freshly ground pepper

    2 tablespoons (¼ stick) butter
    2 medium onions, diced
    2 carrots, thinly sliced
    2 strips fresh pork fat or blanched bacon
    ½ cup dry white wine
    ½ cup chicken stock

    4 Italian plum tomatoes, diced
    ½ cup dry white wine
    ½ cup chicken stock

1 pound orzo,* cooked *al dente* and drained
¼ cup chopped fresh parsley
Freshly grated Parmesan cheese (optional)

Combine all ingredients for parsley pesto in food processor and blend well. Set aside 2 tablespoons pesto (for orzo).

Preheat broiler. Spread boned side of veal with remaining pesto. Roll veal up lengthwise and tie with string every 2 inches. Brush with olive oil and season with salt and pepper. Brown on all sides, about 2 inches from heat source, turning often. Set aside.

Preheat oven to 325°F. Melt butter in shallow flameproof casserole over medium heat. Add onions and carrots and sauté until onion is soft, about 7 minutes. Transfer veal to casserole, spooning vegetables over top. Cover veal with pork fat. Pour ½ cup wine and ½ cup chicken stock into casserole and bring to a boil over medium-high heat. Cover tightly with aluminum foil. Top casserole with lid and bake until meat thermometer inserted in thickest portion of veal registers 175°F, about 1¾ to 2 hours. Transfer meat to serving platter and keep warm.

Skim fat from sauce. Add tomatoes, remaining ½ cup wine and ½ cup chicken stock to casserole and mix well. Bring to boil over medium-high heat. Reduce heat to medium and simmer until sauce thickens, about 8 to 10 minutes. Adjust seasonings to taste. Remove 1 cup sauce and keep warm.

Add reserved pesto, orzo and parsley to casserole and blend well over medium heat. Adjust seasonings to taste. Spoon orzo mixture around veal. Carve veal into ¾-inch-thick slices. Serve immediately with reserved sauce. Pass Parmesan cheese separately.

*Orzo is rice-shaped pasta available in Italian or Middle Eastern food markets.

Arugula Salad with Creamy Dijon Dressing

6 servings

   1 large bunch arugula, rinsed and patted dry
   1 large bunch watercress, rinsed and patted dry
   4 heads Belgian endive
   Creamy Dijon Dressing (see following recipe)

Remove root ends from arugula. Cut watercress crosswise into bite-size pieces. Slice endive lengthwise into thin strips. Combine all greens in salad bowl.

Drizzle about ¾ cup dressing over salad and toss. Taste and add more dressing if necessary.

Escarole can be substituted for arugula and Boston lettuce for Belgian endive.

Creamy Dijon Dressing

Makes 1 cup

   1 small egg yolk, room temperature
   2 teaspoons Dijon mustard
   2 teaspoons white wine vinegar
   ½ teaspoon minced garlic
   ½ teaspoon salt
   ¼ teaspoon freshly ground pepper
   3 drops hot pepper sauce
   1 cup olive oil
   1 teaspoon fresh lemon juice
   1 tablespoon warm water

Combine egg yolk, mustard, vinegar, garlic, salt, pepper and hot pepper sauce in small bowl and blend well. Slowly whisk in oil in thin stream. Blend in lemon juice and water.

Dressing can be prepared 1 day ahead and refrigerated. Reblend before using.

Chocolate Apricot Roll

10 servings

Filling
   ½ pound dried apricots, snipped into small pieces with scissors
   2 cups water
   2 3-inch strips lemon peel
   ½ cup sugar
   3 tablespoons brandy or orange or apricot liqueur
   1 teaspoon fresh lemon juice

Cake
   8 ounces sweet chocolate
   ⅓ cup strong coffee
   2 teaspoons vanilla

   7 egg yolks, room temperature
   ¾ cup sugar
   8 egg whites, room temperature

   Unsweetened cocoa powder

   Powdered sugar or unsweetened cocoa powder
   Whipped cream

The chocolate cake, spread with its apricot filling, is gently rolled lengthwise.

For filling: Combine apricots, water and lemon peel in large saucepan and simmer over medium-low heat until fruit is barely tender, about 10 minutes. Stir in sugar and continue simmering until fruit is tender, about 5 more minutes. Remove from heat and discard lemon peel. Using fork, blend to textured puree. Blend in brandy and lemon juice. Cover and chill at least 2 hours.

For cake: Preheat oven to 350°F. Grease 11 × 15-inch jelly roll pan. Line bottom with waxed paper, extending paper over short ends. Grease paper. Combine chocolate and coffee in medium saucepan and warm over very low heat until chocolate melts. Remove from heat. Stir in vanilla; set aside to cool.

Combine yolks and sugar in medium bowl and beat until pale and light. Stir into cooled chocolate mixture. Beat whites in large bowl until stiff but not dry. Gently stir ⅓ of whites into chocolate mixture, then fold chocolate mixture into remaining whites.

Pour into prepared pan. Bake 10 minutes. Reduce oven temperature to 300°F and continue baking 5 minutes. Remove pan from oven.

Lay large towel on a flat surface and dust with cocoa. Loosen cake around edges with knife and turn out onto towel. Carefully remove paper. Cut off any crisp edges of cake and discard. Beginning on *long* side, gently roll up cake and towel. (Towel prevents cake from sticking to itself.) Transfer to rack and cool completely.

To assemble: Unroll cake and remove cloth. Spread apricot filling evenly over cake, leaving 1-inch border on all sides. Carefully roll cake up lengthwise. *(Can be prepared ahead to this point and refrigerated for several hours or frozen. If refrigerating, let stand at room temperature for 1 hour before serving.)*

Transfer roll to serving dish. Sift powdered sugar or cocoa powder lightly over top. Pipe whipped cream across top of roll, or pass whipped cream separately.

French Country Feast

THE MENU

Mushroom, Fennel and Pepperoni Salad

Chicken with Braised Garlic and Rosemary

Potatoes Boulangère

Vermouth-Glazed Pears

Serves 6

Mushroom, Fennel and Pepperoni Salad, Chicken with Braised Garlic and Rosemary, Golden Potatoes Boulangère, and Vermouth-Glazed Pears served with Frozen Rum Cream.

THE STRATEGY

An informal menu with a distinctly French accent, including Chicken with Braised Garlic and Rosemary, country-style potatoes layered with Gruyère cheese and Vermouth-Glazed Pears served with Frozen Rum Cream. Only the chicken requires any last-minute attention, and the dessert can bake while you are enjoying the main course.

Shopping List

  2 chickens (chickens will be quartered and only
       1½ will be used)
  2 cups chicken stock (total)
  ¾ cup pepperoni, thinly sliced
  1 pound large mushrooms
  1 red bell pepper or 1 pimiento
1½ heads garlic (about 35 cloves)
  8 medium boiling potatoes
  6 medium-size firm ripe pears
    Fennel or celery (1 cup julienne)
    Lemon (for peel)
    Fresh lemon juice
    Parsley
    Lettuce leaves
    Watercress for garnish
1½ sticks butter
1¼ cups grated Gruyère or Swiss cheese
 20 small almond cookies (½ cup crushed)
  ¼ cup chopped almonds
  2 bay leaves
    Salt
    Black pepper
    Olive oil
    Red wine vinegar
    Hot chili pepper
    Dried rosemary
    Fennel seed
  ⅔ cup apricot preserves
    Greek or Niçoise olives
  1 pint extra-rich vanilla ice cream
    Dry white wine
    Sweet vermouth
    Dark rum

Tips

All recipes can be doubled; bake potatoes in separate gratin dishes.

Countdown

1 day ahead
Prepare mushroom salad to point of adding pepperoni and parsley. Refrigerate.

Morning of dinner
Peel and slice potatoes and set aside in bowl of ice water to prevent darkening; add ice to bowl occasionally as other cubes melt.
Grate cheese for potatoes and refrigerate.

About 4 hours before serving
Let ice cream for Frozen Rum Cream soften at room temperature.

About 3 hours before serving
Prepare Frozen Rum Cream and return to freezer.

About 1½ hours before serving
Blanch garlic cloves for chicken; peel and set aside.

About 1 hour before serving
Begin roasting chicken.

About 40 minutes before serving
Assemble Potatoes Boulangère.
Prepare pears and put in oven to bake.

Just before serving
Add pepperoni and parsley to mushroom salad and assemble on plates.
Finish chicken and sauce.
Let rum cream stand at room temperature 10 minutes before dessert time.

Wine Suggestions

A full-bodied oak-aged California Chardonnay such as those made by Chateau St. Jean or Beringer would work well with this supper. Surprisingly enough, so would a slightly chilled French Beaujolais.

French oil, vinegar and vermouth give these recipes a distinctive flair.

THE RECIPES

Mushroom, Fennel and Pepperoni Salad

6 servings

 1 **pound large fresh mushrooms, sliced**
 1 **cup fennel or celery, cut julienne**
 1 **red bell pepper, roasted, peeled and diced, or 1 pimiento, diced**
 1 **cup olive oil**
 2 **tablespoons minced hot chili pepper**
 1 **tablespoon minced garlic**
 ½ **cup red wine vinegar**
 2 **teaspoons fennel seed**
 1½ **teaspoons salt**
 ¼ **teaspoon freshly ground pepper**
 2 **bay leaves, crushed**

 ¾ **cup thinly sliced pepperoni**
 ¼ **cup chopped fresh parsley**
 6 **lettuce leaves**
 Ripe Greek or Niçoise olives

Combine mushrooms, fennel and red pepper in large bowl. Combine oil, hot chili pepper and garlic in 1-quart saucepan and simmer over medium-high heat until garlic is golden, about 10 minutes. Stir in vinegar, fennel seed, salt, pepper and bay leaves and simmer an additional 3 minutes. Remove from heat and cool slightly. Pour over mushrooms and toss well. Cover and refrigerate 4 to 24 hours.

Just before serving, add pepperoni and parsley and toss again. Center lettuce leaf on each salad plate and top evenly with mushroom mixture. Garnish with Greek or Niçoise olives.

Chicken with Braised Garlic and Rosemary

6 servings

1½ **heads garlic (about 35 cloves)**

  6 **tablespoons (¾ stick) butter**
1½ **chickens, quartered**
  2 **teaspoons dried rosemary, crumbled**
     Salt and freshly ground pepper

  ⅓ **cup dry white wine**
  1 **cup chicken stock**
  3 **tablespoons fresh lemon juice**
     Watercress (garnish)

Separate garlic cloves (do not peel) and drop into small saucepan of boiling water. Simmer 2 to 3 minutes. Drain well; slip off skins. Set garlic aside.

Preheat oven to 425°F. Melt butter in shallow roasting pan large enough to accommodate chicken in single layer. Roll chicken in butter and arrange in pan. Sprinkle with rosemary, salt and pepper. Roast 15 minutes. Turn chicken over and scatter garlic cloves over top. Baste with butter. Continue roasting until chicken is golden, about 30 minutes.

Transfer chicken to serving platter. Reserve about 7 garlic cloves and sprinkle remainder over top. Pour off fat from roasting pan. Add wine to pan and bring to boil over medium-high heat, stirring in reserved garlic and scraping up any browned bits. When most of wine has evaporated, add stock and lemon juice and boil rapidly until sauce thickens slightly. Season with salt and pepper to taste. Pour sauce over chicken. Garnish with watercress. Serve immediately, including some sauce, garlic cloves and watercress with each portion of chicken.

Potatoes Boulangère

6 servings

  8 **medium boiling potatoes, peeled and thinly sliced***
  1 **teaspoon salt**
  ¼ **teaspoon pepper**
1¼ **cups grated imported Gruyère or Swiss cheese**
  6 **tablespoons (¾ stick) butter**
  1 **cup chicken stock**

Position rack in upper third of oven and preheat to 425°F. Generously butter 9 × 12 × 2-inch gratin or other baking dish (the larger the pan, the shorter the cooking time). Drain potatoes thoroughly. Arrange half of potatoes in gratin dish. Sprinkle with half of salt, pepper and cheese. Dot with half of butter. Repeat with remaining potatoes, salt, pepper, cheese and butter. Pour stock over top. Bake until potatoes are tender and crust is golden brown, about 30 minutes. Serve immediately.

*Add each potato to bowl of cold water after slicing to prevent darkening and discoloration.

Quartered chicken is rolled in melted butter for Chicken with Braised Garlic and Rosemary.

*The top layer of sliced potatoes
is arranged in the gratin pan for
the Potatoes Boulangère.*

Vermouth-Glazed Pears

Delicious hot or at room temperature.

6 servings

   6 **medium-size firm ripe pears, stems attached**
      Juice and grated peel of 1 lemon
  ⅔ **cup apricot preserves**
  ⅓ **cup sweet vermouth**
  ½ **cup crushed almond cookie crumbs (about 20**
      small cookies)
  ¼ **cup chopped toasted almonds**
      Frozen Rum Cream (see following recipe)

Position rack in center of oven and preheat to 350°F.
Peel pears. Core from bottom; *be careful not to remove stem.* If necessary, remove thin slice from bottom so pears stand upright. Arrange in shallow
6½ × 10-inch baking dish, spacing no more than 1

inch apart. Pour lemon juice over pears. Combine
preserves, vermouth and lemon peel in small saucepan and bring to boil over medium-high heat. Pour
sauce over pears. Sprinkle with crumbs and nuts.
Bake, basting occasionally, until pears are tender
when pierced with knife, about 30 minutes. Transfer
to individual plates and top each serving with generous spoonful of rum cream.

Frozen Rum Cream

Makes 1 pint

   3 **tablespoons dark rum**
   1 **pint extra-rich vanilla ice cream, softened**

Beat rum into ice cream. Freeze. Let stand at room
temperature 10 minutes before spooning onto pears.

Festive Springtime Fare

THE MENU

Springtime Spaghettini

Grilled Salmon with Tarragon Mayonnaise

Positively West Coast Salad

Almond Tulips with Fresh Banana Ice

Serves 6

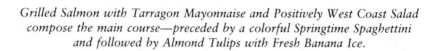

Grilled Salmon with Tarragon Mayonnaise and Positively West Coast Salad
compose the main course—preceded by a colorful Springtime Spaghettini
and followed by Almond Tulips with Fresh Banana Ice.

THE STRATEGY

A lively menu with the flavors of spring: fresh vegetables tossed with pasta, broiled salmon, a colorful salad and a refreshing homemade banana ice served in crunchy almond-enhanced "tulips." It is a delightful meal for friends that is as easy as it is delicious.

Shopping List

- 6 salmon steaks (about ½ pound each), 1 inch thick
- 2 large carrots
- 1 medium zucchini
- 1 small sweet red or green bell pepper
- 1 pound fresh beets (preferably tiny)
- 1 large head red leaf, Boston or romaine lettuce
- 1 ripe avocado
- 1 cup alfalfa sprouts
- 2 large very ripe bananas
  Garlic
  Fresh or dried dill plus dill sprigs for garnish

  Green onion (½ cup minced plus 3 tablespoons finely minced if not using red onion)
  Red onion (see note above)
  Fresh orange juice
  Fresh lemon juice
  Fresh tarragon or fresh parsley and dried tarragon plus tarragon sprigs for garnish
  Lemons or limes for garnish
- 1 stick butter
- 4 eggs (only whites will be used)
- 1 cup whipping cream
  Parmesan cheese
- 1 pound very thin egg noodles (capellini or very thin spaghetti can be substituted)
- ½ cup sliced blanched almonds
- 1 cup superfine sugar
  Candied violets or citron peels for garnish
  Salt
  Black pepper
  Vegetable oil

Nothing but the freshest ingredients for this light and simple springtime dinner.

Olive oil
White wine vinegar
Sugar
All purpose flour
Vanilla extract
Almond extract
2 **cups mayonnaise**
Dijon mustard
1 **9- or 10-ounce package frozen artichoke hearts**
Capers (2 tablespoons chopped)

Tips

Serve frozen tulip cups directly from freezer; do not thaw before using.
All recipes can be doubled.

Countdown

1 week ahead
Prepare almond tulip cups and freeze.

2 days ahead
Make banana ice.

1 day ahead
Blend mayonnaise mixture for salmon and refrigerate.

Prepare Mustard Vinaigrette for salad and refrigerate.
Cut carrot, zucchini and bell pepper for spaghettini into julienne and refrigerate.

Morning of dinner
Ready beets and artichoke hearts for salad and refrigerate.

About 30 minutes before serving
Begin boiling water for pasta.
Sauté garlic and vegetables for pasta and set aside.

About 10 minutes before serving
Assemble salad.
Spread mayonnaise mixture on salmon; preheat broiler.

Just before serving
Cook pasta and finish sauce.
Broil fish.
Let banana ice soften at room temperature 10 minutes before dessert time.

Wine Suggestions

Serve the same fresh, dry white wine throughout this meal: a snappy Sauvignon Blanc or a light Chardonnay from California, a Chablis or Macon from France or a Frascati or dry Orvieto from Italy.

THE RECIPES

Springtime Spaghettini

6 appetizer servings

2 **tablespoons salt**
1 **pound very thin egg noodles***
¼ **cup (½ stick) butter**
2 **teaspoons minced garlic**
2 **large carrots, cut julienne**
1 **medium zucchini, cut julienne**
1 **small sweet red or green pepper, seeded and cut julienne**

1 **cup whipping cream**
½ **cup freshly grated Parmesan cheese**
¼ **cup chopped fresh dill or 1⅓ tablespoons dried dillweed**
½ **teaspoon salt**
¼ **teaspoon freshly ground pepper**

Dill sprigs (garnish)
Additional Parmesan cheese

Bring water to rapid boil in large saucepan over high heat. Add salt and pasta and cook to *al dente*. Meanwhile, melt butter in large skillet over medium-high heat. Add garlic and sauté until garlic just begins to color, about 1 minute. Add vegetables and toss over high heat for 2 minutes. Remove from heat.

Drain pasta. Place vegetables over high heat. Stir in cream, ½ cup Parmesan, dill, salt and pepper. Add pasta to skillet and toss gently to blend. Divide pasta among 6 heated plates. Garnish with dill. Pass additional Parmesan cheese separately.

*If egg noodles are not available, capellini or very thin spaghetti can be substituted.

Grilled Salmon with Tarragon Mayonnaise

6 servings

  2 cups mayonnaise
  ¼ cup chopped fresh tarragon *or* ¼ cup chopped fresh parsley and 2 teaspoons dried tarragon, crumbled
  3 tablespoons finely minced green or red onion
  2 tablespoons fresh lemon juice
  2 tablespoons chopped capers
  ¼ teaspoon freshly ground pepper
     Salt

     Vegetable oil
  6 salmon steaks (about ½ pound each), cut 1 inch thick
     Lemon or lime slices, halved (garnish)
     Tarragon sprigs (garnish)

Combine mayonnaise, tarragon, onion, lemon juice, capers and pepper in large bowl and blend well. Season with salt. Cover and chill 2 to 24 hours.

Arrange rack over grill or broiler pan about 5 inches from heat source. Brush rack with oil. Preheat coals or broiler. Place salmon steaks on rack and spread top of each with 2 to 2½ tablespoons tarragon mayonnaise. Broil 6 minutes. Turn fish over and spread with another 2 to 2½ tablespoons sauce. Broil until tip of knife pierced into middle of steak near center bone meets little resistance, 4 to 6 more minutes. (Fish should be barely opaque with touch of deeper pink color remaining.) Arrange on serving platter. Garnish with lemon or lime slices and tarragon sprigs. Pass remaining tarragon mayonnaise.

Positively West Coast Salad

6 servings

  1 pound fresh beets (preferably tiny), steamed until tender when pierced with fork
  1 9- or 10-ounce package frozen artichoke hearts

  1 large head red leaf, Boston or romaine lettuce, thoroughly chilled
  1 ripe avocado, peeled, pitted and cubed
     Mustard Vinaigrette (see following recipe)
  1 cup alfalfa sprouts
  ½ cup minced green onion (including tops)

Peel beets under cold running water. Remove stems and root ends. Quarter beets if large. Cover and refrigerate. Bring about 1 inch salted water to boil in medium saucepan. Add artichoke hearts and cook until separated and barely tender, 1 to 3 minutes.

Cool quickly under cold water. Drain and refrigerate until ready to use.

Arrange lettuce leaves on large shallow platter. Mound beets, artichoke hearts and avocado in center. Pour dressing over top. Arrange sprouts in circle around vegetables. Sprinkle green onion over salad and serve.

Mustard Vinaigrette

Makes ¾ cup

  9 tablespoons olive oil
  3 tablespoons white wine vinegar
  1 tablespoon Dijon mustard
  ½ teaspoon minced garlic
  ½ teaspoon salt
  ¼ teaspoon freshly ground pepper

Combine all ingredients in jar with tight-fitting lid and shake well. Shake again just before using.

Mustard Vinaigrette can be prepared up to 1 day ahead and refrigerated.

Almond Tulips with Fresh Banana Ice

6 servings

Almond Tulip Cups
  2 egg whites
  ½ cup sugar
  ½ cup sliced blanched almonds
  ⅓ cup all purpose flour
  ¼ cup melted butter
  1½ teaspoons water
  ½ teaspoon vanilla extract
  ¼ teaspoon almond extract
     Dash of salt

Fresh Banana Ice (makes 1½ quarts)
  2 large very ripe bananas
  1 cup superfine sugar
  ¾ cup fresh orange juice
  ¼ cup fresh lemon juice
  2 cups water
  2 egg whites

     Candied violets or citron peels (garnish)

For cups: Position rack in center of oven and preheat to 400°F. Butter and flour baking sheet. Beat egg whites in medium bowl, gradually adding sugar just until frothy; *this is not a meringue, so do not try to form peaks.* Add remaining ingredients and beat well.

Smooth batter into six-inch circles to bake for the Almond Tulips.

Drop about 3 tablespoons batter on each side of prepared sheet, forming 2 circles. Smooth batter with back of spoon until each circle measures about 6 inches across. Bake until edges of cookies brown, about 8 to 10 minutes. Set baking sheet on open oven door (to keep second cookie warm and pliable when the first is being shaped). Remove cookie from sheet using large spatula and quickly fit into custard cup or muffin tin, gently pressing down, fluting and folding edges to fit. Repeat with second cookie. (It may be helpful to use small lemon or lime to press dough into cups without piercing. Since cups will be filled, small holes are no problem.) Repeat baking and shaping cookies with remaining batter. If weather is dry and cookies are to be served the same day, wrap and set aside. If weather is humid or cookies are prepared more than 1 day ahead, wrap airtight and freeze; do not thaw before serving.

For ice (with machine): Puree bananas, sugar, orange juice and lemon juice in processor or blender until smooth. Add water and egg whites and puree again until smooth. Pour into ice-cream maker and freeze according to manufacturer's instructions.

For ice (without machine): Puree bananas, sugar, orange juice and lemon juice in processor or blender until smooth. Add water and egg whites and mix again until smooth. Pour into freezer trays or shallow pans. Freeze until firm. Transfer to processor or blender in batches and mix until smooth. Transfer to bowl and blend well. Return to trays and refreeze.

To serve, let ice stand at room temperature until softened slightly, about 5 to 10 minutes. Arrange each tulip cup in wide-bowled wine glass, in dessert bowl or on plate. Place large scoop of banana ice in each cup. Garnish if desired. Serve immediately. Leftover ice can be frozen several days, although texture may change slightly.

Elegant Dinners

THE HIGH DAYS OF *la grande cuisine* are long over, and their passing is largely unlamented. Who would want to see, much less eat, a dinner like the one Antonin Careme designed for Czar Alexander of Russia? It consisted of ninety dishes served as sixteen separate courses, finishing with ten astonishingly complex pastry creations, one of them so huge that it required a twenty-foot stepladder to decorate it and eight men to carry it. Today such an elaborate display would be considered excessive, ostentatious and probably downright laughable—even for royalty.

But elegance itself never goes out of fashion, and it is possible for cuisine to be *haute* without being overblown and intimidating. For the modern taste, an elegant dinner party is a matter of style rather than size, a careful selection of special dishes rather than a multitude, a simple grace in setting and service rather than the periwigged waiters and gold plates of the czars.

The five unique menus in this chapter are designed for those occasions when you want to pull out all the stops and give a party that is a bit formal, a bit fancy, and perhaps more than a bit romantic. Each is a celebration of elegance in terms of both flavor and appearance. And, perhaps best of all, each is perfectly practical for the cook whose only "helper" is the convenience of the modern kitchen: no servants necessary.

The dishes include such imaginative delicacies as seafood quenelles with a sauce mousseline (page 43); Gourmandise with Sautéed Pine Nuts (page 52); Tomato Granité with Pernod (page 58); Noisettes of Lamb Florentine (page 68); Veal Meatballs with Caper Mayonnaise (page 65); and a Ricotta Almond Torte (page 69). As a bonus, each menu has wine-serving suggestions to help you set just the right tone for a formal dinner, and make your party a sophisticated marriage of good taste and great tastes.

Easy Elegance

THE MENU

Hors d'Oeuvres

Cream of Watercress Soup

Seafood Quenelles Mousseline

Beef Richelieu with Madeira Sauce

Stuffed Turnips

Chestnut Roll

Serves 8

Beef Richelieu with Madeira Sauce is the impressive main course.

THE STRATEGY

This special dinner creates a look of opulence without a lot of fuss. And it presents an opportunity for the wine collector to share his or her enthusiasm by offering different wines with soup, seafood, beef and dessert. Although the beef requires some last-minute attention from the cook, the rest of the meal can be prepared in easy stages, with the dessert, a delicious chestnut-filled cake roll, safely tucked away in the refrigerator long before the guests arrive. Add your own favorite hors d'oeuvres and a simple vegetable, such as stuffed turnips, and the picture is complete.

Shopping List

    1   4-pound beef fillet
    ½   pound tiny shrimp (purchase cooked or cook
        at home)
    ¼   pound scallops
    2 to 3 cups chicken stock or broth (preferably
        homemade)
    1   cup beef broth (preferably homemade)
    3   pounds potatoes
    2   bunches watercress
   12   medium tomatoes
   12 to 16 whole mushrooms (each about 1½
        inches in diameter)
    1   onion (1 tablespoon minced)
        Fresh or freeze-dried shallots
        Parsley sprigs for garnish
        Truffles or duxelles (2 tablespoons finely
        chopped)
   4½   cups whipping cream (or 1 cup half and half
        and 3½ cups whipping cream)
    2   sticks butter
    5   eggs
    1   cup milk
    ¼   cup breadcrumbs
        Cornflakes (½ cup crumbs)
        Arrowroot
        Cake flour
        Baking powder
        Sugar
        Powdered sugar
        Vanilla
        Semisweet chocolate for garnish
        Instant flour
        Salt

Black pepper
Hot pepper sauce
Beau Monde seasoning
Whole nutmeg
Oil
    1   17½-ounce can crème de marrons (chestnut
        puree)
    2   cups clam juice
        Tomato paste
        Dry white wine
        Dry Madeira
        Dark rum

Tips

The following recipes can be doubled: Cream of Watercress Soup and Seafood Quenelles Mousseline (prepare in batches in food processor).

Countdown

3 days ahead
Prepare Madeira Sauce for beef and refrigerate.

1 day ahead
Make Sauce Mousseline for quenelles and refrigerate.

Morning of dinner
Prepare quenelles to point of adding sauce. Let cool, cover and refrigerate.
Bake cake for Chestnut Roll; follow instructions for rolling up. Cool completely.

About 1½ hours before serving
Make Chestnut Butter Cream and assemble Chestnut Roll; refrigerate.

About 1 hour before serving
Cook potatoes and watercress for soup. Puree with onion and transfer to large saucepan.

About 30 minutes before serving
Top quenelles with sauce and put in oven to bake.
Prepare Beef Richelieu; reheat Madeira Sauce.

Just before serving
Add remaining ingredients to potato-watercress puree and finish soup.

Wine Suggestions

Begin with a dry Johannisberg Riesling or Gewurz-traminer, a German Riesling of the "Kabinet" designation or an Alsatian Riesling by Dopff & Irion, Hugel or Trimbach. With the beef serve a full-bodied California Pinot Noir such as one by Acacia, Carneros Creek or Calera, or a French red Burgundy. Conclude with an "Auslese" German Riesling or a slightly sweet California Riesling or Gewurztraminer.

THE RECIPES

Cream of Watercress Soup

8 to 10 servings

1 pound potatoes, peeled and quartered
Boiling salted water

1 cup water
2 bunches watercress, thoroughly washed and dried, stems removed

1 tablespoon minced onion
2 to 3 cups chicken stock or broth (preferably homemade)
1 cup whipping cream *or* half and half
¼ cup (½ stick) butter
Salt and freshly ground pepper
Hot pepper sauce

Cook potatoes in medium saucepan with enough boiling salted water to cover until very tender, about 25 minutes. Drain well and set aside.

In the meantime, bring 1 cup water to boil in large saucepan. Add watercress leaves and cook covered over medium-low heat until tender, about 8 minutes. Drain well.

Transfer watercress to food processor or blender and puree. Add potatoes and minced onion and puree again. Return puree to large saucepan and add remaining ingredients. Bring to boil, reduce heat and simmer 2 minutes. Serve hot immediately.

Consistency of soup may be varied by amount of potato used.

Seafood Quenelles Mousseline

Makes about 18 quenelles

½ pound tiny cooked shrimp
¼ pound scallops
1 egg
1 teaspoon salt
½ teaspoon Beau Monde seasoning
¼ teaspoon freshly grated nutmeg
1½ cups whipping cream
½ cup cornflake crumbs
¼ cup breadcrumbs

Instant flour
Boiling water
Sauce Mousseline (see following recipe)

Place first 6 ingredients in food processor or blender and mix thoroughly. If using processor, with machine running slowly add cream and process until mixture thickens. Add crumbs and continue processing until mixture forms thick paste. If using blender, transfer fish mixture to large bowl. Whip cream separately and gently fold into fish until evenly blended. Add crumbs and mix well to form thick paste. Cover and refrigerate 1 to 2 hours.

Preheat oven to 425°F. Grease large skillet. Generously butter baking dish. On pastry board, flour a circle 8 to 10 inches in diameter. Shape quenelles by dropping a large tablespoon of mixture into center of circle and rolling it back and forth with heel of hand, forming cylinder approximately 1 × 4 inches. Transfer to skillet using spatula. Pour in enough simmering water to allow quenelles to float. Set over medium-low heat and continue simmering gently 3 to 4 minutes. Turn over and cook an additional 3 to 4 minutes. Remove with slotted spoon and drain. Transfer to baking dish and spoon some of sauce over each. Bake 20 to 25 minutes, or until sauce is bubbly.

Sauce Mousseline

Makes about 2 cups

½ cup dry white wine
2 tablespoons chopped fresh shallots or 2
    teaspoons freeze-dried
2 cups bottled or canned clam juice
1 tablespoon tomato paste
1 cup whipping cream
1 cup milk
  Salt and freshly ground pepper

Combine wine and shallots in 2-quart saucepan and simmer 5 minutes. Add clam juice and tomato paste and bring to a boil, stirring occasionally. Continue boiling until reduced to 1 cup. Add cream and milk and reduce to 2 cups, or until slightly thickened, stirring occasionally. Season to taste with salt and pepper. Cool, then cover and refrigerate until ready to use.

Beef Richelieu with Madeira Sauce

4 to 6 servings

Madeira Sauce (see following recipe)

2 pounds potatoes, peeled and shaped into ovals
    approximately 1½ inches in diameter
    Boiling salted water

1 4-pound beef fillet
1 tablespoon oil

12 medium tomatoes
    Salted water

¼ cup (½ stick) butter
12 to 16 whole mushrooms, approximately 1½
    inches in diameter

3 tablespoons butter

Parsley sprigs (garnish)

Prepare Madeira Sauce. *This can be made up to 3 days ahead and refrigerated.*

Preheat oven to 375°F. Cook potatoes in enough boiling salted water to cover until barely tender, about 8 to 12 minutes. Drain well and set aside.

While potatoes are boiling, brown fillet in 1 tablespoon oil in large skillet over high heat. Transfer to roasting pan and bake 25 minutes for rare (meat thermometer should register 125°F to 130°F). When meat is done, remove from oven, cover loosely with foil and keep warm.

While meat is roasting, cook tomatoes in enough salted water to cover over medium-high heat until tender, 5 to 8 minutes. *Do not overcook.* Drain; let cool slightly before peeling. Cover and keep warm.

Melt ¼ cup butter in large skillet over medium-high heat. Add mushrooms and sauté until lightly browned. Remove from skillet and keep warm.

Add remaining 3 tablespoons butter to same skillet and heat over medium-high. Add potatoes and sauté until evenly browned.

To serve, transfer meat to heated platter and surround with vegetables. Degrease pan drippings with paper towel or spoon, add to sauce and reheat. Spoon some of sauce over meat, reserving remainder to pass separately. Garnish with parsley sprigs.

Madeira Sauce

Makes 1¾ cups

1 cup beef broth (preferably homemade)
¼ cup dry Madeira
¼ cup (½ stick) butter
2 tablespoons finely chopped truffles*
2 to 2½ teaspoons arrowroot
  Salt and freshly ground pepper

Combine first 4 ingredients in small saucepan and bring to boil. Reduce heat and simmer 3 minutes. Mix some of sauce with arrowroot and then stir into pan. Continue simmering, stirring frequently, until sauce is consistency of whipping cream, about 20 to 25 minutes. Season with salt and pepper.

*Duxelles may be substituted for truffles.

Chestnut Roll

8 to 10 servings

¾ cup sifted cake flour
1 teaspoon baking powder
¼ teaspoon salt

4 eggs
¾ cup sugar
1 teaspoon vanilla

Powdered sugar

Chestnut-Rum Filling (see following recipe)
Bitter chocolate curls (decoration)

Preheat oven to 400°F. Line bottom of jelly roll pan with well buttered waxed paper or foil. Sift together flour, baking powder and salt. Set aside.

Beat eggs until light and foamy. Continue beat-

Far left: Cake batter for the Chestnut Roll is spread in a jelly roll pan.

Left: Extra Chestnut-Rum Filling tops the finished dessert.

ing, adding sugar gradually, until mixture is thick and at least doubled in volume. Sprinkle dry ingredients over batter and fold gently to combine. Fold in vanilla. Pour into prepared pan and bake 12 to 15 minutes, or until cake is delicately browned and top springs back when lightly touched with fingertip.

Lay large towel flat on a surface, and generously dust with powdered sugar. Loosen cake around edges with knife and turn out onto cloth. Carefully remove paper. Cut off any crisp edges of cake and discard. Beginning on *long* side, gently roll up cake and cloth. (Cloth or towel prevents cake from sticking to itself.) Transfer to rack and cool completely.

When cool, unroll cake and remove towel. Spread top with half of Chestnut-Rum Filling and reroll. Place on serving platter and frost with remaining cream. Decorate with chocolate curls.

Chestnut-Rum Filling

Makes about 3½ cups

  1 **17½-ounce can crème de marrons (chestnut puree)**
  2 **tablespoons dark rum**
  1 **cup whipping cream**

Combine chestnut puree and rum in mixing bowl and blend well. Whip cream separately until soft peaks form. Gently but thoroughly fold into puree.

Make-Ahead French Feast

THE MENU

*Eggplant Tempura-Style with
Red Onion Relish*

Endive-Cress Salad

Boeuf à la Ficelle

Pommes Dauphine

Sautéed Leeks

Gourmandise with Sautéed Pine Nuts

Sorbet au Cabernet with Sliced Kiwi

Langues de Chats

Serves 8

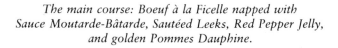

*The main course: Boeuf à la Ficelle napped with
Sauce Moutarde-Bâtarde, Sautéed Leeks, Red Pepper Jelly,
and golden Pommes Dauphine.*

THE STRATEGY

An elegant sit-down dinner with a French spirit. But even a multicourse meal can be easy with a complete party plan. Just follow the instructions in the countdown for spectacular results with a minimum of time and energy. You will be rewarded with a delicious and varied array of dishes—everything from a crisp tempura-style appetizer and refreshing salads, relishes and sorbet to a tender beef roast served with two delectable sauces. Finish with coffee and your favorite chocolates.

Shopping List

3¼- to 3½-pounds well-trimmed fillet of beef
3 quarts beef stock
2 1- to 2-pound eggplants (or 6 to 8 small Japanese eggplants)
3 large tomatoes
1 large green pepper
8 small shallots, plus 6 tablespoons minced
8 small Belgian endive
4 small bunches watercress
1 large red onion (½ needed)
4 onions
4 carrots
4 celery stalks
2 turnips
4 large red bell peppers
2 large potatoes
16 small to medium leeks
2 to 2½ pounds seedless red or green grapes (2½ cups juice)
4 kiwi fruit
2 cups fresh lemon juice
Parsley for garnish
5¼ sticks unsalted butter
½ stick butter
8 gourmandise cheese wedges
12 eggs
2 cups shelled pine nuts
1 cup chopped walnuts
7½ cups sugar
2 cups all purpose flour
1 cup unbleached all purpose flour
Baking powder
Vinegar
Pink peppercorns for garnish (optional)
Vegetable oil plus additional vegetable oil for deep frying

Cottonseed oil for deep frying
Walnut oil
Cider vinegar
Red wine vinegar
White wine vinegar (red wine vinegar can be used)
Salt
Black pepper
Dijon mustard
Whole nutmeg
Vanilla
1 6-ounce bottle liquid pectin
⅔ cup beer
Cabernet Sauvignon
Paraffin for sealing

Special Equipment

Ice cream maker

Tips

The following recipes can be doubled: Endive-Cress Salad, Red Onion Relish, Sauce Moutarde-Bâtarde, Gourmandise with Sautéed Pine Nuts and Langues de Chats.
Recipe for Sautéed Leeks can be halved.
To extract juice from grapes for sorbet, crush fruit in food processor and then squeeze through cheesecloth.

Countdown

1 day ahead
Prepare Red Pepper Jelly.
Prepare Red Onion Relish. Chill.
Prepare batter for Eggplant Tempura-Style to point of adding egg white; chill.
Prepare batter for Pommes Dauphine; cover tightly and refrigerate.
Make Sorbet au Cabernet.
Prepare Sauce Moutarde-Bâtarde; chill.
Clean and slice leeks for Sautéed Leeks.
Cover and refrigerate.
Toast walnuts for Endive-Cress Salad. Store in airtight container.

The ingredients for the sauces, and the fillet of beef suspended over the stock for Boeuf à la Ficelle.

Prepare dressing; cover and chill.

Prepare Langues de Chats. Store at room temperature in airtight container.

Boil stock with vegetables for Boeuf à la Ficelle; cover and chill.

Morning of dinner

Mince shallots for Boeuf à la Ficelle; cover and refrigerate.

Prepare Gourmandise with Sautéed Pine Nuts. Cover and refrigerate.

Peel and slice eggplant for Eggplant Tempura-Style. Set on paper towels.

Day of dinner

Remove fillet for Boeuf à la Ficelle from refrigerator and bring to room temperature.

Steam and cool leeks; chill.

Wash and slice endive and combine with watercress and walnuts; cover and refrigerate.

Slice kiwi fruit for Sorbet au Cabernet; arrange on dessert plates; cover.

2 hours before serving

Complete Eggplant Tempura-Style; set aside and keep warm.

Remove Sauce Moutarde-Bâtarde from refrigerator and bring to room temperature. Reheat and keep warm in top of double boiler set over hot water.

Bring stock to boil for Boeuf.

About 45 minutes before serving

Set first-course and dinner plates on electric hot tray or in low oven.

Have parsley garnish and Red Onion Relish for Eggplant Tempura-Style ready on counter.

Remove gourmandise cheese from refrigerator and set aside.

Steam fillet; remove from pot.

Fry Pommes Dauphine; keep warm.

About 15 minutes before serving

Complete Sautéed Leeks.

Just before serving

Slice meat and keep warm.

Pour dressing over salad and toss.

Wine Suggestions

Serve a stylish, oaky California Chardonnay, such as those made by Jordan, Acacia, William Hill or St. Clement, with the first course. Then an elegant Cabernet Sauvignon, such as the Jordan, Buena Vista or Iron Horse, or a fine red Bordeaux with the beef. Finish with a soft Muscat, a "Late Harvest" Johannisberg Riesling or a Sauternes with dessert.

THE RECIPES

Eggplant Tempura-Style

8 first-course servings

  2 1- to 2-pound eggplants or 6 to 8 small Japanese eggplants, peeled and sliced ⅛ inch thick

Batter
  1 cup all purpose flour
  1 teaspoon baking powder
 ⅔ cup chilled beer
  2 egg yolks, chilled
  1 teaspoon vegetable oil
     Dash of fresh lemon juice

  3 egg whites, room temperature

     Cottonseed oil for deep frying
     Red Onion Relish (see following recipe)
     Parsley sprigs (garnish)

Pat eggplant dry with paper towels.

For batter: Sift flour with baking powder into mixing bowl. Add beer, egg yolks, oil and lemon juice and beat well. *(Batter can be prepared 1 day ahead and chilled.)*

Beat egg whites until peaks form. Fold into batter, blending thoroughly.

Heat oil in skillet or deep fryer to 375°F. Dip eggplant in batter and add to oil. Fry about 3 at a time, turning once, until light golden brown. Remove with slotted spoon or tongs and drain on paper towels. Increase oil temperature to 450°F. Return eggplant in batches and fry until deep golden brown. Drain on paper towels. Serve hot with Red Onion Relish and parsley.

Eggplant can be fried up to 2 hours ahead; keep warm in low oven with door ajar.

The first batch of Eggplant Tempura-Style emerges from the fryer crisped and golden.

Red Onion Relish

Makes about 2 cups

  3 large tomatoes, peeled, seeded and cut into ⅛-inch dice
  1 large green pepper, seeded and cut into ⅛-inch dice
  ½ large red onion, cut into ⅛-inch dice
    Cider vinegar
    Salt and freshly ground pepper

Combine tomato, green pepper and onion in bowl. Add vinegar just to cover and salt and pepper to taste. Chill. *(Can be prepared 1 day ahead.)*

    A few hours before serving, drain well. Serve chilled or at room temperature.

Endive-Cress Salad

8 servings

Dressing
  1 cup walnut oil
  ½ cup red wine vinegar
  6 tablespoons minced shallot
  ¼ cup fresh lemon juice
    Salt and freshly ground pepper

  8 small Belgian endive, sliced crosswise ¼ inch thick
  4 small bunches watercress, tender top part only
  1 cup chopped walnuts, toasted

For dressing: Combine all ingredients for dressing in jar with tight-fitting lid and shake well. *(Can be prepared ahead.)*

    Combine endive, watercress and walnuts and toss lightly. Cover and chill. Just before serving, add dressing to taste and toss gently but thoroughly.

Boeuf à la Ficelle

8 servings

  3 quarts beef stock
  4 onions, quartered
  4 carrots, sliced
  4 celery stalks, sliced
  2 turnips, quartered

  3¼- to 3½-pounds well-trimmed fillet of beef, *room temperature,* securely tied lengthwise and crosswise with string

  8 small shallots, minced (garnish)

    Sauce Moutarde-Bâtarde (see following recipes)
    Red Pepper Jelly (see following recipes)
    Pink peppercorns (optional garnish)

Combine stock, onion, carrot, celery and turnip in large stockpot with side handles. Boil mixture vigorously 30 minutes.

    Tie meat to handles, suspending as closely as possible to broth without actually touching. Cover tightly and let steam until meat thermometer registers 120°F (rare), about 18 to 20 minutes.

    Slip large fork under wrapping strings, then remove meat to platter. Cut strings holding meat. Let rest 5 minutes before carving; *do not remove strings around meat until after it has been carved.* Slice thinly, allowing 2 or 3 slices per serving, or cut into 8 thicker slices. Save juices to moisten each portion. Reassemble slices, wrap with foil and keep warm but serve as soon as possible. Garnish each serving with shallots and accompany with Sauce Moutarde-Bâtarde or Red Pepper Jelly, or both. Sprinkle sauce with pink peppercorns as garnish.

Sauce Moutarde-Bâtarde

8 servings

  1¼ cups (2½ sticks) unsalted butter, cut into small pieces
  6 egg yolks
  ¼ cup fresh lemon juice
    Salt and freshly ground white pepper
  6 to 8 tablespoons Dijon mustard

Combine butter, egg yolks, lemon juice, salt and white pepper with mustard to taste in top of double boiler. Whisk over simmering water until well blended and sauce is warm. *(Can be prepared 1 day ahead and refrigerated, or up to 2 hours before serving and kept warm in double boiler. Cover tightly and stir occasionally with wooden spoon.)*

    If chilled, bring to room temperature and warm in double boiler, whisking constantly. Serve in individual bowls or pass separately in sauceboat.

Red Pepper Jelly

Makes 7 half-pints

  4 large red bell peppers (about), seeded

5½ cups sugar
  ¾ cup vinegar
  ⅓ cup fresh lemon juice
  1 bottle liquid pectin
    Paraffin (for sealing)

Red Pepper Jelly.

Finely chop peppers in processor or run through grinder. Strain, pressing lightly. Measure 2 full cups and ¼ cup pepper juice. Discard remaining juice.

Combine ground peppers, pepper juice, sugar and vinegar in 3- or 4-quart saucepan. Bring to boil, stirring frequently. Remove from heat and let stand 15 minutes. Reheat to boil, stirring frequently. Add lemon juice and return to boil for 1 minute, stirring. Add pectin and let boil 3 minutes, skimming off foam as it accumulates. Pour into jars. Seal with paraffin.

This recipe cannot be doubled.

Pommes Dauphine

8 servings

½ cup (1 stick) plus 1 tablespoon unsalted butter
1 cup cold water
2 teaspoons salt
1 cup all purpose flour
4 eggs
   Freshly grated nutmeg
2 large potatoes (about), cooked and mashed

   Oil for deep frying

Combine butter, water and salt in large saucepan. Place over low heat and stir until butter is melted. Remove from heat and stir in flour. Return to heat and stir constantly to let mixture dry, about 20 seconds. Add eggs 2 at a time and beat on high speed of electric mixer. Season mixture with nutmeg to taste. Measure 2½ cups potatoes and add to mixture, beating well. *(Can be prepared 1 day ahead to this point and refrigerated.)*

Add oil to depth of 3 inches in deep fryer or pot and heat to 375°F. Add potato mixture by small rounded tablespoons and fry until golden brown. Remove with slotted spoon and drain on paper towels. Keep warm on paper towel–lined platter (do not let sides touch) until ready to serve. *Pommes can be cooked 45 minutes ahead.*

Sautéed Leeks

8 servings

16 small to medium leeks, thoroughly rinsed, cut into ½-inch slices (discard tough green stalks)

2 to 4 tablespoons (¼ to ½ stick) unsalted butter

Arrange leeks in steamer basket over boiling water. Cover and steam until tender when pierced with tip of sharp knife, about 7 to 10 minutes. Remove from heat and immediately plunge leeks into ice-cold water.

When ready to serve, drain leeks thoroughly and pat dry with paper towel. Melt butter in large skillet over medium-high heat. Add leeks and sauté until golden, about 5 to 8 minutes.

Gourmandise with Sautéed Pine Nuts

8 servings

¼ cup (½ stick) butter
2 cups shelled pine nuts

8 gourmandise cheese wedges

Melt butter in large skillet over medium-high heat. Add pine nuts and sauté until golden brown. Remove from heat.

Arrange cheese on individual plates and top with sautéed pine nuts.

A pastry bag is used to pipe the Langues de Chats.

Sorbet au Cabernet with Sliced Kiwi

Best made within 24 hours of serving.

Makes about 1 quart

1½ cups sugar
1¼ cups Cabernet Sauvignon
 1 cup water

2½ cups juice from seedless red or green grapes*
   (2 to 2½ pounds grapes)
 1 cup fresh lemon juice, chilled

 4 kiwi fruit, peeled and thinly sliced (garnish)

Combine sugar, wine and water in saucepan and simmer 5 minutes, stirring until sugar is dissolved. Chill.

　　Add grape and lemon juices to syrup. Process in ice-cream maker.

　　Arrange kiwi fruit and scoops of sorbet on individual dessert plates.

*To extract juice from grapes, crush fruit in processor, then squeeze through cheesecloth.

Langues de Chats

Makes about 60 cookies

 ½ cup (1 stick) unsalted butter
 ½ cup sugar
  1 teaspoon vanilla
    Pinch of salt
  2 egg whites
  1 cup unbleached all purpose flour, sifted

Preheat oven to 400°F. Lightly butter baking sheet(s). Dust with flour, shaking off excess. Set aside.

　　Cream butter and sugar in large bowl until light and fluffy. Add vanilla and salt and beat well. Beat in egg whites one at a time. Mix in flour.

　　Spoon mixture into pastry bag fitted with ½-inch plain tip. Holding bag straight up, pipe flat strips onto sheet(s) in 3-inch lengths, spacing 1 inch apart. Bake until edges of cookies are lightly browned, about 5 to 8 minutes.

A Touch of Sophistication

THE MENU

*Shrimp in Mustard Sauce with
Corn Bread Rounds*

Tomato Granité with Pernod

*Medallions of Veal in
Brown Sauce with Port and Ginger*

Paillasson

*Mushroom and Pine Nut Salad
with Raspberry Vinegar Dressing*

Basil Bread

Walnut Tart

Serves 8

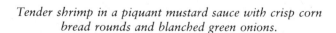

*Tender shrimp in a piquant mustard sauce with crisp corn
bread rounds and blanched green onions.*

THE STRATEGY

A sophisticated menu that combines classic and *nouvelle* French cuisine. While there are some last-minute finishing touches between courses, they involve a minimum amount of time and ensure absolutely the freshest and fullest flavor. The dinner also offers an opportunity to sample some interesting wines to complement the different courses. Top the meal off with an assortment of cheeses.

Shopping List

24 large fresh shrimp (uncooked)
16 3- to 4-ounce medallions of veal (cut ¾ to 1 inch thick)
10 pounds veal or beef bones
16 4-inch-long green onions plus 8 additional for garnish
 2 shallots
 6 ripe tomatoes plus 2 additional for stock
 3 onions
 2 carrots plus additional carrots for 1 cup julienne
 1 leek
 1 celery stalk
 1 head garlic (optional)
 1 head curly endive
 1 head romaine lettuce
 1 head red leaf lettuce
 2 heads Boston or Bibb lettuce
 2 bunches watercress
 1 pound button mushrooms, Japanese tree mushrooms or wild mushrooms
 1 3½-ounce package enoki mushrooms
 1 bunch parsley (stems needed)
   Additional watercress or additional parsley for garnish
   Fresh ginger
   Fresh thyme (2 sprigs) or dried (½ teaspoon)
   Potatoes (2 cups julienne)
   Turnip (1 cup julienne)
   Fresh tarragon (2 teaspoons minced)
   Additional tarragon leaves or parsley leaves for garnish
   Fresh lemon juice
   Fresh chives (⅓ cup minced)
 1 cup milk
4½ sticks butter
 3 sticks unsalted butter
 7 eggs

 8 small wedges Brie
1½ cups buttermilk
3¼ cups whipping cream
 1 cup yellow cornmeal
12 ounces walnuts
 ¾ cup toasted sliced almonds
 ¾ cup pine nuts
 4 cups all purpose flour plus additional flour for kneading
 3 cups pastry flour plus 2 tablespoons pastry flour
 3 cups sugar plus 2 tablespoons sugar
 1 pound semisweet chocolate
 ¾ cup walnut oil
 ⅓ cup raspberry vinegar
 2 bay leaves
   Baking soda
   Dried basil
   Moutarde de Meaux (coarsely ground French mustard)
   Oil
   Salt
   Black pepper
   Whole black peppercorns
   Fresh nutmeg
   Cream of tartar
1½ cups tomato juice
   Tomato paste
 2 cups dry red wine (optional for stock)
   Dry white wine or vermouth
   Pernod (anise liqueur)
   Port

Special Equipment

Electric mixer with dough hook

Tips

Accompany main course with lemon baskets filled with chopped blanched spinach and garnished with thin slivers of lemon peel.

Countdown

1 month ahead
Prepare Brown Stock for veal sauce and freeze.

Crisp vegetables, fresh pink shrimp and tangy French mustard are some of the ingredients for the first course.

Bake Basil Bread and freeze.

Assemble Walnut Tart to point of adding ganache; let cool, wrap tightly and freeze.

3 weeks ahead

Make ganache. Cover and refrigerate.

1 day ahead

Prepare Tomato Granité with Pernod to point noted in recipe.

Bake corn bread for Corn Bread Rounds (do not cut). Wrap tightly and store at room temperature.

Remove Brown Stock from freezer and let thaw in refrigerator overnight.

Remove Basil Bread from freezer and let thaw in refrigerator overnight.

Remove Walnut Tart from freezer and let thaw in refrigerator overnight.

Morning of dinner

Remove ganache from refrigerator and let stand at room temperature.

Remove Walnut Tart from refrigerator and let stand at room temperature.

Cut vegetables for Paillasson into julienne. Set aside in bowl of ice water to prevent potato from darkening; add more ice to bowl occasionally as other cubes melt.

Combine all lettuce leaves and watercress for salad in large bowl and refrigerate.

Afternoon of dinner

Finish Walnut Tart and return to refrigerator.

About 1 hour before serving

Assemble granité on plates and refrigerate to soften.

Begin Paillasson.

About 30 minutes before serving

Place Paillasson in oven to bake.

Cut corn bread into rounds of desired size and place in low oven to warm.

Warm Basil Bread in low oven with Corn Bread Rounds.

About 15 minutes before serving

Prepare shrimp mixture for first course; toast Corn Bread Rounds at this time if desired.

Between first courses and main course

Prepare veal (veal and sauce should only take about 20 minutes total).

Between main course and salad course

Finish salad (about 15 minutes total assembly time).

Remove Walnut Tart from refrigerator and let stand at room temperature until dessert time.

Wine Suggestions

With the shrimp dish serve a crisp, elegant Chardonnay, such as those made by Vichon, Villa Mt. Eden or Monticello, or a white Meursault from Burgundy. With the veal the appropriate wine would be a well-bred California Cabernet Sauvignon or a 1975 or 1979 Bordeaux from a classified chateau. Wind up with a crisp brut or mature Champagne.

THE RECIPES

Shrimp in Mustard Sauce with Corn Bread Rounds

8 servings

 16 4-inch-long green onions

  2 tablespoons oil (or more)
 24 uncooked large fresh shrimp

  2 shallots, minced
 ½ cup dry white wine or vermouth
 ½ cup whipping cream
  1 cup (2 sticks) unsalted butter, cut into small pieces
  2 tablespoons coarsely ground French mustard (Moutarde de Meaux)
     Salt and freshly ground pepper
     Fresh lemon juice

  8 4-inch Corn Bread Rounds (see following recipe)
 ⅓ cup minced fresh chives
  8 2-inch Corn Bread Rounds (optional garnish)
  8 green onions, cut into 5-inch lengths, green ends feathered (garnish)

Blanch 4-inch onions in large saucepan of boiling salted water until crisp-tender, about 3 to 4 minutes. Drain onions well and keep warm.

Shell and devein shrimp. Heat 2 tablespoons oil in heavy large skillet over high heat until very hot. Add shrimp in batches and stir-fry 1 to 2 minutes (shrimp should be slightly undercooked). Remove from skillet using slotted spoon and set aside.

Reduce heat to medium, add more oil to skillet if necessary and sauté shallots 30 seconds. Pour in wine, scraping up any browned bits. Stir in cream. Cook until mixture thickens and coats back of spoon, about 4 to 5 minutes. Reduce heat to low. Gradually whisk in butter; then whisk in mustard *(do not boil)*. Add salt, pepper and lemon juice.

To serve, arrange one 4-inch corn bread round on each of 8 heated plates. Top each round with 2 blanched green onions and 3 shrimp. Nap each with sauce and sprinkle with chives. Garnish with one 2-inch corn bread round and one 5-inch green onion. Serve immediately.

Corn Bread Rounds

8 servings

  1 cup sour milk
  1 teaspoon baking soda
  1 cup all purpose flour
  1 cup yellow cornmeal
  1 teaspoon salt
  2 eggs
  2 tablespoons (¼ stick) unsalted butter, melted

Position rack in lower third of oven and preheat to 450°F. Butter 11 × 17-inch shallow baking pan.

Mix sour milk and soda in small bowl. Combine flour, cornmeal and salt in processor or blender and mix well. With machine running, pour in sour milk, then add eggs and melted butter, blending until just combined. Pour batter into prepared pan, smoothing top. Bake until bread shrinks away from sides of pan and springs back when lightly touched, 10 to 14 minutes. Transfer to rack and cool in pan. Cut bread into eight 4-inch rounds and eight 2-inch rounds.

For sour milk, pour 2 tablespoons vinegar into bottom of 1-cup measure. Fill with milk and stir lightly. Let stand at room temperature until curdled, about 10 minutes.

Bread rounds can be reheated in low oven or crisply toasted before serving.

Tomato Granité with Pernod

8 servings

  6 ripe tomatoes, peeled, cored, seeded, chopped and pureed
  2 egg whites
 1½ cups tomato juice
 ¼ cup fresh lemon juice
  2 tablespoons Pernod
  1 tablespoon tomato paste
  2 teaspoons minced fresh tarragon
 ⅛ to ¼ teaspoon salt

     Fresh tarragon leaves or parsley leaves (garnish)

Combine pureed tomatoes, egg whites, tomato juice, lemon juice, Pernod, tomato paste, tarragon and ⅛ teaspoon salt in medium bowl and blend well. Taste and add more salt and fresh lemon juice as desired. Cover and freeze until granité is hard and icy.

Mushroom and Pine Nut Salad, Basil Bread and assorted cheeses follow the main course.

Let granité thaw slightly at room temperature; then scoop 16 granité balls onto baking sheet. Refreeze at least 1 hour. *(Granité can be prepared 1 day ahead to this point.)*

About 1 hour before serving, arrange tarragon or parsley in nests in 8 serving dishes. Top each with 2 scoops of granité. Refrigerate to soften; serve.

Medallions of Veal in Brown Sauce with Port and Ginger

Lemon baskets filled with chopped blanched spinach and lemon peel are a perfect accompaniment to this dish.

8 servings

Veal
16 3- to 4-ounce medallions of veal, cut ¾ to
    1 inch thick
    Salt and freshly ground pepper
2 tablespoons vegetable oil
4 tablespoons (½ stick) unsalted butter

Brown Sauce
1 cup Port
3 cups Brown Stock (see following recipe)
2 teaspoons freshly grated ginger or to taste
    Salt and freshly ground pepper

    Watercress or parsley (garnish)

For veal: Season each medallion on both sides with salt and pepper. Heat oil and 1 tablespoon butter in large skillet over medium-high heat. Add veal (in batches if necessary; do not crowd) and sauté until medium rare, about 1 to 2 minutes per side. Transfer to heated platter and keep warm.

For brown sauce: Discard any fat in skillet. Add Port to skillet, scraping up any browned bits. Place over medium-high heat and reduce to syrupy glaze. Stir in Brown Stock and ginger and reduce by half. Strain into saucepan. Place over medium heat and cook 1 minute. Whisk in remaining 3 tablespoons butter. Season with salt and pepper.

To serve, nap heated individual plates with sauce. Arrange 2 medallions on each plate. Garnish with watercress or parsley and serve with remaining sauce.

Brown Stock

Makes 3 to 4 quarts

10 pounds veal or beef bones
 3 onions, unpeeled and halved

 2 carrots, scrubbed and cut into 2 or 3 pieces
 2 tomatoes, halved
 2 bay leaves
 2 sprigs fresh thyme or ½ teaspoon dried,
    crumbled
 1 leek, washed thoroughly and cut into thirds
 1 celery stalk, cut into thirds
 1 head garlic, halved horizontally (optional)
 1 tablespoon peppercorns
    Stems from 1 bunch parsley
 2 cups (or more) dry red wine or water

Preheat oven to 500°F. Arrange bones and onion in large roasting pan. Roast, turning 2 or 3 times, until golden brown, about 90 minutes. Set aside.

Combine carrots, tomatoes, bay leaves, thyme,

leek, celery, garlic, peppercorns and parsley stems in large stockpot. Add browned onions and bones. Discard fat from roasting pan, add 2 cups red wine or water and cook over high heat, scraping up any browned bits, about 3 minutes. Add wine mixture to stockpot with enough water to cover by 1 or 2 inches. Bring mixture to boil over high heat. Reduce heat to low and simmer 20 to 30 minutes, skimming foam from surface. Continue simmering at least 8 hours (preferably up to 24), adding more water to stockpot as necessary to keep bones covered.

Pour stock through cheesecloth-lined strainer set over large saucepan. Let cool, skimming off fat as it accumulates. Place stock over medium heat and cook until thickened and full-bodied in flavor, about 1 hour. Let cool. Cover and refrigerate (or freeze) until ready to use.

Paillasson

8 servings

 2 cups potato julienne
 1 cup turnip julienne, blanched
 1 cup carrot julienne
 ¼ cup (½ stick) melted butter
 ½ teaspoon salt or to taste
 ¼ teaspoon freshly ground pepper
    Pinch of freshly grated nutmeg

Preheat oven to 450°F. Combine all ingredients in large bowl and mix well. Turn into 10-inch nonstick skillet, pressing evenly with back of spoon. Cook over medium heat until bottom of vegetables begins to brown, about 10 minutes. Transfer to oven and bake until tender, about 25 to 30 minutes. Invert onto platter and serve.

Mushroom and Pine Nut Salad with Raspberry Vinegar Dressing

8 servings

    Tender inner leaves of 1 head *each* curly endive, romaine and red leaf lettuce, washed and patted dry
    Tender inner leaves of 2 heads Boston or Bibb lettuce, washed and patted dry
 2 bunches watercress, washed, stemmed and patted dry
 ¾ cup walnut oil
 1 pound button mushrooms, Japanese tree mushrooms or wild mushrooms, cleaned, trimmed and patted dry
 ¾ cup pine nuts
 1 3½-ounce package enoki mushrooms
 ⅓ cup raspberry vinegar
    Salt and freshly ground pepper
 8 small wedges of Brie (garnish)
    Basil Bread (see following recipe)

Toss lettuce leaves and watercress in large bowl and set aside. Heat ½ cup walnut oil in large skillet or sauté pan over medium heat. Add button, Japanese or wild mushrooms and sauté until golden, about 5 minutes. Add pine nuts and cook until golden, about 5 minutes. Stir in enoki mushrooms. Pour mixture over lettuce and toss.

Return skillet to medium heat, add remaining ¼ cup oil with raspberry vinegar, salt and pepper and mix well. Cook briefly to heat through. Pour over salad and toss again. Taste and adjust seasoning, adding more oil and vinegar as desired. Divide evenly among 8 serving plates. Garnish each with wedge of cheese and slice of Basil Bread. Serve salad warm.

Basil Bread

Makes one 7- or 8-inch round loaf

 3 cups all purpose flour
 1½ teaspoons baking soda
 ½ to 1 teaspoon dried basil, crumbled or to taste (do not use fresh)
 ½ teaspoon salt
 ¼ teaspoon freshly ground pepper
 2 tablespoons (¼ stick) melted unsalted butter
 1½ cups buttermilk

    Flour

Preheat oven to 450°F. Generously butter 7 (or 8) × 3-inch round pan and set aside. Combine flour, baking soda, basil, salt and pepper in large bowl of electric mixer fitted with dough hook. Mix at medium speed several seconds just to blend. Form well in center of mixture and pour in melted butter. With mixer at medium speed, slowly pour in buttermilk and blend, stopping once or twice to scrape down sides of bowl. Continue mixing until dough comes away from sides of bowl and wraps around hook, about 10 minutes (dough will be quite soft).

Turn dough out onto floured surface and knead until smooth. Shape into round loaf. Transfer dough to prepared pan. Sprinkle top generously with flour to form crust. Bake until golden brown, about 35 to 40 minutes. Transfer to rack to cool.

Walnut Tart

Tart can be baked and frozen (without ganache) one month ahead. Ganache can be prepared three weeks ahead and refrigerated until ready to use.

10 to 12 servings

Ganache
   2 **cups whipping cream**
   1 **pound semisweet chocolate, cut or shaved into very small pieces**

Sugar Dough
   1 **cup plus 2 tablespoons (2¼ sticks) butter, room temperature**
   ½ **cup plus 2 tablespoons sugar**
   2 **eggs**
   3 **cups plus 2 tablespoons pastry flour**
   Pinch of salt

Caramel Filling
2½ **cups sugar**
   1 **cup plus 3 tablespoons water**
   ¼ **teaspoon cream of tartar**
   ¾ **cup whipping cream, room temperature**
   12 **ounces walnuts, coarsely chopped**
   7 **ounces (1¾ sticks) butter, cut into small pieces**

   1 **egg, lightly beaten**

   ¾ **cup toasted sliced almonds**

For ganache: Bring whipping cream to rapid boil in medium saucepan over medium-high heat. Meanwhile, add chocolate pieces to medium bowl. Pour hot cream over chocolate in slow steady stream, stirring constantly until chocolate is melted and mixture is well blended. Refrigerate until well chilled.

For dough: Cream butter with sugar in large bowl until light and fluffy. Add eggs one at a time, beating after each addition. Add flour and salt and stir until mixed. (Dough will be thick and soft.) Wrap dough in plastic and chill at least 30 minutes.

For filling: Combine sugar, water and cream of tartar in medium saucepan, swirling to mix. Bring to boil over high heat and cook without stirring until syrup is rich medium brown and candy thermometer registers 334°F, washing down any crystals on sides of pan with brush dipped in cold water. Remove from heat and let stand 15 seconds. Add whipping cream (mixture will bubble up), swirling saucepan gently until foam subsides; *do not stir.* Gently stir in walnuts. Place butter pieces over mixture and let melt, about 5 minutes. Gently stir in melted butter until just combined. Transfer mixture to large bowl and let cool (or place bowl in ice water and stir until cool).

To assemble: Divide dough in half. Roll half of dough into circle ⅜ inch thick. Press into 9 × 1½-inch round cake pan or 10 × 1-inch tart pan with sloping sides, allowing slight overlap. Pour caramel filling over dough to ¾ full. Brush edges of pastry with beaten egg. Roll remaining dough into circle ⅜ inch thick and arrange over caramel. Roll across pastry with rolling pin to seal edges completely; trim excess pastry. Chill tart 5 minutes before baking.

Position rack in lower third of oven and preheat to 400°F. Bake tart until golden brown, about 40 to 45 minutes. Invert onto baking sheet. If too light in color (tart should be light golden on bottom), return to pan and bake 5 to 10 more minutes. Invert onto serving platter and let cool completely. Bring ganache to room temperature.

Transfer ganache to medium saucepan and swirl over medium heat to remove any chill, about 5 seconds; then pour over cooled tart, letting ganache run over sides. Using spatula, touch up any unglazed areas on sides of tart by gently lifting small amount of ganache from platter and barely pressing onto unglazed area. Carefully press nuts around sides of tart and refrigerate. Let tart stand at room temperature for 30 minutes before serving.

For Special Occasions

THE MENU

Kir Royale with Raspberries

Veal Meatballs with Caper Mayonnaise

Velouté of Fennel

Shrimp Salad with Mushrooms

Minted Pink Grapefruit Ice

Noisettes of Lamb Florentine

Potato Cauliflower Puree

Cardamom Carrots

Ricotta Almond Torte

Serves 8

An elegant setting for an equally elegant main course—Noisettes of Lamb Florentine, Cardamom Carrots, and Potato Cauliflower Puree.

THE STRATEGY

Individual servings of lamb Florentine provide the focal point for this delicious dinner. The party begins with tall glasses of Champagne tinted with crème de cassis and garnished with fresh raspberries. Veal Meatballs with a tangy Caper Mayonnaise accompany the drinks. A smooth Velouté of Fennel begins the dinner. Shrimp tossed in a lively vinaigrette precedes a refreshing grapefruit ice and is followed by the main course, served with a suave potato puree and cardamom-scented carrots. A creamy Ricotta Almond Torte topped with chocolate leaves provides the rich finishing touch.

Shopping List

- ⅔ pound ground veal
- 3 sweet Italian sausages (about 12 ounces)
- 8 cups chicken stock (preferably homemade)
- 20 large shrimp (or 1 to 1½ pounds fresh crabmeat)
- 8 noisettes of lamb (each about 1¼ inches thick), cut from rib chops or sirloin (see recipe footnote)
- Anchovy paste
- 1¼ pounds cauliflower
- 1 medium boiling potato
- 2 pounds carrots
- 1 small orange (1½ tablespoons grated peel)
- 1 small red onion (3 tablespoons finely minced)
- 6 large heads fennel
- 16 snow peas
- 10 large white mushrooms
- 1 cup (½ pint) raspberries
- 2 very large pink or white grapefruit plus additional grapefruit sections for garnish
- 2 pounds fresh spinach
- 1 garlic clove
- 8 lettuce leaves
- Lemon (slices for garnish)
- Fresh lemon juice
- Fresh lime juice
- Cherry tomatoes
- Parsley plus additional parsley for garnish
- Chopped fresh dill or dried dillweed
- Fresh chives for garnish
- Mint leaves for garnish
- 2¾ cups ricotta cheese

- 1 cup crème fraîche or lightly whipped cream
- 2¼ cups whipping cream
- 5 sticks unsalted butter
- 8 eggs
- Parmesan cheese
- 3 ¾-inch slices Italian bread
- 8 slices good quality white bread plus white bread to make 1 cup breadcrumbs
- 20 whole almonds for garnish
- 1¾ cups ground almonds
- ½ cup chopped unsalted macadamia nuts
- 2 cups sugar
- 3 ounces semisweet chocolate plus 3 tablespoons grated
- 2 cups olive oil
- ¼ cup green peppercorns
- 4 cardamom pods
- Corn oil
- All purpose flour
- Capers
- Salt
- Black pepper
- White pepper
- Fresh nutmeg
- Vanilla
- Dijon mustard
- 2 to 3 bottles brut Champagne
- Crème de cassis
- White or green crème de menthe
- Crème de cacao
- Amaretto liqueur
- Dry vermouth
- Camellia or other waxy leaves

Countdown

3 days ahead
Prepare Ricotta Almond Torte to point of adding chocolate leaves. Cover and freeze.

1 day ahead
Mix Caper Mayonnaise and refrigerate.
Make Velouté of Fennel to point noted in recipe and refrigerate.
Mix vinaigrette for shrimp salad and refrigerate.
Poach shrimp for salad and refrigerate.
Blanch snow peas for salad and refrigerate.
Prepare grapefruit mixture for ice and freeze.
Assemble chocolate leaves for dessert garnish and refrigerate or freeze.

Blend Potato Cauliflower Puree to point noted in recipe. Turn into saucepan, cover and refrigerate.

Morning of dinner
Mix veal mixture for meatballs. Cover and refrigerate.
Make croutons for main course. Set aside at room temperature.
Prepare Cardamom Carrots to point noted in recipe and set aside.

About 1½ hours before serving
Mix grapefruit ice in processor and refreeze.

About 30 minutes before serving
Shape meatballs and fry; transfer to 200°F oven.
Rewarm croutons in same low oven with meatballs.
Finish shrimp salad to point of adding vinaigrette.
Place raspberries in Champagne glasses.

Just before serving
Cook spinach for lamb and set aside.
Sauté lamb, transfer to heated platter and keep warm.
Toss shrimp salad with vinaigrette.
Let grapefruit ice soften at room temperature 10 minutes.
Reheat carrots.

Reheat Potato Cauliflower Puree.

As guests arrive
Place velouté over low heat and bring to simmer.
Prepare Kir Royale individually.
Remove torte from freezer and let soften in refrigerator until dessert time.
Arrange meatballs on platter with Caper Mayonnaise.

Between appetizer and soup course
Finish velouté with egg yolks and cream.

Between first course and main course
Finish sauce for lamb and assemble entrées on individual plates.

Just before dessert
Peel leaves from chocolate and arrange atop torte.

Wine Suggestions

Serve a crisp, young Chardonnay or Sauvignon Blanc with the shrimp salad. Follow that with a mature California Cabernet Sauvignon, a fine 1974, 1975 or 1978, or a 1970, 1971 or 1975 Bordeaux from a classified chateau. With dessert serve a well-chilled Asti Spumante or an "Auslese" German Riesling.

THE RECIPES

Kir Royale with Raspberries

16 to 24 servings

  1 cup raspberries
  ¼ cup crème de cassis
  2 to 3 bottles brut Champagne, well chilled

For each serving, place 2 to 3 raspberries in Champagne glass. Add ½ teaspoon crème de cassis to each. Pour Champagne over and serve.

Veal Meatballs with Caper Mayonnaise

Makes about 5 dozen meatballs

  ⅔ pound ground veal
  3 sweet Italian sausages, casings removed (about 12 ounces)

  3 ¾-inch slices stale Italian bread, moistened and squeezed dry
  2 eggs
  ¼ cup freshly grated Parmesan cheese
  3 tablespoons minced fresh parsley
  ½ teaspoon salt
  ¼ teaspoon freshly grated nutmeg
    Freshly ground pepper

  1 cup very fine stale white breadcrumbs
    Olive oil
    Lemon slices
    Parsley sprigs
    Cherry tomatoes
    Caper Mayonnaise (see following recipe)

Combine veal, sausage, Italian bread, eggs, Parmesan, parsley, salt, nutmeg and freshly ground pepper in processor and mix using on/off turns just until well combined; *do not overprocess*. Refrigerate at least 1 hour.

Shape mixture into 1-inch balls. Roll in crumbs. Pour olive oil into heavy large skillet to depth of ½ inch and heat over medium-high heat until very hot (400°F). Add meatballs in batches and fry until golden brown on all sides, about 5 minutes. Remove with slotted spoon and drain on paper towels. *(Meatballs can be prepared ahead and kept warm in 200°F oven for 30 minutes.)* Arrange on serving platter. Garnish with lemon slices, parsley and tomatoes. Pass mayonnaise separately.

Caper Mayonnaise

About 1¾ cups

1½ **cups olive oil**
2 **egg yolks, room temperature**
1 **tablespoon fresh lemon juice**
2 **tablespoons capers, well drained**
1 **to 2 tablespoons anchovy paste**
  Salt and freshly ground pepper

Combine 3 tablespoons olive oil, egg yolks and lemon juice in processor. Blend using on/off turns until mixture thickens slightly. With machine running, pour remaining oil through feed tube in thin stream (mayonnaise will thicken as oil is added). Stir in capers and 1 tablespoon anchovy paste. Taste and add remaining anchovy paste if desired. Season with salt and pepper.

Velouté of Fennel

8 servings

4 **tablespoons (½ stick) unsalted butter**
6 **large heads fennel, trimmed and thinly sliced**

6 **tablespoons (¾ stick) unsalted butter**
6 **tablespoons all purpose flour**
8 **cups chicken stock, preferably homemade**

4 **egg yolks**
¾ **cup whipping cream**
  Salt and freshly ground pepper
  Chopped fresh chives (garnish)

Melt 4 tablespoons butter in large skillet over medium heat. Add fennel, cover and slowly braise until completely softened and lightly browned, stirring occasionally, about 30 minutes. Puree in processor.

Melt remaining butter in large heavy saucepan over medium-low heat. Add flour and stir with wooden spoon until flour is cooked but still light in color, about 15 minutes. Slowly add stock to flour mixture, beating constantly. Bring to boil. Reduce heat to low and simmer gently 30 minutes. Stir in fennel. Pass soup through fine strainer, if desired. *(Can be prepared ahead.)*

Just before serving, bring soup to simmer. Combine egg yolks and cream in small bowl and beat well. *Gradually* add about 1 cup stock to yolk mixture, beating constantly. Slowly blend yolk mixture back into remaining stock. (Be careful not to let soup boil or eggs will curdle.) Season to taste with salt and pepper. Garnish with chives.

If fennel is unavailable, substitute 1 pound celery and 1 tablespoon fennel seed.

Shrimp Salad with Mushrooms

8 servings

20 **large shrimp, shelled and deveined (tails intact)***
   Court bouillon for poaching (about 6 to 8 cups)

16 **snow peas**

10 **large white mushrooms, cleaned and thinly sliced**

½ **cup chopped unsalted macadamia nuts**
3 **tablespoons finely minced red onion**
  Vinaigrette (see following recipe)
8 **lettuce leaves**

Poach shrimp in gently simmering court bouillon until pink, about 3 minutes. Transfer shrimp to bowl using slotted spoon. Let shrimp cool to room temperature, then refrigerate.

Carefully slice 8 largest shrimp in half lengthwise down through tails. Reserve for garnish. Slice remaining shrimp in medallions crosswise, discarding tails. Blanch snow peas in boiling salted water for 2 to 3 minutes. Drain well and pat dry with paper towels. Cut each pod diagonally into 3 pieces.

Combine shrimp, snow peas, mushrooms, macadamia nuts and onion in large bowl. Add vinaigrette to taste and toss gently. Arrange lettuce leaves on individual plates. Mound salad in center. Garnish each serving with 2 reserved shrimp halves. Pass any remaining vinaigrette separately.

*1 to 1½ pounds fresh crabmeat can be substituted for shrimp.

Vinaigrette

About 1½ cups

- **2 tablespoons Dijon mustard**
- **¼ cup lime juice or to taste**
- **2 tablespoons chopped fresh dill or 2 teaspoons dried dillweed**
- **½ cup (8 tablespoons) olive oil**
- **½ cup (8 tablespoons) vegetable or corn oil**
- **Salt and freshly ground pepper**

Combine mustard and ¼ cup lime juice in small bowl and mix well. Add chopped dill. Add oils 1 tablespoon at a time, whisking well after each addition. Add more lime juice if desired. Season to taste with salt and pepper.

Minted Pink Grapefruit Ice

8 servings

- **⅔ cup sugar**
- **2 very large pink grapefruit,* peeled and sectioned (membrane removed)**
- **5 tablespoons white crème de menthe or 2 tablespoons green crème de menthe**
- **¼ cup water**

  Grapefruit sections (garnish)
  Mint leaves (garnish)

Combine sugar, grapefruit, crème de menthe and water in processor and puree (you should have about 3 cups). Let stand 30 minutes. Transfer to shallow glass dish and freeze 4 to 24 hours (mixture must be frozen solid).

Transfer frozen fruit mixture to processor and process with on/off turns until smooth. Return to shallow dish and refreeze 1 to 1½ hours. Let stand at room temperature about 10 minutes before serving to soften slightly. Scoop into bowls and garnish with grapefruit sections and mint leaves.

*White grapefruit can be substituted.

Noisettes of Lamb Florentine

8 servings

Croutons
8 slices good quality white bread, cut into 3-inch circles (use beverage glass or cookie cutter)
½ cup (1 stick) unsalted butter, melted

Spinach
2 pounds fresh spinach, stemmed, washed and lightly shaken
Pinch of salt
¼ cup (½ stick) unsalted butter
1 garlic clove, finely minced

Lamb
3 tablespoons unsalted butter
1½ tablespoons vegetable oil or corn oil
8 noisettes of lamb, about 1¼ inches thick, patted dry*
Salt and freshly ground pepper

Sauce
¾ cup dry vermouth
1 cup whipping cream
¼ cup green peppercorns, rinsed and drained
Parsley (garnish)

For croutons: Preheat oven to 350°F. Brush both sides of bread circles with melted butter. Arrange on baking sheet. Bake until browned, about 10 to 12 minutes on each side. Keep warm.

For spinach: Combine spinach and salt in heavy large casserole or Dutch oven over medium heat and cook until tender, about 5 to 7 minutes. Transfer to strainer and drain, but do not squeeze. Melt ¼ cup butter in casserole over medium-high heat. Add garlic and shake several seconds. Add spinach and sauté, stirring occasionally, 2 more minutes. Season with salt. Remove from heat and set aside.

For lamb: Heat 3 tablespoons butter with oil in heavy large skillet over medium-high heat until foaming. Add noisettes and cook, turning once, about 5

to 6 minutes on each side for medium rare. Season generously with salt and pepper. Transfer noisettes to heated platter and keep warm.

For sauce: Discard fat from skillet. Pour vermouth into skillet, stirring up any browned bits. Boil until liquid is reduced by half. Add cream and peppercorns, crushing peppercorns with back of spoon. Boil sauce until thickened.

To assemble: Arrange croutons on individual plates. Stir spinach 1 minute over high heat to reheat. Divide spinach evenly over croutons. Place noisettes over spinach. Top each with generous tablespoon sauce. Garnish with parsley and serve.

*Have butcher prepare noisettes from 2 rib chops, well trimmed and tied together. If necessary, noisettes can be prepared from sirloin. Remove all fat and tie into neat circle. Each noisette should weigh about ⅓ pound. Flatten noisettes slightly with palm of hand before cooking.

Potato Cauliflower Puree

8 servings

1¼ pounds cauliflower (with 2 inches of stem), broken into small pieces
1 medium boiling potato, peeled and cut into ½- to ¾-inch dice
½ cup whipping cream
½ cup freshly grated Parmesan cheese
3 tablespoons unsalted butter
⅛ teaspoon freshly ground white pepper
Large pinch of freshly grated nutmeg
Salt

Steam cauliflower with potatoes until soft, about 12 minutes. Transfer to processor. Add cream, cheese, butter, pepper and nutmeg and mix until completely smooth. Season with salt to taste. *(Can be prepared ahead to this point and reheated.)*

Cardamom Carrots

8 servings

2 pounds carrots, sliced ¼ inch thick
¼ cup (½ stick) unsalted butter
1½ tablespoons freshly grated orange peel
4 cardamom pods, hulled and seeds pounded in mortar
Salt

Steam carrot slices just until tender, about 5 to 7 minutes; *do not overcook.* Melt butter in heavy large

Ricotta Almond Torte: Ricotta filling is sweetened with grated chocolate.

The filled torte will be chilled until firm.

Chocolate leaves and caramel-dipped almonds decorate the finished torte.

skillet over medium heat. Add carrot, orange peel and cardamom and cook, stirring occasionally, 2 to 3 minutes. Season with salt to taste. *(Can be prepared ahead and reheated over low heat.)* Turn into dish and serve immediately.

Ricotta Almond Torte

8 servings

Toasted Almond Crust
1¾ cups ground toasted almonds
 ¼ cup sugar
 ¼ cup (½ stick) unsalted butter, melted and cooled

⅔ cup sugar
 ¼ cup water
20 whole almonds (garnish)

Ricotta Filling
2¾ cups ricotta cheese
 ¼ cup plus 2 tablespoons sugar
 1 tablespoon crème de cacao
 1 tablespoon amaretto liqueur
 1 teaspoon vanilla
 1 cup crème fraîche *or* lightly whipped cream
 3 tablespoons grated chocolate

Chocolate Leaves
 3 ounces (about) semisweet chocolate
 1 teaspoon butter

Camellia or other waxy leaves

For crust: Preheat oven to 375°F. Butter 9-inch springform pan. Grease small baking sheet. Combine ground almonds, ¼ cup sugar and butter in large bowl and mix. Press almond mixture into bottom and sides of prepared pan. Bake 10 minutes. Cool.

Combine ⅔ cup sugar and water in small heavy saucepan and cook over low heat until sugar is dissolved. Increase heat to medium-high and cook until caramelized (mixture should be rich medium brown). Remove from heat and quickly dip and swirl whole almonds in caramel. Transfer to prepared baking sheet. Set aside for garnish. Quickly pour remaining syrup over crust. Let cool about 30 minutes.

For filling: Combine ricotta, sugar, crème de cacao, amaretto and vanilla in processor and blend until smooth and creamy; *do not overprocess.* Gently blend in crème fraîche. Fold in chocolate. Transfer to prepared crust. Freeze torte for at least 2 hours.*

For leaves: Melt chocolate and butter in top of double boiler. Stir until smooth. Using spoon or spatula, generously coat underside of leaves. Refrigerate or freeze until firm.

Just before serving, loosen crust from pan using sharp knife; remove springform. Gently peel leaves from chocolate, starting at stem end. Arrange leaves and reserved almonds on top.

*If frozen over 2 hours, torte may need to be softened in refrigerator before serving.

Stylish Celebration

THE MENU

Champagne Framboise

Anchovy Puffs

Carrot Soup

*Crown Roast of Lamb with
Wild Rice,
Lamb Meatballs
and Glazed May Apples*

Green Vegetable Medley

Assorted Cheeses

Sage Bread

Green Grape Tart

Chocolate Torte

Serves 8

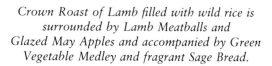

*Crown Roast of Lamb filled with wild rice is
surrounded by Lamb Meatballs and
Glazed May Apples and accompanied by Green
Vegetable Medley and fragrant Sage Bread.*

THE STRATEGY

A colorful selection of springtime dishes—light yet satisfying—all come together with style in this elegant menu. A spectacular crown roast of lamb filled with wild rice, surrounded by lamb meatballs and wreathed with bay leaves is the focal point. A smooth carrot soup, a sauté of fresh vegetables, fragrant sage bread and glazed apples round out the main course. Green Grape Tart and rich Chocolate Torte are the two delectable desserts.

Shopping List

    6 cups (or more) chicken stock
    1 7- to 8-pound crown roast of lamb
    2 pounds ground lamb
    1 2-ounce tube anchovy paste
    2 pounds carrots
    2 large onions
    2 potatoes (about 1 pound total)
    5 shallots
    2 lemons (2 tablespoons finely grated peel plus peel of one whole lemon)
   16 May apples or other small baking apples
    3 pounds fresh green peas (about 3 cups shelled)
    1 pound snow peas
    3 very large cucumbers
    2 garlic cloves
      Seedless green grapes
      Parsley for garnish
      Fresh lemon juice
    1 cup small curd cottage cheese
    8 eggs
  4½ sticks unsalted butter plus additional butter for cake pan
    1 3-ounce package cream cheese
      Wild rice for garnish
    1 cup breadcrumbs
    4 ounces slivered almonds
   ½ cup almonds plus 2 tablespoons ground
    5 cups all purpose flour plus additional for cake pans
 1⅓ cups sugar
    1 bay leaf plus additional bay leaves for decoration
    1 envelope dry yeast
  9½ ounces German's Sweet Chocolate
      Soy sauce

Dijon mustard
Dried rosemary
Dried sage
Ground marjoram
Baking soda
Lard (optional)
Red food coloring
Solid vegetable shortening
Cream of tartar
Olive oil
Salt
Black pepper
1½ cups apple cider
  1 cup currant jelly
 ½ cup apricot preserves
  1 16-ounce can whole raspberries in heavy syrup
  1 to 2 bottles Champagne
    Framboise (raspberry brandy)
    Grand Marnier

Tips

The following recipes can be doubled: Champagne Framboise, Anchovy Puffs, Carrot Soup, Lamb Meatballs, Glazed May Apples, Green Vegetable Medley and Sage Bread (prepare dough in two batches).

Countdown

1 month ahead
Prepare pastry for tart crust and freeze.
Prepare Sage Bread and freeze.

2 days ahead
Divide raspberries and syrup among ice cube trays and freeze.

1 day ahead
Remove pastry for tart from freezer and let thaw in refrigerator overnight.
Prepare Chocolate Torte and refrigerate.
Remove Sage Bread from freezer and let thaw in refrigerator overnight.
Prepare Glazed May Apples and refrigerate.
Bake Anchovy Puffs. Cool completely, transfer to plastic bags and set aside at room temperature.

Prepare Carrot Soup. Cool completely, cover and refrigerate.

Morning of dinner
Cook Lamb Meatballs and drain on paper towels. Set aside at room temperature.
Make Green Grape Tart and set aside at room temperature.
Cook fresh peas and snow peas for vegetable dish and set aside at room temperature.

Afternoon of dinner
Determine desired degree of doneness for lamb and roast accordingly.

About 1 hour before serving
Scoop cucumber with melon baller and set aside on paper towels.

About 30 minutes before serving
Place Lamb Meatballs, Anchovy Puffs and Sage Bread in low oven to rewarm. Cook wild rice for lamb garnish.

About 15 minutes before serving
Rewarm carrot soup over low heat (thin with additional chicken stock if desired).

As guests arrive
Prepare Champagne Framboise.
Place Anchovy Puffs on serving platter.

Just before serving
Finish Green Vegetable Medley.
Fill center of lamb with wild rice; surround with meatballs.

During dinner
Remove Chocolate Torte from refrigerator and let stand at room temperature 20 minutes before dessert time.

Wine Suggestions

Since this meal starts with an aperitif and the first course is soup, only a Cabernet Sauvignon to serve with the lamb is needed. However, this wine should be quite special. An older California "Reserve" such as a Mondavi, Sterling, Martini or Beaulieu, or a 1964, 1966 or 1970 Bordeaux from one of the better estates would be perfect.

THE RECIPES

Champagne Framboise

A simple aperitif that can be adapted for any number of guests.

8 servings

  1 **16-ounce can whole raspberries in heavy syrup**
     Framboise
     Chilled Champagne

Divide raspberries and syrup among ice cube trays and freeze solidly. Place 1 cube in each of 8 Champagne or other stemmed glasses. Add 1 to 3 teaspoons Framboise to each glass and fill with Champagne. Serve immediately.

Anchovy Puffs

Makes about 5 dozen

  1 **3-ounce package cream cheese, room temperature**
  ½ **cup (1 stick) unsalted butter, room temperature**
  1 **cup all purpose flour**
  1 **2-ounce tube anchovy paste**

Beat cheese with butter until well blended. Add flour and mix thoroughly. Transfer dough to plastic bag and flatten into disc. Chill.

Preheat oven to 400°F. Roll dough out on lightly floured surface to thickness of about ⅛ inch. Cut into 2-inch rounds using cookie or biscuit cutter. Spread each with anchovy paste. Fold over and crimp edges with fork. Transfer to baking sheet and bake until lightly golden, about 8 to 10 minutes.

A minced parsley monogram adds an artistic touch to each serving of the Carrot Soup.

Carrot Soup

8 servings

 3 tablespoons unsalted butter
 2 pounds carrots, chopped
 2 large onions, sliced
 2 potatoes (about 1 pound), peeled and chopped
 1 bay leaf
 6 cups (or more) chicken stock

 Salt and freshly ground pepper
 Minced fresh parsley (garnish)

Melt butter in Dutch oven or other large saucepan over low heat. Add carrot and onion. Cover with circle of waxed paper and let sweat about 8 minutes. Add potatoes, bay leaf and chicken stock to cover. Simmer, covered, until vegetables are tender, about 40 minutes. Discard bay leaf.

Puree soup in batches in processor or blender. Return to saucepan and season with salt and pepper to taste. Place over medium heat and bring to boil, stirring occasionally. Ladle into bowls and garnish with minced parsley.

Additional chicken stock can be added to puree if thinner soup is preferred.

Crown Roast of Lamb

8 servings

 Lemon juice
 1 7- to 8-pound crown roast of lamb, all fat removed
 Salt and freshly ground pepper

 ½ cup Dijon mustard
 2 tablespoons soy sauce

 2 garlic cloves, minced
 1 teaspoon dried rosemary leaves, crumbled
 ¼ teaspoon ground marjoram

 Freshly cooked wild rice
 Lamb Meatballs (see following recipe)
 Glazed May Apples (see following recipe)
 Wreath of bay leaves (decoration)

Preheat oven to 325°F. Moisten paper towel with lemon juice and rub over lamb. Insert meat thermometer into meatiest section of roast, being careful not to touch bone. Place on rack in roasting pan and sprinkle with salt and pepper to taste. Cover tips of bones with foil to prevent burning; crumple additional foil and place in center of roast to help retain shape. Roast until thermometer registers 120°F.

Meanwhile, combine next 5 ingredients in small bowl and blend well. When 120°F temperature is reached, discard foil from center of roast and paint inside of meat generously with mustard mixture. Continue roasting until thermometer registers 130°F to 135°F, depending on desired doneness.

To serve, fill center of lamb with wild rice. Ring meatballs around outside and surround with glazed apples. Decorate with wreath of bay leaves.

Lamb Meatballs

Makes about 45 meatballs

 2 tablespoons (¼ stick) unsalted butter
 5 shallots, minced
 2 pounds ground lamb
 1 cup fresh breadcrumbs
 ¼ cup chopped fresh parsley
 1 egg, lightly beaten
 2 tablespoons finely grated lemon peel
 ½ teaspoon ground marjoram
 Salt and freshly ground pepper

 1 tablespoon unsalted butter
 1 tablespoon olive oil

Melt 2 tablespoons butter in small skillet over medium heat. Add shallot and sauté until softened. Transfer to large bowl and add lamb, breadcrumbs, parsley, egg, lemon peel, marjoram, salt and pepper and blend well. Form mixture into balls about the size of chestnuts.

Heat remaining butter with oil in large skillet over medium-high heat. Add meatballs in batches and sauté until browned on all sides and cooked as desired. Drain on paper towels. Reheat in low oven before serving.

Glazed May Apples

8 servings

16 May apples or other small baking apples, peeled but *not* cored
2 tablespoons sugar or to taste
1½ cups apple cider

1 cup currant jelly, melted
Red food coloring

Preheat oven to 300°F. Arrange apples in large, shallow baking dish and dust with sugar. Pour in cider. Bake, basting several times, until apples are tender when pierced with fork but still hold their shape, 30 to 45 minutes.

Transfer apples to shallow serving platter. Add jelly to juices in baking dish and blend well. Tint with food coloring. Pour over apples to glaze. Let cool, then refrigerate. Serve chilled.

Green Vegetable Medley

8 servings

3 pounds fresh green peas, shelled (about 3 cups peas)
1 pound snow peas, trimmed

3 very large cucumbers
2 tablespoons (¼ stick) unsalted butter
Salt and freshly ground pepper

Cook fresh green peas in boiling salted water until crisp-tender. Remove with slotted spoon (or strainer) and transfer to colander. Run under cold water until cool; drain well and set aside. Cook snow peas in same water until crisp-tender. Transfer to colander and run under cold water until cool; drain well.

Halve cucumbers and discard seeds. Using very small melon baller, scoop out as many cucumber balls as possible. Melt butter in large skillet over medium-high heat. Add snow peas and sauté briefly just to barely heat through. Add green peas and cucumber balls and sauté until heated through. Season with salt and pepper and toss lightly. Transfer to heated dish and serve immediately.

Sage Bread

Makes 1 loaf

2½ cups all purpose flour
1 tablespoon sugar
2 teaspoons dried sage, crumbled
1 teaspoon salt
¼ teaspoon baking soda
1 package dry yeast
¼ cup warm water (105°F to 115°F)
1 cup small curd cottage cheese
1 egg
1 tablespoon lard or unsalted butter, melted

Generously grease 2-quart round baking dish. Combine first 5 ingredients in medium bowl and blend well. Combine yeast and water in measuring cup and let stand until foamy, about 10 minutes. Combine cottage cheese and egg in processor or blender and beat until smooth. Transfer to large bowl of electric mixer. Add lard and yeast and blend well. Add flour a small amount at a time, beating well after each addition (dough will be stiff). Cover with towel and let stand in warm, draft-free area until doubled, about 1 hour.

Punch dough down. Turn out onto work surface and knead 1 minute (dough will be sticky but should not require additional flour).

Transfer to prepared dish. Cover dough and let rise in warm, draft-free area until doubled in size, about 40 minutes.

Preheat oven to 350°F. Bake loaf until top is browned and bread sounds hollow when tapped with finger, about 35 to 40 minutes. Turn out onto rack and let cool before slicing and serving.

Green Grape Tart

8 to 10 servings

Crust
1 cup sifted all purpose flour
½ teaspoon salt
⅓ cup vegetable shortening, chilled
3 tablespoons cold water

Almond Cream Filling
6 tablespoons sugar
2 egg yolks
¼ cup (½ stick) unsalted butter, room temperature
½ cup ground almonds
Finely grated peel of 1 lemon

An exceptional finish: irresistible Chocolate Torte and liqueur-glazed Green Grape Tart served with espresso.

½ **cup apricot preserves**
¼ **cup Grand Marnier**
Green grapes

For crust: Sift flour with salt into large bowl. Cut in shortening until mixture resembles coarse meal. Sprinkle with water and toss with fork until uniformly moistened. Form dough into ball. Transfer to plastic bag and flatten into disc. Refrigerate for at least 1 hour.

Preheat oven to 400°F. Roll dough on lightly floured surface to thickness of ⅛ inch. Fit into 9-inch tart pan, easing and pressing into place around bottom and sides. With kitchen shears, trim dough ¼ inch beyond pan. Crimp edge, extending ¼ inch above pan to allow for shrinkage during baking.

Line pastry with parchment or waxed paper. Fill with dried beans or rice and bake 15 minutes. Remove from oven; discard paper and beans. Reduce oven temperature to 350°F and let crust cool while preparing filling.

For filling: Combine sugar and yolks in medium bowl and beat until pale yellow. Beat in butter. Blend in nuts and lemon peel. Pour into crust and bake until center is golden and filling is set, about 10 minutes.

Meanwhile, combine preserves and liqueur in processor or blender and mix well. Remove tart from oven. Working from outer edge, arrange grapes over top in single layer, covering filling completely. Brush with preserve mixture. Cool before serving.

Chocolate Torte

8 to 10 servings

Torte
 Melted butter and flour

¾ **cup sugar**
 4 egg yolks
¾ **cup (1½ sticks) unsalted butter**
 6 ounces (1½ bars) German's Sweet Chocolate
¼ **cup all purpose flour, sifted**

2 tablespoons ground blanched almonds

4 egg whites
   Pinch of cream of tartar
   Pinch of salt

Chocolate Glaze
3½ ounces German's Sweet Chocolate
 3 tablespoons water
 3 tablespoons unsalted butter, room temperature
 4 ounces slivered almonds, lightly toasted

For torte: Preheat oven to 375°F. Coat 8-inch round cake pan with melted butter. Cut circle of waxed paper to fit bottom of pan; brush with butter. Sprinkle with flour, shaking out excess.

Combine ⅔ cup sugar and yolks in large bowl and whisk or beat with electric mixer until pale yellow. Melt butter with chocolate in top of double boiler over gently simmering water, stirring until smooth. Remove from heat. Add yolk mixture and blend well. Thoroughly stir in flour and almonds.

Beat egg whites in medium bowl until foamy. Add cream of tartar and salt and continue beating until soft peaks form. Add remaining sugar a tablespoon at a time and beat until stiff. Stir ¼ of whites into chocolate mixture to loosen; fold in remaining whites. Turn batter into prepared pan, tapping pan on counter so mixture is smooth on top. Bake until outside edges of cake are dry but center is still moist, about 30 minutes. Let cool *completely* before inverting onto serving platter.

For glaze: Melt chocolate with water in top of double boiler, stirring until smooth. Remove from heat. Blend in butter 1 tablespoon at a time, beating well after each addition. Pour over top of cake, tilting platter until glaze completely covers top and sides. Sprinkle almonds around top of cake about 1 inch from edge. Chill thoroughly. Let stand at room temperature about 20 minutes before serving.

Light Meals

NOT LONG AGO, the term "light meal" usually meant a summer luncheon or a Sunday night supper, something that was preceded or followed by a meal that was anything but light. The notion of lightness was often equated with dullness or skimpiness, and was almost never deemed appropriate for entertaining.

Much has changed in recent years, and now a light menu is not only acceptable but also very welcome as the principal meal of the day. Diet-conscious guests are delighted to be presented with a dinner that is based on fresh ingredients and natural flavors rather than on complex preparations and heavy masking sauces. Even those not concerned with calories and inches will find a light meal a refreshing change of pace.

The menus in this chapter are all aimed at entertaining with a light touch, whatever the season and whether the occasion is casual or formal. Seafood is featured in each menu, either as the centerpiece, in a supporting role or—in the first dinner, Shellfish Festival (page 81)—as every course but dessert. Fish and shellfish predominate partly because they are so nutritious and low in calories, and partly because they lend themselves to especially attractive presentations and an extraordinary variety of preparations. Here we have, for example, everything from oyster *dolmades* with lemon and caviar (page 83) and chilled, elegant lobster with curried mayonnaise (page 93) to a dramatic seafood *paella* (page 101) to scallopine of fresh salmon served with a Mexican *salsa verde* (page 116); there's even an unusual Bloody Mary made with clam juice and minced clams (page 83). All of these are complemented by soups, salads, breads and light desserts.

You and your guests certainly do not have to be dieting to enjoy these menus; they are all deliciously satisfying. But the advantage of great light meals is that they let you feel virtuous and have fun at the same time.

Shellfish Festival

THE MENU

Clam Bloody Mary

*Fresh Oyster Dolmades
with Lemon and Caviar*

Mussels à la Nage

Bombay Bread

Boudin Blanc de Bretagne

King Crab Stir-Fry

Clam Pilaf

*Lobster Fricassee Primavera
with Beurre Blanc*

*Iced Pear and Apricot Soufflé
with Raspberry Sauce*

Serves 12

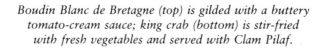

*Boudin Blanc de Bretagne (top) is gilded with a buttery
tomato-cream sauce; king crab (bottom) is stir-fried
with fresh vegetables and served with Clam Pilaf.*

THE STRATEGY

A great new idea for entertaining—a shellfish party that is a seafood lover's delight. The collection of international dishes includes Greek-style oyster dolmades with lemon and caviar, an herbed boudin blanc and a zesty King Crab Stir-Fry. Iced Pear and Apricot Soufflé is the refreshing finish.

Shopping List

24 large oysters
 5 dozen mussels
1¼ pounds medium shrimp
 1 pound scallops
 1 pound king crab legs
 4 1½-pound lobsters
 2 dozen littleneck or cherrystone clams
 1 cup chicken broth
 ¼ cup fish stock or additional clam juice
 4 large green onions plus ⅓ cup sliced
30 large perfect, flat spinach leaves
 1 lemon (for garnish) plus 7 tablespoons fresh lemon juice plus peel of 2 lemons
 1 large leek
 2 medium onions
 4 large garlic cloves
 3 large tomatoes
 5 large shallots plus 2 tablespoons minced
 6 large mushrooms
 1 ounce dried oriental black mushrooms
 6 small zucchini
 1 medium celery root
 ½ pound green beans (julienne)
 6 large carrots
 2 large turnips
10 small dried apricots
   Fresh parsley for garnish (sprigs plus 1 tablespoon minced) plus ¼ cup minced
1½ to 2½ cups whipping cream
 9 eggs
4¾ sticks unsalted butter
 3 tablespoons butter
1½ cups long-grain converted rice
 5 tablespoons fresh fine breadcrumbs (one 1-ounce slice bread)
   Cornmeal
 2 cups bread flour
 1 cup unbleached all purpose flour
 1 envelope dry yeast

¾ cup plus 2 tablespoons sugar
¼ cup white wine vinegar
   Safflower oil
   Peanut oil (or additional safflower oil)
   Worcestershire sauce
   Hot pepper sauce
   Salt
   Black pepper
   White pepper
   Ground red pepper
   Whole nutmeg
   Curry powder
   Ground oregano
 2 envelopes unflavored gelatin
 1 6½-ounce can minced clams
 1 16-ounce can tomatoes
 1 46-ounce can tomato juice plus additional tomato juice (optional; see recipe for Clam Bloody Mary)
 2 8-ounce bottles clam juice plus additional ½ cup clam juice (optional; see recipe for Fresh Oyster Dolmades)
 2 29-ounce cans pear halves
 1 8-ounce can water chestnuts
   Oyster sauce (3 tablespoons)
   Black caviar (1 tablespoon)
   Pimiento (2 teaspoons finely diced)
   Tomato paste (1 tablespoon)
 1 10-ounce package frozen raspberries
1½ cups vodka (or more to taste; see recipe for Clam Bloody Mary)
3½ cups dry white wine or dry vermouth
   Pear brandy (eau de poire)
   Kirsch (optional; see recipe for Raspberry Sauce)

Tips

The following recipes can be doubled: Clam Bloody Mary, Mussels à la Nage, Clam Pilaf.

Oyster sauce is available in oriental markets.

Countdown

1 month ahead
Prepare Bombay Bread and freeze.

1 week ahead
Make boudin blanc and freeze.

1 day ahead
Mix Clam Bloody Mary to point of adding vodka and refrigerate.

Remove Bombay Bread from freezer and defrost in refrigerator overnight.

Remove boudin blanc from freezer and defrost in refrigerator overnight.

Make Iced Pear and Apricot Soufflé and refrigerate.

Prepare Raspberry Sauce and refrigerate.

Morning of dinner
Prepare Fresh Oyster Dolmades to point noted in recipe and refrigerate.

Make Mussels à la Nage and refrigerate.

Mix tomato, wine and cream sauce for boudin blanc to point of adding butter. Set aside at room temperature.

Soak mushrooms for stir-fry; drain, trim and cut as directed.

Cook and shell clams for pilaf. Strain liquid and set aside at room temperature (wrap clams in dampened cheesecloth to keep moist).

Fix vegetables for Lobster Fricassee Primavera and set aside at room temperature.

About 40 minutes before serving
Finish Clam Pilaf.

Prepare Beurre Blanc for Lobster Fricassee Primavera; set pan in larger pan of hot water to keep warm.

About 15 minutes before serving
Rewarm Mussels à la Nage over low heat.

Just before serving
Add vodka to Clam Bloody Mary.
Finish Oyster Dolmades.
Rewarm sauce for boudin blanc and add butter.
Finish King Crab Stir-Fry.
Cook Lobster Fricassee Primavera.
Place Beurre Blanc for lobster over very low heat and rewhisk to blend if necessary.

Wine Suggestions

This entire feast should be accompanied by crisp, dry white wines. A white Bordeaux (the green bottle tells you it's dry) such as Chevalier de Vedrines or Maître d'Estournel would be fine, as would a California Sauvignon Blanc such as those made by Kenwood or Dry Creek. You might even try a dry Chenin Blanc like the ones made by Hacienda or Lakespring or a young Frascati from Italy.

THE RECIPES

Clam Bloody Mary

12 servings

    1 6½-ounce can minced clams, undrained
    4 large green onions (2 ounces total), minced
    1 16-ounce can tomatoes, undrained
    1 46-ounce can tomato juice
    2 8-ounce bottles clam juice
    2 tablespoons fresh lemon juice
 1½ teaspoons Worcestershire sauce
    6 drops hot pepper sauce or to taste
       Salt and freshly ground pepper
 1½ cups (12 ounces) vodka or to taste
       Additional tomato juice (if cocktail requires thinning)

Puree clams with liquid in processor or blender. Transfer to 3-quart pitcher (preferably glass); stir in onion. Cut tomatoes crosswise and remove seeds. Puree with liquid in processor or blender. Add to pitcher with remaining ingredients except vodka and additional tomato juice. Taste and adjust seasoning. Refrigerate at least 2 hours or overnight. Just before serving, add vodka, and tomato juice if needed.

Fresh Oyster Dolmades with Lemon and Caviar

12 servings

    3 quarts water
    1 tablespoon salt
   30 large perfect, flat spinach leaves, stems trimmed

Oyster Dolmades and light Clam Bloody Marys begin the meal.

24 large oysters with their liquor
½ cup clam juice (if necessary to supplement oyster liquor)

    Salt and freshly ground white pepper
    Freshly grated nutmeg

2 tablespoons (¼ stick) unsalted butter
3 tablespoons fresh lemon juice
1 tablespoon black caviar
2 teaspoons finely diced pimiento
1 lemon, scored and thinly sliced (garnish)

Bring water to boil with salt in 4-quart saucepan. Add spinach and cook 30 seconds. Drain and carefully transfer leaves (do not tear) to bowl of ice water.

Combine oysters with their liquor (and clam juice if necessary) in small saucepan. Over high heat, sim-mer oysters until barely cooked (just beginning to become firm). Drain well.

Spread spinach leaves on towel. Place an oyster off center toward top of each leaf. Season lightly with salt, pepper and nutmeg. Wrap each oyster by folding tip of leaf over first, then two opposite sides. Roll oyster toward stem end of leaf to make neat package. *(Can be made early in the day and refrigerated.)*

Melt butter in large skillet over medium heat. Arrange dolmades seam side down and reheat until just barely warm, about 3 to 4 minutes. Transfer to serving dish. Add lemon juice to skillet and heat through. Pour into small bowl and stir in caviar. Spoon sparingly over dolmades. Dot each with 1 to 2 pieces pimiento and garnish dish with lemon.

Mussels à la Nage

Although mussels are usually cooked at the last minute, this recipe can be prepared ahead and reheated quickly either in a microwave or over direct heat.

12 servings

  5 dozen mussels (always buy a few extra, since usually some must be discarded)
  2 tablespoons salt
  1 large leek (8 ounces) (including greens), thinly sliced
  1 medium onion (3 ounces), thinly sliced
  1 large garlic clove, halved
1½ cups dry white wine or dry vermouth
  ¾ cup water
  2 teaspoons salt
    Freshly ground pepper

  ½ cup (1 stick) unsalted butter, chilled and cut into 4 pieces
  1 large tomato (6 ounces), peeled, seeded, juiced and outer shell cut into ½-inch dice
  1 tablespoon minced fresh parsley (garnish)

Wash mussels in cold water, discarding any that are open. Transfer to 2-quart bowl, cover with water and add 2 tablespoons salt; let stand 30 minutes. Drain well; scrub mussels as clean as possible by rubbing one against the other to remove beards and dirt. Transfer to 3-quart saucepan. Add leek, onion, garlic, wine or vermouth, water, 2 teaspoons salt, and pepper. Cover and cook over high heat 6 to 8 minutes, stirring after 4 minutes to bring opened mussels on the bottom to the top.

When mussels are all open (discard any that simply refuse to open), transfer to serving dish using slotted spoon. Boil liquid for 3 minutes. Reduce heat to medium; add butter pieces and let melt by shaking pan. Discard garlic. Stir in diced tomato. Taste and adjust seasoning. Pour sauce over mussels and garnish with parsley.

Bombay Bread

Delicately flavored with curry, this bread is wonderful with shellfish.

Makes 2 baguettes

  1 envelope dry yeast
  1 tablespoon sugar
  1 cup plus 2 tablespoons warm water (105°F to 115°F)

    Cornmeal

  2 tablespoons (¼ stick) unsalted butter
  2 tablespoons minced shallot
  2 cups bread flour (10 ounces)
  1 cup unbleached all purpose flour (5 ounces)
1¼ teaspoons salt
  ½ teaspoon curry powder

  1 egg
  ½ teaspoon salt

Combine yeast, sugar and water and let stand until foamy, about 10 minutes.

Oil large bowl and double French bread pans; sprinkle pans with cornmeal.

Melt butter in small skillet over low heat. Add shallot and cook until softened, about 10 minutes. Transfer to processor and add flours, salt and curry. With machine running, pour yeast through feed tube and mix until dough is moist and smooth, about 40 seconds. (If using mixer or blending by hand, work yeast in gradually and knead 8 to 12 minutes.) Transfer dough to oiled bowl, turning to coat entire surface. Cover bowl with damp towel and let stand in warm draft-free area until dough is doubled, about 1 hour.

Punch dough down. Turn out onto heavily floured board and work in enough flour so dough is easy to handle and no longer sticky. Divide dough in half. Roll one-half into rectangle on floured board. Roll into oblong loaf (as for jelly roll), pinching ends and seam tightly. Place seam side down in prepared pan. Repeat with remaining dough. Cover loaves lightly with damp cloth and let stand in warm area until almost doubled, about 45 minutes.

Position rack in center of oven and preheat to 425°F. Slash tops of loaves with sharp knife. Beat egg with salt and brush over loaves, being careful not to drip glaze onto pan. Bake until loaves are golden brown and sound hollow when tapped on bottom, about 25 to 30 minutes. Remove bread from pans and let cool on wire rack before slicing.

Boudin Blanc de Bretagne (Seafood Sausages with Tomato, Wine and Cream Sauce)

These sausages make an elegant presentation when sliced and served over several spoonfuls of the delicious sauce. Can be made ahead and frozen.

12 servings

2 tablespoons (¼ stick) unsalted butter
6 large mushrooms (¼ pound total), minced
1 large shallot (½ ounce), minced
5 tablespoons fresh fine breadcrumbs (one 1-ounce slice of bread, crust removed)

1 tablespoon oil (preferably safflower)
1¼ pounds medium shrimp, shelled and deveined (reserve shells for sauce)

1 pound scallops
1½ teaspoons salt
½ teaspoon hot pepper sauce
½ teaspoon freshly grated nutmeg
Freshly ground white pepper
2 egg whites
1 to 2 cups whipping cream, well chilled

Tomato, Wine and Cream Sauce
1 cup dry white wine or vermouth
2 large shallots (1 ounce total), minced
Reserved shrimp shells, washed and drained
2 large tomatoes (14 ounces total), peeled, seeded and diced
1 tablespoon tomato paste
1 teaspoon sugar
½ cup whipping cream
½ teaspoon salt
Freshly ground pepper
Freshly grated nutmeg
4 tablespoons (½ stick) unsalted butter, chilled and cut into 4 pieces

Melt butter in small skillet over medium-high heat. Add mushrooms and shallots and cook until softened, about 8 minutes. Transfer to processor or blender; add breadcrumbs and mix well. Let cool in container.

Heat oil in medium skillet over high heat. Add ¾ pound shrimp and cook, stirring constantly, until opaque, removing immediately with slotted spoon. Chop coarsely with knife. Let cool, then refrigerate until ready to use.

Add scallops to processor (or to blender in batches) and puree. Add remaining ½ pound shrimp with salt, hot pepper sauce, nutmeg and pepper and puree again, scraping sides of container as necessary.

Add egg whites and mix well. With machine running, *gradually* add cream through feed tube (use only what mixture will absorb) and blend thoroughly. Transfer to large bowl. Drain chopped cooked shrimp if necessary and pat dry with paper towels. Fold gently into scallop mixture.

Generously butter 4 large pieces of heavy duty foil (each about 14 inches long). Spoon ¼ of fish mixture into each piece of foil, patting into cylinder. Roll to enclose. Twist ends tightly to seal. Place sausages in large skillet(s) and cover with cold water. Set small lid over sausages to weight down and keep immersed. Cover with regular lid, bring water to 180°F and cook about 15 to 20 minutes; do not boil (water should just be shivering, not even simmering). Remove from heat and let sausages stay in water for approximately 10 minutes.

Remove sausages from water and unwrap carefully. Discard any accumulated liquid. Transfer to buttered dish, cover with waxed paper and keep warm in 160°F oven while preparing sauce.

For sauce: Combine wine, shallots and reserved shells in 1-quart nonaluminum saucepan. Simmer 15 minutes; strain. Return liquid to saucepan. Add tomatoes, tomato paste and sugar and simmer, stirring occasionally, until mixture is reduced to 1¼ cups. Add cream and seasoning and simmer 5 minutes longer. Transfer to processor or blender and puree. Return to saucepan and reheat. Add butter 1 piece at a time, whisking constantly until butter is incorporated. Taste and adjust seasoning.

To serve, slice sausages into ½-inch pieces. Spoon some of sauce onto serving platter. Arrange overlapping slices of sausage in circle over sauce. Serve immediately with remaining sauce.

King Crab Stir-Fry

12 servings

1 ounce dried oriental black mushrooms

2 tablespoons peanut or safflower oil
2 large garlic cloves, halved
6 small zucchini (1½ pounds total), unpeeled, scored and cut into ⅛-inch slices
1 pound king crab legs, cut into 1-inch chunks
1 8-ounce can water chestnuts, drained and cut into ⅛-inch slices
3 tablespoons bottled oyster sauce*
⅓ cup sliced green onion
Clam Pilaf (see following recipe)

Rinse mushrooms; place in small bowl, cover with hot water and let stand until softened, about 20 minutes. Drain well. Remove any tough stems (reserve for soup); cut larger mushrooms in half.

Heat oil with garlic in wok or skillet over medium-high heat. Cook only until garlic begins to brown, then remove pieces. Increase heat to high, add zucchini and cook until crisp-tender, stirring frequently. Add crab, water chestnuts and mushrooms and cook, stirring gently, until heated through, about 3 to 5 minutes. Add oyster sauce and cook another minute, stirring gently. Transfer to platter and garnish with green onion. Serve with Clam Pilaf.

*Available in oriental markets.

Clam Pilaf

12 servings

  2 dozen littleneck or cherrystone clams
  1 cup dry white wine or dry vermouth
  1 cup water

  3 tablespoons butter
  1 medium onion (3 ounces), minced
  1 large garlic clove, minced
1½ cups long-grain converted rice
  1 cup chicken broth
    Salt and freshly ground pepper

½ teaspoon ground oregano
¼ cup minced fresh parsley

Line strainer with double thickness of damp cheesecloth and set over medium bowl. Wash clams thoroughly, discarding any that are open. Transfer to 4-quart saucepan. Add wine and water and bring to boil over high heat. Cover and cook until clams open, about 8 to 10 minutes, stirring after 4 minutes. Strain liquid; set clams aside.

Melt butter in heavy 2-quart saucepan over medium heat. Add onion and garlic and sauté until softened but not browned, about 10 minutes. Add 2 cups clam liquid, rice, broth, salt and pepper and bring to boil. Stir through once, reduce heat, cover and simmer until all liquid is absorbed and rice is tender, about 15 minutes.

Meanwhile, shell clams; halve littlenecks or quarter cherrystones (you should have a generous cup of clams).

When rice is done, remove from heat; add clams and oregano and stir gently with fork. Let stand covered 10 minutes. Taste and adjust seasoning; stir in parsley. Transfer to serving dish.

Lobster Fricassee Primavera with Beurre Blanc

12 servings

  2 quarts water
  1 tablespoon salt
  1 medium celery root (8 ounces)
½ pound green beans, cut julienne into 2-inch lengths

  6 large carrots (tips trimmed), cut into 1¾-inch lengths and turned* (24 turned carrots)
  2 large turnips, cut into 1¾-inch lengths ½ inch wide and turned* (24 turned turnips)

Beurre Blanc
¼ cup white wine vinegar
¼ cup fish stock or clam juice
  2 large shallots (2 ounces), minced
  1 cup (2 sticks) unsalted butter, chilled and cut into tablespoon-size pieces
    Pinch of ground red pepper
    Salt and freshly ground pepper

  4 tablespoons (½ stick) unsalted butter
  4 1½-pound lobsters, cooked, shelled and cut into 2-inch chunks (about 1½ pounds meat)
    Salt
    Pepper

    Parsley sprigs (garnish)

Bring water to boil with salt in 4-quart saucepan over high heat. Peel celery root; cut julienne into 2-inch lengths. Immediately add to pan and return water to boil. Let boil 30 seconds. Remove with slotted spoon (maintain water at boil) and transfer to large bowl of ice water. Add beans to pan and boil 30 seconds. Remove with slotted spoon (maintain water at boil) and transfer to bowl of ice water.

Add carrots to pan and boil 4 minutes. Remove with slotted spoon (maintain water at boil) and add to ice water. Add turnips to pan and boil 2 minutes. Transfer to ice water using slotted spoon. When vegetables are completely cool, drain well and set aside.

For beurre blanc: Combine vinegar, stock and shallots in small saucepan and cook over medium heat until liquid is reduced to 3 tablespoons. Whisk in butter 1 piece at a time, making sure each piece is completely incorporated before adding the next; *do not boil.* Remove from heat and season with red pepper, salt and pepper. Keep warm.

To assemble: Melt 2 tablespoons butter in *each* of two 8-inch skillets over medium-high heat. Add

vegetables to one skillet and lobster to the other. Cook both until heated through. Season to taste with salt and pepper.

Place lobster in center of serving platter or individual plates. Arrange vegetables over top. Spoon some of beurre blanc over vegetables and garnish with parsley. Pass remaining beurre blanc.

If beurre blanc needs reheating, warm gently (do not boil), whisking constantly.

*"Turning" refers to carving the vegetables uniformly into oval pieces, usually 1½ to 1¾ inches in length. The trimmings can be used in soups and stocks.

Iced Pear and Apricot Soufflé with Raspberry Sauce

12 servings

    2 29-ounce cans pear halves, well drained
    2 envelopes (2 scant tablespoons) unflavored
       gelatin

    ½ cup sugar
    4 egg yolks
    10 small dried apricots (1 ounce total), finely
       minced
       Peel of 2 lemons
    3 tablespoons pear brandy (eau de poire)
    2 tablespoons fresh lemon juice

    6 egg whites
    ⅛ teaspoon salt
    ¼ cup sugar
       Raspberry Sauce (see following recipe)

Cut piece of foil long enough to encircle 5- to 6-cup soufflé dish with 1-inch overlap. Fold in half lengthwise. Oil one side. Wrap around dish oiled side in with collar extending at least 4 inches above rim. Tie or tape firmly.

Cut 2 pear halves into ¼-inch dice; set aside. Puree remaining pears with gelatin. Transfer to large saucepan and cook over medium heat until reduced to about 1 cup, about 45 minutes.

Combine ½ cup sugar with egg yolks, apricots and lemon peel in processor or large bowl of electric mixer and blend until mixture is thick and pale yellow. Add 2 tablespoons hot pear puree and blend well. Add remaining puree with brandy and lemon juice and mix thoroughly. Transfer to large bowl (if necessary) and fold in diced pears. Refrigerate until mixture begins to thicken.

Beat egg whites with electric mixer until foamy. Add salt and continue beating until whites are stiff and glossy. Add remaining sugar and beat 5 seconds. Stir ¼ of whites into pear mixture and mix well. Fold in remaining whites, blending gently but thoroughly. Spoon into prepared dish. Refrigerate until completely set, several hours or overnight. Serve with Raspberry Sauce.

Raspberry Sauce

    1 10-ounce package frozen raspberries, thawed
       (undrained)
    1 tablespoon kirsch (optional)

Pulverize raspberries in processor or blender for at least 1 minute. Strain, if desired. Stir in kirsch. Cover and chill until ready to serve.

A warm loaf of Bombay Bread complements the main course—Lobster Fricassee Primavera.

Cool and Casual

THE MENU

Chilled Cream of Watercress Soup

Lobster with Curried Mayonnaise

Rice and Vegetable Salad

Cucumber-Stuffed Tomatoes

Cheese and Fruit

Serves 4

Chilled Cream of Watercress Soup served in elegant china at a table gleaming with silver and crystal begins a memorable dinner.

THE STRATEGY

Here is an ideal menu for summer—light, refreshing and easy to prepare. Complete this sophisticated luncheon with a selection of imported cheese and seasonal fruit.

Shopping List

      8 rock lobster tails
      3 cups defatted chicken broth
      1 large bunch watercress plus sprigs
         (for garnish)
      4 medium cucumbers plus ½ cup peeled, seeded
         and chopped
     ½ cup pea pods
     10 large radishes
      2 small red peppers
      4 medium tomatoes
         Celery (¼ cup chopped)
         Parsley (1 teaspoon chopped plus 1½ teaspoons
         minced)
         Fresh lemon juice
         Bibb lettuce
         Green onion tops (½ cup chopped)
   1¼ cups whipping cream

      1 cup sour cream
      1 tablespoon butter
      4 eggs
   1½ cups cooked rice
   2½ cups oil
         Cider vinegar (4 tablespoons)
         Flour
         Sugar
         Salt
         White pepper
         Black pepper
         Ground red pepper
         Paprika
         Curry powder
         Beau Monde seasoning
         Celery salt
         Dried dillweed
         Hot pepper sauce
      6 ripe olives

Tips

All these recipes can be doubled.

The ingredients compose a bright still life.

Countdown

1 day ahead

Prepare Chilled Cream of Watercress Soup to point of adding remaining cream. Cover and chill.

Cook lobster for main course. Let cool, cover and refrigerate.

Mix curried mayonnaise for lobster. Cover and refrigerate.

Cook rice for Rice and Vegetable Salad. Let cool, cover and refrigerate.

Blend vinaigrette for Rice and Vegetable Salad. Cover and refrigerate.

Halve tomatoes for Cucumber-Stuffed Tomatoes. Scoop out pulp, turn tomato shells upside down onto paper towels and refrigerate.

Morning of luncheon

Combine rice, vegetables and vinaigrette for salad; cover and refrigerate.

Prepare cucumber and assemble Cucumber-Stuffed Tomatoes.

Line individual plate with lettuce leaves for lobster; refrigerate.

Just before serving

Whip remaining cream for garnish for soup.

Arrange lobster tails on plates.

Wine Suggestions

This relaxed luncheon calls for a snappy Gewurztraminer from California—try those by Monterey Vineyards or Grand Cru; from Alsace, look for wines made by Dopff & Irion, Hugel or Trimbach. An Alsatian Riesling might also do the trick or perhaps a dry Johannisberg Riesling from California.

THE RECIPES

Chilled Cream of Watercress Soup

4 servings

    3 cups defatted chicken broth
    1 tablespoon butter
    1 tablespoon flour
 1¼   cups whipping cream
       Salt and freshly ground pepper
    1 large bunch watercress, leaves and stems finely chopped

       Watercress sprigs (garnish)

Bring broth to simmer in medium saucepan. Meanwhile, melt butter in small skillet over medium-high heat. Add flour and stir constantly until smooth. Add to broth, mixing well. Continue simmering 6 to 8 minutes, stirring several times. Blend in 1 cup cream, salt and pepper. Add watercress and cook until heated through, *but do not boil*. Remove from heat and cool slightly. Cover and chill thoroughly.

Just before serving, whip remaining cream. Pour soup into chilled bowls and garnish with cream and watercress.

Lobster with Curried Mayonnaise

4 servings

    4 egg yolks
    1 teaspoon sugar
    4 dashes ground red pepper
    2 dashes paprika
    2 tablespoons fresh lemon juice
    2 tablespoons cider vinegar
    2 cups oil
  ½   teaspoon curry powder or to taste
       Salt

    8 rock lobster tails, cooked, chilled, shells loosened
       Bibb lettuce

Combine yolks, sugar, pepper and paprika in small bowl of electric mixer and beat until very thick and light in color. Combine lemon juice and vinegar. Gradually add to yolks alternately with oil, beating constantly. Stir in curry and salt. Cover and chill well.

Place lobster tails on lettuce-lined plates. Spoon mayonnaise over; pass remainder separately.

Rice and Vegetable Salad

4 servings

1½ cups cooked rice, chilled
 ½ cup chopped green onion tops
 ½ cup peeled, seeded and chopped cucumber
 ½ cup pea pods, lightly steamed
 ¼ cup chopped celery
10 large radishes, thinly sliced
 6 ripe olives, thinly sliced
 2 small red peppers, chopped
 1 teaspoon chopped fresh parsley
 ¼ teaspoon Beau Monde seasoning
 ¼ teaspoon celery salt

   Salt and freshly ground pepper
 ½ cup oil
 2 tablespoons cider vinegar
 2 tablespoons fresh lemon juice
1½ teaspoons salt
 1 teaspoon sugar
 ½ teaspoon paprika
 ¼ teaspoon freshly ground pepper

Combine first 11 ingredients with salt and pepper in large bowl and toss lightly. Combine remaining ingredients in small bowl or jar with tight-fitting lid and blend well. Pour over rice and toss gently. Cover and chill well.

Cucumber-Stuffed Tomatoes

4 servings

  4 medium cucumbers
  4 medium tomatoes

  1 cup sour cream
1½ teaspoons dillweed
1½ teaspoons minced fresh parsley
 ½ teaspoon hot pepper sauce
   Pinch of freshly ground white pepper
   Salt and freshly ground pepper

Peel, seed and thinly slice cucumbers. Transfer to colander and let drain. Halve tomatoes and scoop out pulp. Turn upside down and drain well.

Combine cucumber with remaining ingredients and blend well. Fill tomato halves with cucumber and arrange on platter. Chill well before serving.

Back to front: Rice and Vegetable Salad, Cucumber-Stuffed Tomatoes, Watercress Soup and Lobster with Curried Mayonnaise.

Easy Buffet for Friends

THE MENU

Wine and Champagne Punch

Tomatoes Pesto

Benne Biscuits

Malibu Paella

Monkey Bread

*Mélange of Frozen Desserts
with Fresh Fruit*

Gingersnaps

Serves 16

*The special paella includes fresh crayfish, clams,
shrimp, snow peas and prosciutto.*

THE STRATEGY

A spectacular paella is the centerpiece for this relaxed dinner. Easy accompaniments—homemade bread, tomatoes dressed with pesto and Benne Biscuits for nibbling with Wine and Champagne Punch—round out the menu. A trio of refreshing desserts, fresh fruit and spicy gingersnaps complete the picture nicely.

Shopping List

    4 dozen large shrimp
    4 whole chicken breasts
    1 pound cooked ham
   16 hot Italian sausages
    6 dozen fresh clams or mussels (or combination)
   32 crayfish
   32 thin slices prosciutto
    1 gallon Fish Stock or 8 cups bottled clam juice
    5 kiwi fruit
    3 pears
    3 apples
   16 large strawberries
    2 cups tightly packed fresh basil leaves (or 1 cup basil leaves and 1 cup parsley)
    2 pints cherry tomatoes
    1 medium onion
    4 large onions
    1 large lemon plus 8 lemons for garnish plus ½ cup fresh lemon juice
    2 tablespoons finely chopped parsley
   10 parsley stems
    8 large artichokes
    4 dozen medium mushroom caps
    1 large green pepper
    1 large red pepper
    3 sprigs fresh thyme or 2 teaspoons dried
    7 garlic cloves plus 1½ teaspoons pressed
    8 medium-size ripe tomatoes (or one 28-ounce can whole tomatoes)
  1½ cups fresh green peas (about 1½ pounds unshelled)
  1½ pounds snow peas
      Leaves of 4 branches fresh thyme or ¼ teaspoon dried

      Leaves of 4 branches fresh oregano or ¼ teaspoon dried
      Fresh oregano leaves or chopped fresh parsley for garnish
      Fresh ginger (four ¼-inch slices)
    5 ounces extra-sharp cheddar cheese
    ½ cup grated Parmesan cheese
    2 cups whipping cream
    4 cups (1 quart) milk
    4 eggs
    6 sticks unsalted butter
    2 sticks butter
    8 cups long-grain white rice
    2 tablespoons pine nuts
    ¾ cup benne seed (unhulled sesame seed; available at natural food stores)
    1 cup plus 2 tablespoons olive oil
    1 envelope dry yeast
    ⅔ cup plus 1 tablespoon sugar
    ⅓ cup superfine sugar
  1½ cups firmly packed light brown sugar
    6 cups sifted bread flour
    ¼ cup blackstrap or dark molasses
  2⅔ cups sifted all purpose flour
      Baking soda
      Salt
      Black pepper
      Ground red pepper
      Cinnamon
      Pickling spices (1 tablespoon)
    1 teaspoon ground saffron or 2 teaspoons crushed saffron threads
      Ground ginger
      Ground cloves
    2 bay leaves
      Dough for 9-inch pie crust
    1 tablespoon chopped preserved ginger in syrup
    2 15-ounce jars mangoes in syrup
    3 10-ounce packages frozen raspberries in syrup
    8 750-milliliter bottles Fumé Blanc
    1 750-milliliter bottle late harvest Johannisberg Riesling
    1 750-milliliter bottle Champagne
    ¾ cup pear brandy

1½ cups dry white wine
  Framboise (raspberry brandy) (optional)

Tips

If preparing Fish Stock, add the following:
  8 pounds fish bones from nonoily fish (halibut, whitefish, sole or sea bass)
  4 large onions
  8 shallots
    Fresh thyme
    Parsley stems
    Sliced mushroom stems (optional)
1½ sticks unsalted butter
  ¼ cup vegetable oil
  1 quart dry white wine
 16 6-inch bamboo skewers

Special Equipment

Block of ice or decorative ice mold (for punch bowl)
Punch bowl and cups
Ice cream maker

Countdown

1 month ahead
Prepare Benne Biscuits and Gingersnaps and store in separate containers with tight-fitting lids in cool, dry place.
Prepare Fish Stock for Malibu Paella; freeze.

2 days ahead
Make ice mold for Wine and Champagne Punch and freeze.
Prepare pesto sauce for Tomatoes Pesto; store in jar and refrigerate.
Shell peas for Malibu Paella and refrigerate.
Peel, seed and chop tomatoes for Malibu Paella; cover with plastic wrap and refrigerate.
Prepare mixtures for ice cream and sorbets; cover and refrigerate.

1 day ahead
Prepare court bouillon for Malibu Paella.

Cook, peel and devein shrimp and store in cooled court bouillon in refrigerator.
Cook artichokes for Malibu Paella. Reserve leaves; quarter bottoms and discard chokes; cover with plastic wrap and refrigerate.
Poach sausage for Malibu Paella. Wrap tightly and store in refrigerator.
Cook peas and store in cooled cooking liquid in refrigerator.
Prepare julienne of ham and prosciutto for Malibu Paella; cover with plastic wrap and refrigerate.
Transfer Fish Stock to refrigerator to thaw.

Day of the dinner
Make fruit skewers for Wine and Champagne Punch and refrigerate.
Prepare Tomatoes Pesto and chill.
Prepare Monkey Bread.
Process mixtures for Ginger Ice Cream, Raspberry Sorbet and Mango Sorbet.
Make individual scoops of desserts and store in freezer.
Cook crayfish in court bouillon.

Just before guests arrive
Make Wine and Champagne Punch.

30 minutes before serving Paella
Warm plates and ramekins.
Cover artichoke leaves and bottoms with foil and warm in oven.
Fry sausage and keep warm in oven.
Sauté mushrooms.
Prepare rice mixture.
Cook clams.
Make clam butter sauce.
Warm peas.
Warm shrimp in court bouillon.
Warm crayfish in court bouillon.
Reheat mushrooms.

Wine Suggestions

The paella, which has meat and seafood in it, will accommodate practically any dry wine. Perhaps the best would be an oak-aged Sauvignon Blanc (Fumé Blanc) from California or an equally weighty Chardonnay. A Soave or Verdicchio from Italy would also work nicely.

THE RECIPES

Wine and Champagne Punch

16 servings

  5 kiwi fruit, peeled and sliced
  3 pears, cored and cut into chunks
  3 apples, cored and cut into chunks
 16 large strawberries, hulled and halved
     Block of ice or decorative ice mold
  8 750-milliliter bottles Fumé Blanc, well chilled
  1 750-milliliter bottle late harvest Johannisberg Riesling, well chilled
  1 750-milliliter bottle Champagne, well chilled
 ¾ cup pear brandy

Thread fruit evenly onto sixteen 6-inch bamboo skewers. Place ice in center of punch bowl. Add chilled wine, Champagne and brandy and mix gently. To serve, ladle punch into goblets and garnish with skewered fruit.

Wine and Champagne Punch.

Tomatoes Pesto

Drain tomatoes cut side down on paper towels before adding pesto.

16 servings

  2 cups tightly packed fresh basil leaves or 1 cup basil leaves and 1 cup fresh parsley
 ½ cup olive oil
  2 tablespoons pine nuts
  3 garlic cloves, chopped
 ½ teaspoon salt
     Freshly ground pepper
 ½ cup freshly grated Parmesan cheese
  2 pints cherry tomatoes, halved

Combine basil, oil, pine nuts, garlic, salt and pepper in processor or blender and mix until smooth. Stir in Parmesan. *(Pesto can be prepared several days ahead, covered tightly and refrigerated.)* Spoon small amount of pesto onto each tomato half. Set aside in refrigerator until ready to serve.

Benne Biscuits

Makes about 35 dozen tiny biscuits

 ¾ cup benne seed (unhulled sesame seed)*

     Dough for 9-inch pie crust
  5 ounces extra-sharp cheddar cheese, grated
 ½ teaspoon freshly ground red pepper
  1 to 2 teaspoons ice water (optional)

     Salt

Preheat oven to 350°F. Arrange seed in shallow layer in large pan. Roast 30 minutes, stirring every 10 minutes. Taste seed; if not toasted, continue roasting, testing every 5 minutes (not more than 15 minutes). Do not overtoast or seed will be bitter. Retain oven temperature at 350°F.

    Combine dough, cheese and ground red pepper in large bowl and blend well. Stir in benne seed. If dough is too dry to incorporate seed, add 1 to 2 teaspoons ice water and mix well.

    Divide dough in half. Turn half out onto lightly floured surface or pastry cloth and pat gently to flatten slightly. Lightly flour top of dough. Roll out to thickness of ⅛ inch. Using sharp knife or fluted pastry wheel, cut dough into ⅝-inch squares. Transfer squares to ungreased baking sheet. Bake just until lightly browned, about 4 minutes. Cool 5 minutes. Repeat with remaining dough. Sprinkle biscuits with salt before serving. *(Can be prepared up to 1 month ahead. Store in container with tight-fitting lid in cool, dark place. Reheat for several minutes in 350°F oven.)*

*Unhulled sesame seed is available at natural food stores. Do not substitute white sesame seed, which becomes oily when heated and will not toast properly.

Malibu Paella

16 servings

Court Bouillon
 2 quarts water (or more)
 1 medium onion, sliced
 1 large lemon, peeled and sliced
10 parsley stems
 1 tablespoon pickling spices
 3 sprigs fresh thyme or 2 teaspoons dried, crumbled
 4 dozen large shrimp, tails intact (about 2 pounds)

Paella
 8 large artichokes
¼ cup fresh lemon juice
 1 teaspoon salt

16 hot Italian sausages (do not prick casings)
 Olive oil for frying

¼ cup (½ stick) unsalted butter
 2 tablespoons olive oil
 4 dozen medium mushroom caps
 1 tablespoon fresh lemon juice

 1 gallon Fish Stock (see following recipe) or 8 cups bottled clam juice mixed with 8 cups water
½ cup olive oil
 4 large onions, chopped
 1 large green pepper, seeded and cut into thin strips
 1 large red pepper, seeded and cut into thin strips
 4 garlic cloves, pressed or minced
 8 cups long-grain white rice
 4 whole chicken breasts, halved, skinned, boned and cut into bite-size pieces
 1 pound cooked ham, cut julienne
 8 medium-size ripe tomatoes, peeled, seeded and chopped or one 28-ounce can whole tomatoes, drained and chopped

 1 teaspoon ground saffron *or* 2 teaspoons crushed saffron threads, dissolved in ¼ cup hot Fish Stock
 2 bay leaves
 Leaves of 4 branches fresh thyme or ¼ teaspoon dried, crumbled
 Leaves of 4 branches fresh oregano or ¼ teaspoon dried, crumbled
 Salt and freshly ground pepper

1½ cups fresh green peas (about 1½ pounds unshelled)
1½ pounds snow peas, strings removed

 3 cups water
1½ cups dry white wine
 2 tablespoons finely chopped parsley
1½ teaspoons pressed garlic
 6 dozen fresh clams or mussels or combination, scrubbed and debearded
 2 cups (4 sticks) unsalted butter
 tablespoons fresh lemon juice

32 crayfish, freshly cooked (optional garnish)

32 thin slices prosciutto, cut julienne
 Fresh oregano leaves or chopped fresh parsley
 8 lemons, quartered (garnish)

For court bouillon: Combine 2 quarts water, sliced onion, sliced lemon, parsley stems, pickling spices and thyme in stockpot and bring to boil over high heat. Reduce heat and simmer 30 minutes. Increase heat and return to boil. Add shrimp and, if necessary, enough additional boiling water to cover shrimp. Return to boil. Cook just until shrimp turn pink, about 2 minutes. Using slotted spoon, quickly transfer shrimp to large bowl of very cold water to stop cooking process. Set court bouillon aside to cool to room temperature.

Meanwhile, drain shrimp well; peel and devein, leaving tails intact. Transfer shrimp to large bowl. Strain cooled court bouillon over shrimp. *(Court bouillon and shrimp can be prepared up to 1 day ahead and refrigerated.)*

For paella: Combine artichokes, ¼ cup lemon juice and 1 teaspoon salt with enough water to cover in large nonaluminum saucepan. Place over medium-high heat and simmer until tender, about 35 to 45 minutes. Invert artichokes on paper towels and drain well. Remove outer leaves and reserve. Cut out chokes and discard. Trim bottoms, cutting each into 4 wedges. *(Artichokes can be prepared 1 day ahead to this point. Cover with plastic wrap and refrigerate until ready to use.)* Transfer wedges and leaves to baking dish. Cover with aluminum foil and keep warm in very low oven.

Cover sausages with water in large skillet. Place over medium-high heat and bring to boil. Reduce heat and simmer gently 7 minutes. (*Sausage can be prepared 1 day ahead to this point.*) Drain well on paper towels. Heat oil in dry skillet over medium-high heat. Add sausage and fry until lightly browned. Slice sausage into ½-inch rounds. Keep sausage warm in low oven.

Melt ¼ cup butter with 2 tablespoons olive oil in heavy large skillet over medium-high heat. Add mushrooms and 1 tablespoon lemon juice and stir constantly until mushrooms are completely coated with butter. Reduce heat, cover and cook slowly 5 minutes. Set aside.

Preheat oven to 375°F. Bring Fish Stock to boil in large saucepan over medium-high heat. Meanwhile, heat ½ cup olive oil in heavy large casserole or stockpot over medium heat. Add chopped onion, green and red pepper strips and 4 garlic cloves to oil. Cover and cook just until transparent, stirring occasionally, about 10 minutes; *do not brown*. Add rice and cook until opaque, about 1 to 2 minutes. Pour boiling Fish Stock over rice. Add chicken, ham, tomatoes, saffron, bay leaves, thyme and oregano with salt and pepper to taste. Bring to boil, stirring gently. Cover and transfer to oven. Bake for 22 minutes.

Over medium-high heat, bring to boil enough salted water to cover shelled peas. Add peas, reduce heat and simmer until crisp-tender, about 5 minutes. Using slotted spoon, transfer peas to bowl of cold water to stop cooking process. Set cooking liquid aside to use later for reheating peas. Repeat process with snow peas, using fresh salted water. (*Peas can be prepared 1 day ahead to this point. Let cooking liquids cool completely, then return peas to liquids. Store in refrigerator until ready to reheat.*)

Combine 3 cups water, 1½ cups dry white wine, 2 tablespoons finely chopped parsley and 1½ teaspoons pressed garlic in large saucepan over medium-high heat and bring to boil. Add half of clams and let simmer 5 minutes. Remove opened clams and continue simmering until all clams open; discard any clams that do not open after 20 minutes. Transfer clams to heated platter and keep warm. Repeat process with remaining clams. Add 2 cups unsalted butter and 1½ tablespoons lemon juice to cooking liquid and continue simmering until butter is melted. Set clam butter aside.

To assemble: Warm 16 large buffet plates and 16 small ramekins in low oven. Arrange ramekins in center of each plate. Fill each ramekin with about ¼ cup clam butter. Spoon rice mixture around ramekins, dividing evenly.

Bring liquid reserved from peas to boil in medium saucepan. Place shelled peas in strainer. Lower into boiling liquid for 10 seconds to reheat. Repeat process with snow peas. Bring reserved court bouillon to boil. Add shrimp and crayfish and warm 1 minute. Drain well. Reheat mushrooms.

Divide sausage evenly among plates. Arrange 2 crayfish, 3 shrimp, 4 clams, 3 mushroom caps and 2 artichoke wedges on each plate. Sprinkle evenly with fresh peas. Top with snow peas, dividing evenly. Arrange artichoke leaves, pointed ends out, around rim of each plate. Sprinkle with prosciutto julienne and fresh oregano leaves or chopped parsley. Garnish each serving with 2 lemon wedges and serve.

Fish Stock

Makes about 1 gallon

- ¾ cup (1½ sticks) **unsalted butter**
- ¼ cup **vegetable oil**
- 8 pounds **fish bones (from nonoily fish such as halibut, whitefish, sole or sea bass), cut into chunks**
- 4 large **onions, thinly sliced**
- 8 **shallots, chopped**
- 1 quart **dry white wine**
- 1 **bouquet garni (bay leaf, fresh thyme and parsley stems)**
  Sliced mushroom stems (optional)

Melt butter with oil in stockpot over medium heat. Add fish bones, onion and shallot. Cover and cook 10 minutes; do not allow onion to brown. Stir in white wine and simmer until most of moisture evaporates. Add bouquet garni, mushroom stems and enough cold water to cover. Simmer until richly flavored, about 30 minutes, skimming occasionally. Strain stock, pressing fish and vegetables lightly with back of spoon to extract as much liquid as possible. Cool to room temperature. Discard fat from surface. (*Can be prepared ahead and refrigerated up to 3 days or frozen up to 1 month.*)

Monkey Bread

16 servings

    1 tablespoon sugar
    1 envelope dry yeast
    ½ cup warm water (105°F to 115°F)
    2 cups milk, scalded
    1 cup (2 sticks) unsalted butter
    2 teaspoons salt
    6 cups sifted bread flour
    3 eggs (room temperature), beaten

Oil large bowl and set aside. Sprinkle sugar and yeast over water in small cup and stir until dissolved. Combine scalded milk, ¼ cup butter and salt in another large bowl and mix well. Let cool to 105°F to 115°F. Stir in yeast mixture. Add 4 cups flour with eggs and beat until well blended. Add remaining flour and knead briskly until dough is smooth and elastic, about 10 minutes. Rub hands with small amount of oil. Form dough into ball. Lightly coat top of dough with oil. Transfer to prepared bowl. Cover and let stand in warm, draft-free area until doubled in bulk, about 1½ to 2 hours.

Punch dough down. Knead in bowl 2 minutes. Turn dough out onto lightly floured surface or pastry cloth. Pat or roll to thickness of 1 inch. Cut dough into 1½-inch squares.

Melt remaining ¾ cup butter. Cool to 85°F. Dip each square of dough into melted butter. Arrange dough in large angel food cake pan (without removable bottom). Cover with greased waxed paper and let stand in warm, draft-free area until doubled, 1 to 1½ hours.

Position rack in center of oven and preheat to 400°F. Bake bread until tester inserted in center comes out clean, about 35 minutes (if top begins browning too quickly, cover loosely with foil). Invert onto rack and let cool at least 30 minutes before serving.

Ginger Ice Cream

The following three frozen desserts are served together, garnished with fresh fruit and accompanied by Gingersnaps. The prepared desserts can be scooped into balls the day of the dinner and refrozen on parchment-lined baking sheets. If assembling ahead, let each soften in refrigerator only 5 minutes before serving.

Makes about 1 quart

    2 cups milk
    2 cups whipping cream
    4 ¼-inch slices peeled fresh ginger
    ⅔ cup sugar

    1 tablespoon chopped preserved ginger in syrup,
      drained

Combine milk, cream and fresh ginger in large saucepan over low heat. When bubbles begin to appear around edge of pan, begin stirring constantly for about 5 minutes; *do not allow mixture to boil.* Remove from heat. Discard ginger slices. Add sugar and stir until dissolved. Cool to room temperature.

Stir in preserved ginger. Refrigerate until very cold. *(Ice cream can be prepared several days ahead to this point, covered and refrigerated until ready to process.)* Transfer mixture to ice cream maker and process according to manufacturer's instructions. Turn into container and freeze. Let soften in refrigerator 20 minutes before serving.

Raspberry Sorbet

Makes about 1 quart

    3 10-ounce packages frozen raspberries in syrup,
      thawed
    ⅓ cup superfine sugar
    2 tablespoons framboise (raspberry brandy)
      (optional)
    1 tablespoon fresh lemon juice

Place undrained raspberries in very fine strainer set over bowl and mash well with back of spoon to extract as much pulp and juice as possible; discard seeds. Add sugar, brandy and lemon juice to berries and blend well. Refrigerate until very cold. *(Sorbet can be prepared several days ahead to this point, covered and refrigerated until ready to process.)* Transfer raspberry mixture to ice-cream maker and process according to manufacturer's instructions. Turn into container and freeze. Let sorbet soften in refrigerator for about 20 minutes before serving.

Mango Sorbet

Makes about 1 quart

2 15-ounce jars mangoes in syrup
1 teaspoon fresh lemon juice

Combine undrained mangoes and lemon juice in processor or blender and mix until smooth. Strain if desired. Turn mixture into bowl and refrigerate until very cold. *(Sorbet can be prepared several days ahead to this point, covered and refrigerated until ready to process.)* Transfer mango mixture to ice cream maker and process according to manufacturer's instructions. Turn into container and freeze. Let soften in refrigerator 20 minutes before serving.

Gingersnaps

Makes about 30 dozen cookies

1½ cups firmly packed light brown sugar
¼ cup blackstrap or dark molasses
1 egg, room temperature
1 cup (2 sticks) butter, melted and slightly cooled
2⅔ cups sifted all purpose flour
2 teaspoons ground ginger
1½ teaspoons ground cloves
1½ teaspoons cinnamon
1½ teaspoons baking soda
⅜ teaspoon salt

Granulated sugar

Combine brown sugar, molasses and egg in large bowl and mix well. Beat in butter. Stir in flour, ginger, cloves, cinnamon, baking soda and salt. Turn dough out onto lightly floured surface and shape into 4 long logs. Roll logs back and forth several times. Cut each in half crosswise. Shape logs to diameter of about ⅝ inch. Freeze until thoroughly chilled, about 1 hour.

Preheat oven to 350°F. Lightly grease baking sheet (preferably nonstick). Pour sugar into pie plate to depth of about ¼ inch. Remove one log from freezer and cut into ¼-inch slices. Dip slices into sugar, turning several times to coat entire surface and pressing dough to spread and flatten to thickness of about ⅛ inch. Transfer slices to prepared sheet, spacing about 1 inch apart. Bake until lightly browned but still soft, about 6 to 8 minutes. Let cool until almost hard, about 30 seconds. Using spatula, quickly transfer cookies to sheet of waxed paper; *if cooled too long, cookies will cling to pan and break when removed.* (If cookies harden before removal from baking sheet, return to oven for about 30 seconds.) Sprinkle with sugar. Repeat with remaining dough. *(Cookies can be prepared up to 1 month ahead. Store in container with tight-fitting lid in cool, dry place.)*

Ginger Ice Cream, Raspberry and Mango Sorbets are accompanied by homemade Gingersnaps.

Dieters' Dinner Party

THE MENU

Stuffed Beet Salad

Salmon with Apples,
Pears and Limes

Brown Rice Milanese

Green Beans—Open Sesame

Buttermilk Strawberry Sherbet

Serves 6

A dramatic table setting and a beautiful beginning—
Stuffed Beet Salad.

THE STRATEGY

A delicious low-calorie, no-salt dinner. The colorful and tempting dishes include a bright Stuffed Beet Salad, salmon steaks garnished with sautéed fresh fruit and herbed rice tossed with Romano cheese. You and your dieting companions don't even have to give up dessert: The Buttermilk Strawberry Sherbet is a smooth and satisfying finish.

Shopping List

    6 salmon steaks (each 1¼ inches thick)
    6 large beets (each about 3½ inches in diameter)
    3 carrots
    1 medium tomato or 6 cherry tomatoes
    1 medium Spanish onion
    1 cucumber
    2 oranges
    2 limes
    1 apple
    1 pear
    2 shallots
    1 garlic clove
    1 pound green beans
    4 large mushrooms
    1 lemon (only juice and peel of ½ lemon will be used)
    4 cups fresh strawberries (unsweetened frozen strawberries can be substituted) plus additional strawberries (optional garnish)
       Parsley (optional garnish)
       Green onion (optional garnish)
    3 cups buttermilk
    4 eggs
    ½ stick butter
    1 cup grated Romano cheese
    1 cup short-grain brown rice
    ½ cup sesame seed
    ¾ cup safflower oil
    ¼ cup red wine vinegar
    6 tablespoons honey
       Vanilla
       Black pepper
       Dried tarragon
       Dried chives
       Dried dillweed
       Nutmeg

Sesame oil
Tamari sauce

Tips

All these recipes can be doubled (prepare sherbet in two batches).

Countdown

1 day ahead
Prepare Buttermilk Strawberry Sherbet and freeze.
Assemble beets for salad to point of adding vegetables. Refrigerate.

Morning of dinner
Prepare Brown Rice Milanese to point of adding cheese. Set aside at room temperature.
Add vegetables and reserved beet pulp to dressing for salad. Refrigerate.

About 20 minutes before serving
Rewarm brown rice over low heat.
Prepare salmon.

About 10 minutes before serving
Prepare Green Beans—Open Sesame.

Just before serving
Add Romano cheese to rice and toss lightly until melted.
Blend oranges into vegetable mixture and fill beets.

Just before dessert
Spoon sherbet into goblets or wineglasses and garnish with strawberries (if desired).

Wine Suggestions

A crisp white wine would be best with this light meal. Try Italian Trebbiano or Soave, German Riesling or Chenin Blanc from California. If you are really concerned about the dietary properties of this dinner, you might want to choose a light, low-calorie wine, such as those by Almaden or Paul Masson.

THE RECIPES

Stuffed Beet Salad

6 servings

   6 large unpeeled beets (about 3½ inches in diameter)

 ¾ cup safflower oil
 ¼ cup red wine vinegar
   2 tablespoons dried tarragon
 ½ teaspoon freshly ground pepper

   3 carrots, cut into ¼-inch dice
   1 medium tomato or 6 cherry tomatoes, chopped
   1 medium Spanish onion, cut into ¼-inch dice
   1 unpeeled cucumber, cut into ¼-inch dice
   2 oranges, peeled and cut into ½-inch wedges
     Minced fresh parsley and chopped green onion (optional garnish)

Boil beets in generous amount of water in covered saucepan for 1 hour or until tender. Drain well. Trim tops and bottoms from beets so they will stand upright; slip off skins. Using small spoon or melon baller, hollow out beets, leaving shell about ½ inch thick. Place half of pulp in processor; dice or slice remainder and set aside.

Add oil, vinegar, tarragon and pepper to processor and mix well. Cover and refrigerate overnight. Chill beets.

Add carrot, tomato, onion, cucumber and reserved beet pulp to dressing and marinate at least 30 minutes. When ready to serve, add oranges and toss lightly. Fill beets with mixture. Garnish each serving with parsley and green onion.

Salmon with Apples, Pears and Limes

6 servings

   6 salmon steaks cut to thickness of 1¼ inches
   2 tablespoons (¼ stick) butter
     Freshly ground pepper
   2 limes, thinly sliced (including ends)
   1 unpeeled apple, halved, cored and thinly sliced
   1 unpeeled pear, quartered, cored and thinly sliced

Preheat broiler. Place salmon on broiler pan. Melt butter in large skillet over low to medium heat. Sprinkle with pepper. Add lime slices and turn to coat with butter. Add apple and pear and sauté until butter is absorbed by fruit, about 5 minutes; *fruit should be tender but not browned.* Remove lime ends from skillet and rub over salmon, simultaneously squeezing juice. Broil about 5 inches from heat source until browned on both sides, about 7 minutes per side. Serve immediately with sautéed fruit.

Squeeze lime ends over salmon before broiling.

Slice mushrooms for Green Beans–Open Sesame.

Calorie wise and delicious, Salmon with Apples, Pears and Limes, Brown Rice Milanese and Green Beans-Open Sesame.

Brown Rice Milanese

6 servings

  2 tablespoons (¼ stick) butter
  2 shallots, chopped
  1 garlic clove, minced
  3 tablespoons dried chives
  ½ teaspoon dried dillweed
  1 cup short-grain brown rice
  2 cups cold water
  1 cup freshly grated Romano cheese

Melt butter in large skillet or shallow heatproof casserole over medium heat. Add shallot and garlic and sauté until tender. Add chives and dillweed and sauté an additional 1 to 2 minutes. Stir in rice and sauté until it begins to crackle. Add water and bring to boil. Reduce heat to low, cover and simmer 45 minutes (do not remove cover during cooking time). Remove from heat and add cheese, tossing lightly until cheese is melted.

Rice can be cooked ahead to point of adding cheese. Heat before adding Romano.

The tempting dessert is Buttermilk Strawberry Sherbet.

Green Beans–Open Sesame

6 servings

  1 pound green beans, cut julienne
  3 tablespoons tamari sauce*
  1 tablespoon sesame oil
  ¼ teaspoon nutmeg
  4 large mushrooms, sliced
  ½ cup sesame seed, toasted

Steam beans until crisp-tender, about 10 minutes. Meanwhile, combine tamari, oil and nutmeg in large skillet over low to medium heat. Add mushrooms and sauté until just tender. Add beans and toss lightly. Add sesame seed and toss again. Serve immediately.

*Similar to soy sauce but less salty, tamari sauce is available at oriental markets, natural food stores and some supermarkets.

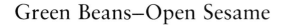

Buttermilk Strawberry Sherbet

6 servings

  3 cups buttermilk
  6 tablespoons honey
  2 teaspoons vanilla
    Juice and peel of ½ lemon
  4 cups fresh or unsweetened frozen strawberries, quartered

  4 egg whites
    Sliced strawberries (optional garnish)

Combine buttermilk, honey, vanilla, lemon juice and peel in processor or blender and mix well. Transfer to 9 x 13-inch baking pan. Blend in berries. Cover and freeze until firm.

Transfer to large mixing bowl and stir with wooden spoon to loosen. Beat whites until stiff. Add to frozen mixture, stirring until sherbet is softened. Return to freezer until solid. Spoon into goblets or wine glasses and garnish with sliced strawberries.

Slim Cuisine With Style

THE MENU

Crustless Spinach Quiche

Crudités with Fresh Tomato Sauce

*Scaloppine of Salmon
with Mexican Green Sauce*

Spiced Chicken Strips

Sesame Broccoli

Broiled Leg of Lamb

Carrot Puree

Chocolate Sherbet

Frozen Lemon Cream

Serves 6 to 10

*Front to back: Broiled Leg of Lamb bordered with Carrot
Puree, Sesame Broccoli surrounding Spiced Chicken Strips,
and light Chocolate Sherbet and Frozen Lemon Cream.*

THE STRATEGY

Light, low-calorie and easy-to-make dishes are the focus of this buffet. Create a beautiful crudité centerpiece and surround with the remaining slimming fare: crustless quiche, salmon in a zesty Mexican sauce, broiled chicken and lamb and two bright vegetable dishes. Frozen Lemon Cream, served in attractive lemon cups, and a sherbet especially for chocolate lovers round out the menu.

Shopping List

1 2-pound piece of salmon
3 pounds boned, skinned chicken breasts
1 6- to 7-pound leg of lamb (have butcher bone and trim)
1 medium onion
1 large onion
1 small onion plus additional onion (1 cup paper-thin slices)
1¼ pounds tomatoes
2½ pounds carrots
½ pound turnips
4 large leaves of romaine lettuce
1 whole head garlic plus 2 cloves plus 2 additional small cloves
1 parsley sprig plus 2 tablespoons chopped
1 large bunch broccoli
5 large lemons plus juice and finely grated peel of 2 lemons (about ½ cup juice) plus an additional 3 tablespoons fresh lemon juice
2 tablespoons fresh lime juice
Fresh ginger (one 1-inch piece)
Fresh dill (1 teaspoon) (dried oregano can be substituted)
Fresh parsley, tarragon or dill (1 tablespoon chopped)
Selection of fresh vegetables for crudités
¾ pound Muenster cheese
5 eggs
3 cups lowfat ricotta cheese
¾ cup lowfat plain yogurt
6 cups nonfat milk
¼ cup fresh breadcrumbs
3 ounces blanched almonds
¼ cup red wine vinegar plus additional 4 teaspoons red wine vinegar or tarragon vinegar
½ cup safflower oil
⅔ cup olive oil
Peanut oil
Sesame oil
Vegetable oil
½ cup sesame seed
32 peppercorns
5 bay leaves
1 tablespoon capers
8 whole cloves
1½ cups sugar
1¾ cups unsweetened cocoa
Catsup
Soy sauce
Salt
Coarse salt (optional)
Black pepper
Ground red pepper
Fennel seed
Ground cumin
Ground cilantro, also known as coriander or Chinese parsley
Cinnamon
Vanilla bean
Honey
Paprika
Seeds from 8 cardamom pods
1 10-ounce package frozen spinach
¼ cup saké

Tips

For an attractive presentation, arrange Sesame Broccoli around rim of large platter and fill center with Spiced Chicken Strips. Sprinkle with additional sesame seed if desired.
For a Frozen Orange Cream variation of the lemon dessert, use one 6-ounce can frozen orange juice concentrate and 1½ teaspoons grated orange peel in place of lemon juice and peel. Reduce sugar to ¼ cup.
All these dishes can be doubled.

Countdown

About 2 weeks ahead
Prepare Fromage Blanc for Carrot Puree and refrigerate.

2 days ahead
Make court bouillon for Mexican Green Sauce and
     refrigerate.

1 day ahead
Prepare Frozen Lemon Cream and freeze.
Ready lemon shell "serving containers" for Frozen
     Lemon Cream; freeze.
Prepare Fresh Tomato Sauce for crudités to point
     of adding oil. Refrigerate.
Make Chocolate Sherbet and freeze.
Combine ingredients for lamb marinade; add meat
     and refrigerate.

Morning of buffet
Scoop Frozen Lemon Cream into lemon shells and
     refreeze.
Cut up raw vegetables, the crudités, for Fresh To-
     mato Sauce dip. Transfer to plastic bags and
     refrigerate.
Prepare Mexican Green Sauce and set aside at
     room temperature.
Mix Carrot Puree and set aside at room
     temperature.
Blend marinade for chicken; add chicken and
     refrigerate.

Afternoon of buffet
Bring lamb and marinade to room temperature.
Combine dressing ingredients for broccoli and set
     aside at room temperature.

About 1 hour before serving
Cook broccoli; drain well and cool to room
     temperature.
Prepare Crustless Spinach Quiche.

About 30 minutes before serving
Finish Broiled Leg of Lamb.

About 15 minutes before serving
Rewarm Carrot Puree over low heat.
Rewarm Mexican Green Sauce over low heat.
Assemble crudités and Fresh Tomato Sauce attrac-
     tively on platter.

Just before serving
Broil chicken for Spiced Chicken Strips.
Toss broccoli with dressing.
Cook salmon; spoon sauce onto plates and arrange
     salmon over sauce.

Wine Suggestions

Serve a fresh, dry Gewurztraminer or Johannisberg
Riesling with the salmon. Try one by Joseph Phelps,
Chateau St. Jean or Gundlach-Bundschu. With the
lamb, serve a medium-weight Cabernet Sauvignon,
such as those by Iron Horse, Jordan or Beringer.

THE RECIPES

Crustless Spinach Quiche

6 to 8 servings

   1   tablespoon vegetable oil
   1   large onion, chopped
   1   10-ounce package frozen spinach, thawed and
        squeezed to remove as much moisture as
        possible

   5   eggs
   ¾   pound Muenster cheese, grated
        Salt and freshly ground pepper

Preheat oven to 350°F. Butter 9-inch pie plate. Heat
oil in skillet over medium-high heat. Add onion and
sauté until wilted. Add spinach; cook until excess
moisture is evaporated. Let cool.
     Beat eggs in bowl. Add cheese. Stir into onion-
spinach mixture and season to taste with salt and
pepper. Turn into pie plate. Bake until tester comes
out clean, 40 to 45 minutes.

Fresh Tomato Sauce

Makes about 3½ cups

   1¼ pounds tomatoes, peeled and chopped
   4   teaspoons red wine vinegar or tarragon
        vinegar
   1   tablespoon chopped fresh parsley, tarragon or
        dill
   ½   teaspoon salt
   ¼   teaspoon freshly ground pepper
   ¼   cup safflower oil

Combine all ingredients except oil in processor or
bowl and mix well. Just before serving, add oil a
small amount at a time and mix until blended.

Two easy first courses: Crustless Spinach Quiche and Scaloppine of Salmon with Mexican Green Sauce.

Scaloppine of Salmon with Mexican Green Sauce

8 to 10 servings

  1 2-pound piece salmon, skinned and boned

    Mexican Green Sauce (see following recipe)

  1 to 2 tablespoons peanut oil
    Coarse salt (optional)

Slice salmon into pieces no more than ¼ inch thick. Place between two pieces of aluminum foil and pound *very lightly.*

Spoon sauce onto heated dinner plates; set aside and keep warm.

Heat large nonstick skillet. Add enough oil just to coat bottom. Cook salmon in 2 or 3 batches about 25 seconds on first side and 15 seconds on the other. Blot with paper towels and place on sauce. Sprinkle lightly with salt if desired.

Mexican Green Sauce

Makes about 2 cups

Court Bouillon
  ½ pound carrots, sliced
  ½ pound turnips, sliced
  ½ small onion, sliced
 12 peppercorns
  2 tablespoons fresh lime juice
  2 bay leaves
  1 teaspoon salt
  4 cups water

Sauce
  ½ small onion, coarsely chopped
  3 ounces blanched almonds, ground
  ¼ cup fresh breadcrumbs
  4 large romaine leaves, torn into pieces
  2 garlic cloves
  1 tablespoon capers
  1 parsley sprig
1¾ cups court bouillon
  ¼ cup safflower oil
    Pinch of ground red pepper

For court bouillon: Combine all ingredients in saucepan and simmer uncovered for 30 minutes. Strain.

For sauce: Combine first seven ingredients in blender and add enough bouillon to mix into smooth puree. Turn into saucepan and add remaining bouillon and oil. Simmer gently, stirring occasionally, for about 10 minutes. Stir in red pepper to taste.

Spiced Chicken Strips

For attractive presentation, arrange Sesame Broccoli around outer edge of large platter and fill center with these flavorful morsels of chicken. Sprinkle additional sesame seed over chicken.

8 buffet servings; 6 main-course servings

Marinade
     1   medium onion, coarsely chopped
     1   whole head garlic, peeled
     5   tablespoons peanut oil
  ¼   cup red wine vinegar
     3   tablespoons catsup
     2   tablespoons fennel seed
     2   tablespoons ground cumin
  1½ to 2 tablespoons paprika
  20   whole peppercorns
     1   1-inch piece fresh ginger, peeled and chopped
         Seeds from 8 cardamom pods
     8   whole cloves
     2   teaspoons ground cilantro
     2   teaspoons salt
     1   teaspoon cinnamon
  ¼   teaspoon ground red pepper

     3   pounds boned, skinned chicken breast, cut into strips about 1½ to 2 inches long and ½ inch wide

Combine all ingredients for marinade in blender and mix to smooth paste.

Place chicken in large bowl. Add marinade and stir to coat thoroughly. Cover and chill 4 to 6 hours.

Position rack so meat will be about 6 inches from heat source and preheat broiler. Spread chicken in shallow baking pan and broil until firm to the touch, about 4 minutes.

Sesame Broccoli

6 servings

     1   large bunch broccoli, broken into florets, stems peeled

  ½   cup sesame seed, toasted
  ¼   cup saké
  1½   tablespoons soy sauce
     2   teaspoons sesame oil
     2   teaspoons honey

Cook broccoli in boiling salted water until crisp-tender. Drain thoroughly. Let stand until cooled to room temperature.

Combine remaining ingredients in large bowl. Before serving, add broccoli and toss to mix well.

1. *Chicken strips are marinated.* 2. *Pieces are put in pan and broiled* (3) *until firm.* 4. *Broccoli is tossed with sesame seed and* (5) *arranged on platter.* 6. *Spiced chicken fills the center.*

1. *Lamb is carved into ¼ slices and arranged on a platter (2) with the Carrot Puree. 3. Pureed carrots, nonfat milk and Fomage Blanc are blended, poured into a pastry bag (4) and piped onto platter (5).*

Broiled Leg of Lamb

10 servings

Marinade
  1 cup onion sliced paper thin
  2 small garlic cloves, minced
  3 tablespoons fresh lemon juice
  3 bay leaves, crumbled
  2 tablespoons chopped fresh parsley
  1 teaspoon dried oregano or fresh dill
  1 teaspoon salt
  ½ teaspoon freshly ground pepper
  ⅔ cup olive oil

1 6- to 7-pound leg of lamb, boned, trimmed of all fat and fell

Combine ingredients for marinade. Spread lamb flat in dish and pour marinade over. Cover and refrigerate 24 hours, turning several times.

Leave meat in marinade and bring to room temperature. Position rack so meat will be 4 to 6 inches from heat source and preheat broiler. Transfer lamb directly from marinade onto rack over broiler pan (reserve marinade). Broil lamb 15 minutes on first side; turn and broil 12 minutes longer. Carve against grain into slices ¼ inch thick. Serve with marinade on the side.

Carrot Puree

6 servings

  2 **pounds carrots, thinly sliced**
  2 **teaspoons salt**
  3 **tablespoons Fromage Blanc (see following recipe)**
  ½ **cup nonfat milk**

Cook carrots in boiling salted water until tender, 15 to 20 minutes. Drain well. Puree half of carrots, Fromage Blanc and milk in processor. Repeat. Warm through if needed.

Fromage Blanc

  3 **cups lowfat ricotta cheese**
  ¾ **cup lowfat plain yogurt**

Combine ingredients in processor or blender and mix until smooth. Transfer to jar. Cover and let stand at room temperature about 6 hours. Refrigerate for at least 10 hours before using.

Fromage Blanc is an excellent low-calorie substitute for cream in cooking and will keep in refrigerator for about 2 weeks.

Chocolate Sherbet

Makes about 20 ¼-cup servings

1¾ **cups unsweetened cocoa**
  1 **cup sugar**
  ⅛ **teaspoon salt**
3½ **cups nonfat milk**
    Vanilla bean

Combine cocoa, sugar and salt in medium saucepan and mix well. Gradually stir in milk. Split vanilla bean, scrape out seeds and add with bean to pan. Place over medium heat and bring just to boil, stirring constantly. Reduce heat and simmer, stirring constantly, 5 minutes. Let cool, then remove vanilla bean. Pour into shallow pan and freeze.

Spoon into processor and mix or beat by hand until smooth. Return to freezer, if needed, or scoop into dishes and serve.

Frozen Lemon Cream

Makes about 10 ¼-cup servings

  2 **cups nonfat milk**
  ½ **cup sugar**
    Juice and finely grated peel of 2 lemons (about ½ cup juice)

  5 **large lemons**

Combine milk, sugar, lemon juice and peel and stir until sugar is completely dissolved. Pour into shallow pan and freeze.

Meanwhile, cut lemons in half lengthwise; remove pulp. Freeze shells.

Spoon frozen lemon mixture into processor and mix or beat by hand until smooth. Return to freezer until partially frozen. Scoop into shells and refreeze until ready to serve.

Frozen Orange Cream variation: Substitute one 6-ounce can frozen orange juice concentrate for lemon juice; add 1½ teaspoons orange peel and ¼ cup sugar.

Regional American Menus

So MUCH HAS BEEN said and written of late about the "new" American cooking that we sometimes seem in danger of forgetting the bounty represented by the older, more traditional American cuisine. Actually this is not one homogeneous cuisine but many different ones, each reflecting a distinct regional or ethnic character, all deeply rooted in the country's "melting pot" history. Think, for example, of the chowders, clambakes and Indian pudding of New England; the Brunswick stew, fried chicken and chess pies of the Deep South; the corn fritters, dumplings and hearty wheat and rye breads of the Midwest and Great Plains; the orange- and nut-flavored chicken dishes and avocado salads of California; jambalaya, filé gumbo and roasted oysters from the bayou country of Louisiana; and even the *maloo*, roast pig and *poi* of the Hawaiian luau. In its variety and interest, American regional cookery is every bit as multifaceted as the cuisines of, say, China and India.

The dinner party menus in this chapter are all based on American themes. One features the flavors of Colonial Maryland (page 123), including Peanut Soup, Bourbon Squash Rings and a very different—and attractive—version of stuffed ham, as well as the original American "cocktail," Fish House Punch. Another is an especially hearty dinner in the Tex-Mex style of the Southwest (page 153)—tortillas, tamales, enchiladas, chili, refried beans, buñuelos and a refreshing Margarita Ice—all as much fun to make as they are to eat. A third menu celebrates the local delicacies of the Pacific Northwest (page 139), including Cream of Lentil Soup and, of course, salmon—here with a *nouvelle* touch of raspberry beurre blanc and lime butter sauce.

Our classic supper from the South (page 131) includes Country Ham with Red Eye Gravy, biscuits, Likker Pudding and a trio of delicious pies. Then, for a look at the eclectic tastes of the Rocky Mountains (page 147), there is a buffet that begins with a powerful grog and goes on to, among other favorites, jalapeños en escabeche and an intriguing variation on chili, Bowl of the Wife of Kit Carson.

In addition to being great entertaining fare, each of these menus can be seen as a lesson in history and geography. But don't worry: Your guests won't fall asleep during the lesson.

Colonial Feast Updated

THE MENU

Spindled Oysters

Fish House Punch

Peanut Soup

Southern Maryland Stuffed Ham

Corn and Cabbage Salad

Bourbon Squash Rings

Pickled Herb Carrots

Stone-Ground Corn Rolls

Old St. Mary's Syllabub

Chocolate Torte

Serves 8

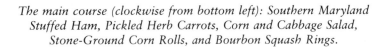

The main course (clockwise from bottom left): Southern Maryland Stuffed Ham, Pickled Herb Carrots, Corn and Cabbage Salad, Stone-Ground Corn Rolls, and Bourbon Squash Rings.

THE STRATEGY

Here is a unique dinner party featuring a collection of traditional American foods. The centerpiece of the menu is a delicious ham stuffed with a fragrant mixture of green onion, kale and watercress. Two desserts—a classic colonial syllabub and a delectable Chocolate Torte—round out the meal in style.

Shopping List

24 oysters
12 strips bacon
 1 12- to 15-pound corned or fresh ham
 1 quart chicken stock (preferably homemade)
 1 medium onion
 1 celery stalk
 3 pounds kale
 1 pound green onions
 1 pound field cress or watercress
 2 medium heads cabbage plus 3 cups shredded
 2 large acorn squash
 ½ cup dried sweet corn or kernels from 2 large ears fresh corn

 5 sprigs fresh thyme (or ½ teaspoon dried)
 1 garlic clove
 1 pound tender young carrots
   Green pepper (¾ cup chopped)
   Fresh parsley
   Juice and peel of 1 dozen lemons (about 3 cups juice) plus juice of 1 lemon plus lemons for garnish plus additional fresh lemon juice (optional)
 2 cups half and half
 2 cups milk
 6 cups whipping cream
 6 eggs
1½ sticks butter
 3 sticks unsalted butter
 ¾ cup stone-ground cornmeal
 3 to 3½ cups plus 1 teaspoon sugar
 6 cups unbleached all purpose flour
2⅔ cups plus 1 tablespoon all purpose flour
 ½ cup powdered sugar
 1 pound plus 2 tablespoons dark brown sugar
 ¾ cup unsweetened cocoa
 3 squares semisweet chocolate

Ingredients for this menu displayed in a Colonial kitchen.

½ cup solid shortening
1 envelope yeast
½ cup white vinegar
⅔ cup white wine vinegar
½ cup olive oil
1 bay leaf
 Salt
 Black pepper
 Whole mustard seed
 Celery seed
 Ground red pepper
 Dry mustard
 Dijon mustard
 Whole nutmeg
 Cinnamon
1½ cups creamy peanut butter
1 cup Madeira
1 quart Jamaica rum
1 quart brandy
⅔ cup dry white wine
 Bourbon to taste (see recipe for Bourbon
 Squash Rings)
12 bamboo skewers

Countdown

3 days ahead
Prepare Chocolate Torte to point noted in recipe.
Make Pickled Herb Carrots.

1 to 2 days ahead
Prepare Southern Maryland Stuffed Ham and refrigerate.

Morning of dinner
Prepare Fish House Punch and set aside at room
 temperature.

About 3 hours before serving
Begin Stone-Ground Corn Rolls.
Make Old St. Mary's Syllabub.

About 1½ hours before serving
Remove ham from refrigerator and let stand at
 room temperature.
If using dried sweet corn for salad, steep in boiling
 water as directed.

About 1 hour before serving
Prepare Peanut Soup.
Finish Chocolate Torte and refrigerate.

About 30 minutes before serving
Assemble and broil Spindled Oysters.
Finish Corn and Cabbage Salad.
Assemble and bake Bourbon Squash Rings.

About 15 minutes before serving
Bake Stone-Ground Corn Rolls.
If serving carrots hot, rewarm gently over low
 heat.
Strain Fish House Punch. Transfer to punch bowl
 or pitcher for serving.

Wine Suggestions

After you have finished the punch, serve a briefly
chilled light red wine such as a French Beaujolais (this
is appropriate, since the only wine available in Colonial times was from Europe), a California Gamay
Beaujolais or an Italian Bardolino.

THE RECIPES

Spindled Oysters

8 servings

12 strips bacon, cut in half lengthwise
24 uncooked oysters
 Chopped fresh parsley
 Lemon wedges (garnish)

Preheat broiler. Cook bacon in large skillet over medium-high heat just until transparent. Wrap each oyster in 1 piece bacon and spear onto skewer. Repeat
with remaining oysters and bacon, spearing several
oysters onto each skewer. Transfer to broiler pan;
broil until bacon is crisp. Remove skewer. Arrange
wrapped oysters on serving platter, spearing each with
toothpick if desired. Sprinkle with parsley. Surround
oysters with lemon wedges. Serve immediately.

Potent Fish House Punch and succulent Spindled Oysters.

Fish House Punch

Makes about 5 quarts

  3 quarts water
  1 pound dark brown sugar
      Juice and peel of 1 dozen lemons
      (about 3 cups juice)
  1 quart Jamaica rum
  1 quart brandy
      Crushed ice

Combine water and sugar in heavy large saucepan over medium-low heat and cook until sugar dissolves, shaking pan occasionally. Increase heat to medium-high and boil syrup 2 minutes. Combine lemon juice and peel in large bowl. Pour hot syrup over. Let cool. Stir in rum and brandy. Strain before using. Serve over crushed ice.

Peanut Soup

8 servings

 ½ cup (1 stick) butter
  1 medium onion, finely chopped
  1 celery stalk, finely chopped
  1 tablespoon all purpose flour
  1 quart chicken stock (preferably homemade)
  2 cups half and half
1½ cups creamy peanut butter
      Salt and freshly ground pepper
      Fresh lemon juice (optional)
      Lemon slices dusted with minced fresh parsley
      (garnish)

Melt butter in heavy 4-quart saucepan over medium-low heat. Add onion and celery and sauté until onion is transparent, about 10 minutes. Add flour and stir 3 minutes. Pour in chicken stock. Bring mixture to rapid boil, stirring constantly. Continue boiling until mixture is slightly thickened and smooth. Reduce heat to low, cover partially and simmer gently about 20 minutes. Strain stock into another saucepan (discard vegetables). Whisk in half and half and peanut butter. Season with salt and pepper. Taste and add lemon juice if desired. Place over low heat and simmer about 5 minutes. Ladle into tureen or individual bowls. Garnish with lemon slices. Serve hot.

Southern Maryland Stuffed Ham

If ham is purchased enclosed in burlap bag, use bag instead of cheesecloth when wrapping stuffing around ham.

10 to 12 servings plus leftovers

- 3 pounds kale (thickest stems discarded), chopped
- 1 pound green onion, chopped
- 1 pound field cress (if available) or watercress, chopped
- 2 medium heads cabbage, cored and chopped
- 3 to 4 tablespoons whole mustard seed
- 2 tablespoons celery seed
- 3 tablespoons plus 1 teaspoon ground red pepper (or more to taste)
- 1 tablespoon plus 1 teaspoon salt

- 1 12- to 15-pound corned ham*

Combine kale, onion, field cress, cabbage, mustard seed, celery seed, red pepper and salt in large bowl.

Remove all skin from ham except near hock. Trim all but ½-inch layer of fat from ham. Pierce ham using long, slender, sharp knife, driving knife straight down and stopping 1 inch from bottom. Repeat, spacing staggered rows of slits 1 to 1½ inches apart, until entire ham is covered with slits.

Fill each slit with vegetable mixture until stuffing can be seen at top. Spread layer of stuffing on piece of cheesecloth large enough to surround ham. Set ham on cheesecloth. Pat remaining stuffing over top of ham. Bring cheesecloth up and around ham, distributing stuffing evenly, and secure with strong twine. Transfer ham to large pot. Add enough hot water to cover. Place over medium-high heat and bring to boil. Reduce heat, cover and simmer about 15 minutes per pound. Remove lid and let ham cool to room temperature in liquid. *(Ham can be prepared 1 to 2 days ahead and refrigerated. Remove from refrigerator about 1½ hours before serving.)* To serve, cut ham into thin slices vertically across grain to expose stuffing.

*Fresh ham can be substituted for corned.

Corn and Cabbage Salad

8 servings

- 1½ cups boiling water
- ½ cup dried sweet corn*
- 3 cups shredded cabbage
- ¾ cup chopped green pepper
- ½ cup white vinegar
- ¼ to ½ cup sugar (or to taste)
- ½ teaspoon dry mustard
  Salt and freshly ground pepper

1. *Remaining stuffing is arranged around ham.* 2. *Cheesecloth bag is tied before simmering.*
3. *Ham is carved vertically to reveal mosaic of stuffing.*

Combine water and corn in medium saucepan and let stand about 1 hour. Stir in cabbage and green pepper. Add vinegar, sugar and mustard and blend well. Season with salt and pepper to taste. Cover, place over medium-low heat and simmer 30 minutes. Turn into dish and serve immediately.

*Kernels from 2 large ears of corn can be substituted for ½ cup dried corn. Add to cabbage in last 3 minutes of cooking.

Bourbon Squash Rings

8 servings

 2 large acorn squash, cut into ½-inch rings and seeded
   Bourbon
 ¼ cup (½ stick) butter, melted
 2 tablespoons brown sugar
 ¼ teaspoon freshly grated nutmeg

Preheat oven to 375°F. Line baking dish with aluminum foil. Arrange squash rings in single layer on foil. Prick with fork. Brush rings generously with bourbon. Let stand 5 minutes to absorb liquor. Brush evenly with melted butter. Sprinkle with brown sugar and nutmeg. Bake until tender, about 20 minutes. Serve immediately.

Pickled Herb Carrots

8 servings

 ⅔ cup dry white wine
 ⅔ cup white wine vinegar
 ½ cup olive oil
 1 teaspoon sugar
 1 teaspoon salt
 5 fresh thyme sprigs, minced, or ½ teaspoon dried, crumbled
 3 fresh parsley sprigs, minced
 1 garlic clove, minced
 1 bay leaf
 ⅛ teaspoon ground red pepper
 ⅔ cup water
 1 pound tender young carrots, cut into ¼-inch julienne
 1½ tablespoons Dijon mustard

Combine wine, vinegar, oil, sugar, salt, thyme, parsley, garlic, bay leaf and pepper in large skillet. Stir in ⅔ cup water. Place over medium-high heat and bring to boil. Add carrots and continue boiling until carrots are just crisp-tender, 20 to 25 minutes. Stir in mustard, blending thoroughly. Cover and let marinate in cool place 2 to 3 days. Serve hot or cold.

Stone-Ground Corn Rolls

Makes about 32 rolls

 2 cups milk
 ¾ cup stone-ground cornmeal
 ½ cup sugar
 ½ cup solid shortening
 1½ teaspoons salt
 2 eggs, beaten
 1 package yeast dissolved in ¼ cup warm water
 6 cups unbleached all purpose flour

Grease baking sheets. Combine milk and cornmeal in large saucepan over low heat and cook, stirring frequently, until thick, about 15 minutes. Add sugar, shortening and salt and mix well. Cool to lukewarm. Blend in eggs and yeast. Slowly mix in flour. Knead until smooth, about 12 minutes. Pinch off 1½- to 2-inch-diameter balls of dough and arrange on prepared sheets. Let rise in warm, draft-free area until doubled, about 1½ to 2 hours.

Preheat oven to 375°F. Bake rolls 15 minutes. Serve immediately.

Old St. Mary's Syllabub

8 servings

 2 cups whipping cream
 ¼ cup sugar
 1 cup Madeira
   Juice of 1 lemon
 2 egg whites

Chill 8 wine glasses. Whip cream and sugar in medium bowl until stiff. Stir in ½ cup Madeira with lemon juice, blending well. Beat egg whites in another bowl until soft peaks form. Fold whites into cream mixture. Pour 1 tablespoon Madeira into each chilled glass. Spoon cream over top, dividing evenly among glasses. Refrigerate several hours before serving.

The finishing touch is put on the torte.

Chocolate Torte and creamy Old St. Mary's Syllabub.

Chocolate Torte

16 servings

2⅔ cups all purpose flour
  2 cups sugar
1½ cups (3 sticks) unsalted butter, room
      temperature
  2 eggs, room temperature
  1 tablespoon cinnamon

  4 cups whipping cream
  ¾ cup unsweetened cocoa
  ½ cup powdered sugar
  3 squares semisweet chocolate, grated

Tear fourteen 9½-inch-long sheets of waxed paper. Stack sheets and, using 9-inch pie pan as guide, cut waxed paper into circles.

Combine 2 cups flour with sugar, butter, eggs and cinnamon in large bowl of electric mixer and mix at low speed until well blended. Increase speed to medium and continue to beat until very light and fluffy, about 3 minutes. Stir in remaining ⅔ cup flour to form soft dough.

Preheat oven to 375°F. Dampen large baking sheet with moist cloth. Arrange 2 waxed paper circles on baking sheet. Spread about ⅓ cup dough in very thin layer over each waxed paper circle, almost covering entire surface. Bake until edges of cookies are lightly browned, about 8 to 10 minutes.

Transfer baking sheet to wire rack and cool 5 minutes. Carefully remove cookies with waxed paper circles attached and set on another wire rack to cool completely. Repeat with remaining dough, stacking cookies on flat plate. *(Torte can be prepared up to 3 days ahead to this point. Wrap cookies tightly in plastic. Store in cool, dry place.)*

Combine cream, cocoa and sugar in large bowl of electric mixer and beat at medium speed until soft peaks form. Arrange 1 cookie on flat platter and carefully peel off waxed paper. Spread about ½ cup filling over entire surface of cookie. Repeat layering of cookies, ending with filling. Top with chocolate. Refrigerate torte for about 30 minutes before serving to facilitate slicing.

Classic Southern Supper

THE MENU

Smoked Cornish Hens

Country Ham and Red Eye Gravy

Carolina Biscuits

Likker Pudding

Cabbage Braised in Vermouth with Pecans

Corn Pudding

Minted Vegetables

Lemon Chess Pie

Buttermilk Pie

Strawberry-Glazed Sherry Pie

Serves 12

Clockwise from right: Corn Pudding, Country Ham and Red Eye Gravy, Cabbage Braised in Vermouth with Pecans, and Carolina Biscuits.

THE STRATEGY

Here is a Southern supper in the classic tradition—everything from Country Ham and Red Eye Gravy and Carolina Biscuits to Corn Pudding and Buttermilk Pie. Complement the meal with pitchers of sweetened iced tea.

Shopping List

        6   1½-pound Cornish hens
        6   whole slices sugar-cured ham (cut ⅜ inch thick)
        2   garlic cloves
        2   lemons plus finely grated peel of 1 lemon plus 2 tablespoons fresh lemon juice
        3   medium yams or sweet potatoes (6 cups grated)
        1   large cabbage
        4   cups fresh corn kernels (about 8 to 10 small ears) (or use frozen or canned)
        1   pound cucumbers (about 3 medium)
        1   pound carrots (about 6 medium)
        1   pound zucchini (about 2 medium to large)
        1   pint fresh strawberries
     ½   cup seedless raisins
            Onions (1 cup thinly sliced plus 1 cup finely chopped)
            Fresh mint leaves (2 tablespoons coarsely chopped)
     ½   cup buttermilk
    2½   cups milk plus an additional ¾ to 1 cup (or additional buttermilk)
        2   cups half and half
      22   eggs
        4   cups whipping cream
    5½   sticks butter
        1   cup pecan halves
     ½   cup blanched slivered almonds
        4   cups plus 2 teaspoons sugar plus additional pinches of sugar for pastry dough
    2½   cups self-rising flour
        1   cup plus 2 tablespoons solid shortening
    4½   cups plus 2 tablespoons all purpose flour
            Vanilla
            Salt
            Black pepper
            White pepper
            Dried rosemary (¼ cup)
            Cinnamon

            Dillweed
            Whole nutmeg
     ½   cup red currant jelly
     ½   cup bourbon or rum
     ½   cup dry vermouth
     ½   cup dry sherry

Special Equipment

Hickory chips
Charcoal briquets
Smoker or covered gas grill

Tips

Frozen or canned drained corn kernels can be substituted for fresh in Corn Pudding.
The following recipes can be doubled: Smoked Cornish Hens, Country Ham and Red Eye Gravy and Minted Vegetables.

Countdown

1 month ahead
Prepare Smoked Cornish Hens and freeze.
Prepare dough for pie crusts and freeze.

2 days ahead
Remove pastry dough from freezer and let thaw in refrigerator overnight.

1 day ahead
Remove Cornish hens from freezer and let thaw in refrigerator overnight.
Prepare Lemon Chess Pie; refrigerate if serving chilled.
Make Buttermilk Pie; refrigerate if serving chilled.
Fix Strawberry-Glazed Sherry Pie and refrigerate; do not decorate with berries or glaze.

Morning of dinner
Prepare glaze for Sherry pie and set aside at room temperature.
Cut carrots for Minted Vegetables and refrigerate.
Cut cucumber and zucchini for Minted Vegetables and refrigerate separately from carrots.

Cut up cabbage for Cabbage Braised in Vermouth and refrigerate.

Let Cornish hens stand at room temperature until ready to serve.

About 2 hours before serving
Prepare Likker Pudding to point of adding bourbon.

Set berries on Sherry pie and brush with glaze (reheat glaze briefly to liquefy if necessary). Refrigerate.

About 1 hour before serving
Make Carolina Biscuits.
Prepare Corn Pudding.

About 30 minutes before serving
Prepare Country Ham and Red Eye Gravy.

Just before serving
Finish Minted Vegetables.
Finish cabbage dish.
Add bourbon to Likker Pudding.

Wine Suggestions

With the smoked hens serve a smoky California Sauvignon Blanc (Fumé Blanc) or a white Bordeaux from France. Matching ham with wine is difficult, but in this case a light red such as a Beaujolais, Napa Gamay or a good dry Burgundy should work well.

THE RECIPES

Smoked Cornish Hens

12 servings

  2 to 4 cups hickory chips
10 pounds charcoal briquets

  2 garlic cloves, lightly crushed
  2 lemons, cut in half
  6 1½-pound Cornish hens
  ¼ cup salt
  ¼ cup dried rosemary, crumbled
  1 tablespoon freshly ground pepper

To prepare smoker: Soak hickory chips in water 30 to 45 minutes. Meanwhile, arrange charcoal in bottom of smoker. Ignite and allow to burn until gray ash forms, about 45 to 60 minutes.

For hens: Rub garlic and lemon in cavity of each hen. Combine salt, rosemary and pepper in small bowl. Rub about ⅓ into cavities. Rub another ⅓ beneath skin, lifting skin as much as possible but taking care to avoid tearing. Sprinkle exterior of hens with remaining seasoning. Truss birds.*

When charcoal is ready, drain hickory chips. Sprinkle about 1 cup over briquets. Arrange hens breast side up in smoker and cook according to manufacturer's directions, adding hickory chips as needed. After 45 minutes turn hens breast side down and cook 30 minutes. Turn hens breast side up and continue cooking until juices in cavities run clear and meat thermometer registers 185°F, about 15 to 30 minutes.

Serve hot, at room temperature or chilled.

Smoked hens can be frozen up to 1 month. Serve at room temperature.

If smoker is unavailable, a covered gas grill can be used. Arrange charcoal in bottom of barbecue on one side only and preheat 5 minutes. Arrange hens on opposite side of grill. Cover and cook per recipe.

*To truss hens: Use single thin string to avoid marking the skin. Insert needle through back and tie. Draw legs together and forward, make a figure eight and tie, pulling legs snugly together. Do not draw string across breast of hen.

The bird is trussed and seasoning is sprinkled over top.

Curing Country-Style Ham

Ideally the temperature should be from 35°F to 45°F during curing. For each day the temperature averages below freezing, add an extra day to the curing schedule. Keep a calendar record during the process.

The most desirable ham for curing is called a "long cut," not the short, bell-shaped cut. It should be rounded on all sides with no loose pieces.

For the sugar cure, use ¼ brown sugar to ¾ salt. Use 1¼ ounces of this mix per pound of ham. Saltpeter is often added to produce a redder color, but is not necessary. Weigh the ham and use the exact amount for curing. Apply ⅓ of the mix each time, rubbing some on the shank end and into the bone. Apply evenly without hard rubbing, putting as much as will stay on the surface. Apply again on the third day, and once more on the tenth day. Store uncovered on a shelf or table.

At the end of the curing period, brush or wash mixture off, pat ham dry and transfer to a large paper bag, leaving the top open. Place in a loose white muslin bag (or old, clean pillowcase) to protect from flies and other insects. Tie bag at top and hang from wire or string inserted through shank end, keeping temperature in the curing area at 35°F to 50°F, for another 30 days. Ham will then be succulent for the next 8 months. Beyond that it will become saltier, harder and much less appetizing.

After curing, ham can be coated with pepper if desired (or add pepper to curing mix). Rinse off curing mixture and pat ham dry. Use about ¼ cup of freshly ground pepper for every 25 pounds of ham. Proceed as outlined above for hanging and storing a cured ham.

A 20-pound ham will, as salt penetrates and water comes out, result in a 14- to 15-pound country-style cured ham.

If ham is not to be smoked, just brush off excess cure. It may be rinsed, but this is not necessary.

If ham is to be smoked, remove it from the cure and soak in cold water for 1 to 2 hours to remove salt accumulated on surface and prevent salt streaking. After soaking, hang ham to dry. Heat provided during smoking will remove some of the moisture absorbed during soaking process.

Keep cured ham under refrigeration for at least 20 to 30 days after curing.

Country Ham and Red Eye Gravy

Sugar-cured ham is too salty for the average palate, though many "born and raised" Southerners prefer it just as it is. To remove excess salt, soak the trimmed ham slices in milk for at least 30 minutes or up to 3 or 4 hours.

12 servings

   6 whole slices sugar-cured ham, cut ⅜ inch thick

   1 cup hot water

For ham: Trim all skin from ham; trim fat, leaving only ⅜-inch rim. Save small piece of trimmed fat to render for cooking. Halve slices and remove bone.

Add reserved fat to heavy large skillet and let render over high heat. Remove trimming and discard. Add ham in batches (do not crowd) and fry until fat is amber and meat is lightly browned, about 2 minutes per side. *(Heat may need to be reduced to medium-high as last batches are being cooked so pan juices will not burn.)* Remove and keep warm.

For gravy: When all ham is fried and removed from pan, pour half of pan drippings into warmed gravy boat. Return skillet to medium-high heat and add hot water. Bring to boil, stirring to incorporate all bits of ham and drippings, and let boil 30 seconds. Continue stirring and add to drippings in gravy boat. Serve immediately.

Carolina Biscuits

Makes 24 small or 16 large biscuits

 2 cups self-rising flour, sifted
 ⅔ cup vegetable shortening
 ¾ to 1 cup milk or buttermilk

Preheat oven to 450°F. Grease large baking sheet and set aside.

Combine flour and shortening in mixing bowl and blend until size of small peas, using fingertips, two knives or pastry blender. Add enough milk to make dough soft and slightly sticky.

Shape dough into ball. Turn out onto lightly floured surface and knead briefly until dough is pliable, flouring hands to prevent dough from sticking. *For hand shaping:* Pinch dough off in pieces the size of small lemon. Pat gently into round, dome shape, smoothing top lightly with fingertips.

Using biscuit cutter: Roll dough out on lightly floured surface to thickness of ½ inch. Cut into rounds using biscuit cutter, measuring cup or inverted glass.

Transfer biscuits to prepared sheet and bake until golden brown, about 12 to 15 minutes. Serve hot.

Likker Pudding

Delicious with turkey as well as ham

12 servings

2½ cups milk
 3 medium yams or sweet potatoes (about 6 cups grated)

 3 eggs
 1 cup sugar
 2 teaspoons cinnamon
 ½ cup blanched slivered almonds
 2 tablespoons (¼ stick) butter
 ½ cup bourbon or rum

Preheat oven to 300°F. Butter shallow 2-quart baking dish. Add milk. Peel yams or sweet potatoes; grate directly into milk to prevent darkening.

Beat eggs, gradually adding sugar. Add cinnamon, then almonds. Add to yams and mix well. Dot with butter. Bake until pudding is set, about 1½ hours. Just before serving, pour bourbon or rum over top.

Carolina Biscuits and Country Ham with Red Eye Gravy.

Cabbage Braised in Vermouth with Pecans

12 servings

- 1 large cabbage

- ¼ cup (½ stick) butter
- 1 cup thinly sliced onion
- ½ cup dry vermouth
- 1 teaspoon dillweed
- 1 teaspoon salt
- ¼ teaspoon freshly ground white pepper
- 1 cup pecan halves, toasted

Cut cabbage in half through root end. Place cut side down on work surface and, starting at top end, slice into strips ¼ to ½ inch wide. (You should have 8 to 10 cups of sliced cabbage.)

Melt butter in 12-inch skillet over medium-high heat. Add cabbage and onion and cook, stirring frequently, until vegetables are well coated with butter, about 2 to 3 minutes. Add vermouth and seasoning and continue cooking, stirring frequently, 3 to 5 minutes longer. Add pecans and stir until heated, about 1 minute. Taste and adjust seasoning. Serve hot.

Corn Pudding

12 servings

- ¼ cup (½ stick) butter
- 1 cup finely chopped onion

- 8 eggs
- 4 cups whipping cream
- 2 teaspoons salt
- ½ to 1 teaspoon freshly grated nutmeg
- 4 cups fresh corn kernels (about 8 to 10 small ears), or use frozen or canned

Preheat oven to 350°F. Butter shallow 3-quart baking dish. Melt butter in large skillet over medium-high heat. Add onion and sauté until transparent.

Combine eggs and cream in large bowl and beat lightly. Add salt, nutmeg, corn and onion (and any butter remaining in skillet) and mix well.

Pour mixture into prepared dish. Set in larger dish and add enough hot water to come 1 inch up sides of baking dish. Bake until pudding is set, about 45 to 50 minutes. Serve hot.

Minted Vegetables

12 servings

- 1 pound carrots (about 6 medium), no more than 1 inch in diameter, cut diagonally into ¾-inch slices
- 1 cup water
- 2 teaspoons sugar
- 1 teaspoon salt

- 1 pound cucumbers (about 3 medium), peeled, halved lengthwise, seeded and cut diagonally into ¾-inch slices
- 1 pound zucchini (about 2 medium to large), halved lengthwise and cut diagonally into ¾-inch slices
- 3 tablespoons butter, cut into pieces
- 2 tablespoons coarsely chopped fresh mint leaves

Combine carrots, water, sugar and salt in 5-quart saucepan or Dutch oven. Cover and bring to boil over high heat. Reduce heat to medium-high and cook 5 minutes. Uncover and cook mixture for an additional 5 minutes.

Increase heat to high, add cucumber and zucchini and boil until water is almost evaporated and vegetables are crisp-tender, about 4 to 6 minutes. Add butter and stir until melted and liquid has evaporated. Remove from heat, add mint and toss well. Serve hot.

Lemon Chess Pie

8 servings

- 1 cup boiling water
- ½ cup seedless raisins

- ¼ cup (½ stick) butter
- 1 cup sugar
- 2 eggs
- 2 tablespoons fresh lemon juice
- 1 teaspoon vanilla
  Finely grated peel of 1 lemon

- 1 baked 8-inch pie crust (see following recipe)
- 1 egg white, lightly beaten

Pour boiling water over raisins and let stand about 30 minutes to plump.

Meanwhile, cream butter with sugar. Add eggs and beat well. Add lemon juice, vanilla and peel and mix well. (Lemon juice will cause filling mixture to have curdled appearance.)

Position rack in lower third of oven and preheat to 350°F. Brush pastry with egg white to waterproof crust. Let dry 2 minutes. Drain raisins and stir into filling. Pour into pastry. Bake until filling is firm and golden brown, about 45 minutes. (If pie begins to brown too much, reduce oven temperature to 325°F.) Serve at room temperature or chilled.

Pie Crust

Makes enough for an 8- or 9-inch pie

1½ cups all purpose flour, sifted
 ½ teaspoon salt
     Pinch of sugar
  6 tablespoons (¾ stick) butter
  2 tablespoons plus 1 teaspoon vegetable shortening
  4 to 5 tablespoons cold water

Combine flour, salt and sugar in large mixing bowl. Add butter and shortening in tablespoon-size pieces and cut into flour, using pastry blender or two knives, until mixture is size of small peas. Add water 1 tablespoon at a time and blend quickly with one hand, gathering dough into a mass. Wrap with waxed paper and chill dough for at least 20 minutes.

When ready to bake, position rack in lower third of oven and preheat to 400°F. Flour work surface and rolling pin and roll dough into circle ⅛ inch thick. Fit into pie pan or flan ring and refrigerate about 15 minutes.

Line crust with foil and weight with dried beans or rice. Bake 12 minutes. Discard foil and beans. Continue baking until bottom of pastry is lightly golden, about 5 minutes longer. Let crust cool completely before filling.

Buttermilk Pie

8 to 10 servings

 ½ cup (1 stick) butter
1½ cups sugar
  2 tablespoons all purpose flour
  3 eggs
 ½ cup buttermilk
  1 teaspoon vanilla

  1 baked 9-inch pie crust (see preceding recipe)
  1 egg white, lightly beaten

Position rack in lower third of oven and preheat to 350°F. Melt butter in small saucepan over low heat. Blend sugar and flour in large bowl. Add melted butter and mix well using wooden spoon. Add eggs one at a time, beating well with wooden spoon after each addition. Stir in buttermilk and vanilla.

Brush pastry with egg white to waterproof crust.

Let dry 2 minutes. Pour in filling. Bake until filling is set, about 45 minutes. Cool 20 minutes. Serve warm, at room temperature or chilled.

Strawberry-Glazed Sherry Pie

8 to 10 servings

  3 eggs
  2 cups half and half
 ½ cup dry Sherry
 ½ cup sugar
  1 baked 9-inch pie crust (see recipe this page)

Strawberry Glaze
 ½ cup red currant jelly
  2 teaspoons hot water

  1 pint whole fresh strawberries, stems removed

Position rack in lower third of oven and preheat to 325°F. Lightly beat eggs in mixing bowl just enough to incorporate whites and yolks. Add half and half, Sherry and sugar and stir until sugar is dissolved. Brush pastry with egg white to waterproof crust. Let dry 2 minutes. Pour in filling. Bake until custard is set, 1 to 1½ hours. Let cool. Chill.

For glaze: Combine jelly and water in small saucepan over low heat and cook, stirring constantly, until jelly is melted and mixture is smooth.

Arrange strawberries, pointed side up, in concentric circles over top of pie. Using pastry brush, lightly coat berries with glaze. Chill before serving.

The pies are stored in an old-fashioned "pie safe."

Pacific Northwestern Party

THE MENU

Cream of Lentil Soup

Crusty French Bread

*Poached Salmon with Raspberry Beurre
Blanc and Lime Butter Sauce*

Rack of Lamb Moutarde

Creamy Carrot Timbales

Zucchini with Pesto Sauce

Warm Goat Cheese Salad

Lemon Tarts with Caramel

Serves 6

*Clockwise from right: Cream of Lentil Soup, Veal and Tomato
Sauce for Rack of Lamb Moutarde accompanied by Creamy Carrot
Timbales, Warm Goat Cheese Salad, Zucchini with Pesto Sauce,
and a basket of Crusty French Bread.*

THE STRATEGY

The fresh foods of the Pacific Northwest—rosy salmon, bright raspberries and tender lamb—combine in this elegant dinner. A sophisticated Cream of Lentil Soup begins the meal, and a Warm Goat Cheese Salad provides a tangy refresher between the main course and dessert.

Shopping List

  1 9- to 12-pound whole fresh salmon
  2 racks of lamb
2½ pounds veal bones
  ¼ pound salt pork
  1 quart chicken stock
  3 leeks
  1 large onion
  2 medium onions
  5 small onions
  3 medium potatoes
  1 head red leaf lettuce
  2 heads Belgian endive (optional; see recipe for Warm Goat Cheese Salad)
  1 pound carrots plus 5 small carrots plus 3 large carrots
  4 garlic cloves
  3 large tomatoes
  6 small zucchini
    Thyme
    Celery (1 cup sliced plus 1 stalk cut up)
    Parsley (2 medium sprigs plus additional sprigs to taste for sauce)
    Shallots (½ cup minced)
    Finely minced peel of 1 lime plus 2 tablespoons fresh lime juice plus additional lime slices for garnish
    Finely grated peel and juice of 1 lemon plus lemon peel and lemon slices for garnish
    Watercress for garnish
    Fresh raspberries (optional garnish)
    Fresh basil leaves (2 cups chopped)
  1 cup half and half
  6 2-ounce rounds goat cheese
3½ cups whipping cream plus additional whipping cream for garnish
  9 eggs
4¼ sticks unsalted butter
  3 sticks butter plus additional butter for sautéing zucchini

  1 cup freshly grated Parmesan cheese
    Sour cream for garnish
  1 pound (2¼ cups) lentils
  3 tablespoons pine nuts
 15 black peppercorns
  2 envelopes dry yeast
  7 cups unbleached all purpose flour
  3 cups all purpose flour plus additional flour for kneading bread dough
1⅚ cups sugar
  ¾ cup walnut oil
  ¼ cup white wine vinegar (preferably tarragon)
  ½ cup raspberry vinegar
  ½ cup olive oil
    White wine vinegar (6 tablespoons)
    Peanut oil
    Salt
    Black pepper
    White pepper
    Prepared mustard (preferably stone-ground)
    Dijon mustard
    Light soy sauce
    Dark soy sauce
    Ground sage
    Ground ginger
    Dried marjoram
    Whole nutmeg
    Cornstarch
    Bay leaves
    Raspberry jam (2 tablespoons strained)
    Tomato paste
    Candied violets and candied mimosa (for decoration)
  4 cups dry white wine

Special Equipment

Six baguette bread pans or 3 French bread pans
Fish poacher (optional; large stockpot can be substituted)
Six ½-cup timbale molds (optional; custard cups can be substituted)
Six 2- to 3-inch tart pans

Tips

All the recipes can be doubled.

Countdown

1 month ahead
Bake Crusty French Bread and freeze.
Make pâte brisée dough for lemon tarts and freeze.
Prepare stock for veal and tomato sauce; let cool, then freeze.

1 week ahead
Prepare pesto sauce for zucchini. Transfer to jar. Cover with ¼ inch olive oil and refrigerate.

1 day ahead
Prepare lentil-potato mixture for soup and puree. Return to stockpot; let cool. Refrigerate.
Remove stock from freezer and let thaw in refrigerator overnight.
Remove French bread from freezer and let thaw in refrigerator overnight.
Remove pâte brisée dough from freezer and let thaw in refrigerator overnight.
Mix vinaigrette for salad and refrigerate.
Cut zucchini into julienne and refrigerate.

Morning of dinner
Finish veal and tomato sauce for lamb and set aside at room temperature.
Shape and bake pastry shells for lemon tarts. Set aside at room temperature.
Prepare salmon to point noted in recipe and refrigerate.
Make carrot puree for timbales to point noted in recipe and refrigerate.
Let goat cheese for salad stand at room temperature to soften.
Prepare caramel for tarts. Pour into bottoms of tart shells and let cool to room temperature.

About 2 hours before serving
Remove pesto sauce from refrigerator and bring to room temperature.
Prepare lemon filling for tarts.

Spoon into tart shells and refrigerate.
Remove vinaigrette for salad from refrigerator and let stand at room temperature.
Remove salmon from refrigerator and let stand at room temperature.

About 1 hour before serving
Finish Creamy Carrot Timbales.

About 30 minutes before serving
Warm French bread in low oven if desired.
Arrange lettuce leaves and endive on individual plates.
Rewarm sauce for lamb over low heat.
Prepare lamb racks.
Place zucchini in colander and salt lightly; let drain.
Rewarm lentil puree for soup over very low heat. Bring sour cream for soup garnish to room temperature.

Just before serving
Finish lentil soup.
Bake goat cheese for salad.
Prepare sauces for salmon.
Sauté zucchini and toss with pesto sauce.

Just before dessert
Whip cream for tarts and decorate.

Wine Suggestions

With the salmon serve a full-flavored Chardonnay such as those by Burgess, Markham or Washington's own Chateau Ste. Michelle. Lamb is usually at its best with Cabernet Sauvignon. Use Chateau Ste. Michelle's or a fairly full-bodied version by Inglenook, Beringer or other California producer. Finish with a "late harvest" Johannisberg Riesling, an "extra dry" Champagne, or a crisp Asti Spumante.

THE RECIPES

Cream of Lentil Soup

6 to 8 servings

   1 pound (2¼ cups) lentils

   1 quart (4 cups) water
   1 quart (4 cups) chicken stock
   ¼ pound salt pork, diced
   3 leeks (white part with bit of green), washed

and coarsely chopped
   2 medium onions, chopped
   3 medium potatoes, peeled and sliced
      Salt and freshly ground pepper

   2 cups whipping cream
   2 tablespoons (¼ stick) butter
      Sour cream, room temperature (garnish)
      Grated lemon peel (garnish)

Soak lentils for 1 hour in large bowl with enough water to cover.

Drain lentils. Add to 6-quart stockpot with 1 quart water, stock, pork, leeks, onion and potatoes. Season lightly with salt and pepper. Bring mixture to boil over medium-high heat. Reduce heat and simmer until lentils are cooked, about 1½ to 2 hours.

Discard salt pork. Transfer mixture in batches to processor or blender and puree. Return soup to pot and bring to boil. Stir in cream and boil about 3 to 4 minutes. Taste and adjust seasoning. Blend in butter. Ladle into individual bowls. Garnish with dollop of sour cream and sprinkling of lemon peel.

Crusty French Bread

Makes 6 baguettes or 3 large loaves

   2 **envelopes dry yeast**
  ½ **cup warm water (105°F to 115°F)**

   7 **cups unbleached all purpose flour**
2¼ **cups warm water (105°F to 115°F)**
   4 **teaspoons salt**

   Flour

Generously grease large bowl. Lightly oil 6 baguette bread pans or 3 French bread pans. Sprinkle yeast over ½ cup warm water and stir until dissolved. Let stand until foamy, about 5 minutes.

Combine 5 cups flour and 2¼ cups warm water in another large mixing bowl. Add yeast and remaining 2 cups flour. Stir in 4 teaspoons salt.

Turn dough out onto lightly floured surface and knead until smooth and elastic, adding flour as necessary to prevent sticking, about 8 to 10 minutes. Transfer dough to greased bowl, turning to coat all surfaces. Cover with plastic wrap and let stand in warm, draft-free area until doubled in volume, about 1 to 1½ hours.

Punch dough down. Transfer to work surface and knead gently 1 to 2 minutes. Return to greased bowl, turning to coat all surfaces. Let stand in warm, draft-free area until doubled, 3 hours.

Turn dough out onto work surface. Divide into 6 or 3 equal pieces. Flatten 1 piece into rectangle. Fold long edge over ⅓; fold over remaining long edge as for business letter to form narrow rectangle. Pinch edges together to seal. Repeat with remaining dough. Roll each rectangle into 18-inch cylinder using rocking motion. Transfer to prepared pans. Cover and let rise until doubled, about 1½ hours.

Preheat oven to 450°F. Arrange shallow roasting pan in lower rack of oven and fill halfway with water.

Holding tip of sharp knife on the bias, make three diagonal slashes across top of each baguette or loaf. Transfer bread to oven and spray generously with water. Spray two more times at 3-minute intervals to steam. Bake *baguettes* until crust is brown, about 30 minutes. (Bake *loaves* 5 to 10 minutes longer.) Remove bread from oven and brush surface with ice water. Turn out onto wire racks and let cool sufficiently before slicing.

Poached Salmon with Raspberry Beurre Blanc and Lime Butter Sauce

6 servings

   4 **cups dry white wine**
   2 **cups water**
   1 **cup sliced celery**
  10 **peppercorns**
   4 **small onions, sliced**
   4 **small carrots, sliced**
   2 **medium parsley sprigs**
   1 **large bay leaf**
  ¼ **teaspoon salt**
   1 **9- to 12-pound whole fresh salmon, cleaned and patted dry**

Raspberry Beurre Blanc
  ½ **cup raspberry vinegar**
  ¼ **cup minced shallot**
   4 **tablespoons (¼ cup) whipping cream**
   1 **cup (2 sticks) unsalted butter, cut into 16 pieces**
   2 **tablespoons raspberry jam, strained**

Lime Butter Sauce
   6 **tablespoons white wine vinegar**
  ¼ **cup minced shallot**
   2 **tablespoons fresh lime juice**
   4 **tablespoons (¼ cup) whipping cream**
   1 **cup (2 sticks) unsalted butter, cut into 16 pieces**
     Finely minced peel of 1 lime

     Watercress (garnish)
     Lime or lemon slices (garnish)
     Fresh raspberries (optional)

A small thin knife facilitates skinning salmon.

Raspberry Beurre Blanc and Lime Butter Sauce add color.

Combine first 9 ingredients in large stockpot or fish poacher and bring to simmer over medium heat. Add salmon and poach 45 minutes to 1 hour; *do not allow poaching liquid to boil.* Transfer salmon to work surface to drain and firm. Remove head and discard. Using sharp knife, gently free salmon skin beginning at head, then peel off by hand, working toward tail. Remove thin layer of dark flesh. Transfer salmon to platter. *(Salmon can be prepared several hours ahead and refrigerated. Be sure to bring to room temperature before serving.)*

For Raspberry Beurre Blanc: Combine vinegar and shallot in small saucepan. Cook over medium-high heat until vinegar is reduced to 2 tablespoons. Add cream and continue cooking until liquid is reduced to 2 tablespoons. Remove from heat. Whisk in 2 or 3 pieces of butter one piece at a time. Return saucepan to low heat and cook, whisking in remaining butter, until mixture is consistency of light mayonnaise. Whisk in strained raspberry jam.

For Lime Butter Sauce: Combine vinegar, shallot and lime juice in small saucepan. Cook over medium-high heat until liquid is reduced to 2 tablespoons. Add cream and continue cooking until liquid is reduced to 2 tablespoons. Remove from heat. Whisk in 2 or 3 pieces of butter one piece at a time. Return saucepan to low heat and cook, whisking in remaining butter, until mixture is consistency of light mayonnaise. Blend in minced lime peel.

To serve, garnish salmon with watercress, lime or lemon slices and raspberries. Serve with sauces.

Rack of Lamb Moutarde

6 servings

Veal and Tomato Sauce
2½ pounds veal bones, cut up

  1 large onion, sliced
  2 carrots, sliced
  1 garlic clove
    Bouquet garni (thyme, parsley and bay leaf)

  2 tablespoons peanut oil
  1 small carrot, finely chopped
  1 small onion, finely chopped
  3 fresh tomatoes, chopped
1½ teaspoons tomato paste
  1 celery stalk, cut up
    Parsley sprigs
  5 peppercorns, lightly crushed

Lamb
  2 racks of lamb, *all fat* removed
 ¼ cup Dijon mustard
1½ teaspoons light soy sauce
1½ teaspoons dark soy sauce
  1 garlic clove, minced
 ½ teaspoon ground sage
 ½ teaspoon dried marjoram, crumbled
 ⅛ teaspoon ground ginger

For sauce: Preheat oven to 475°F. Spread bones on large baking sheet. Roast, turning once or twice until well browned, about 45 minutes.

Combine bones, onion, sliced carrot, garlic and bouquet garni in large stockpot with enough water to cover. Place over high heat and bring to vigorous boil. Reduce heat and boil gently about 4 hours, skimming foam from surface.

Strain stock through fine sieve set over large bowl (you should have about 2 cups of brown veal stock). Let stock cool. Remove and discard any fat from surface. Set stock aside. *(Stock can be prepared ahead and refrigerated or frozen. Reheat when ready to use.)*

Heat oil in medium saucepan over medium heat. Add carrot and onion and sauté until golden. Reduce heat to low. Add remaining ingredients with cooled veal stock and simmer until reduced by half. Strain through fine sieve into small mixing bowl, pressing vegetables with back of spoon to extract as much liquid as possible. Keep warm.

For lamb: Preheat oven to 400°F. Arrange lamb racks on baking sheet, bone side down. Combine remaining ingredients in small bowl, blending well. Coat meat thoroughly with mixture. Roast lamb until tender, about 15 to 20 minutes. Transfer racks to platter and serve. Pass sauce separately.

Creamy Carrot Timbales

6 servings

  1 **large carrot**

  1 **pound carrots, sliced**
  3 **tablespoons all purpose flour**

  4 **eggs**
  1 **cup whipping cream**
  ¾ **teaspoon salt**
  ½ **teaspoon freshly ground white pepper**
    Freshly grated nutmeg

Preheat oven to 375°F. Butter six ½-cup timbale molds. Line each with circle of waxed paper; butter paper. Set aside.

Cut thickest part of large carrot into six ⅛-inch slices. Scallop edges of each slice to resemble flower. Blanch slices in boiling salted water until tender. Remove with slotted spoon (retain water at boil) and drain well. Set 1 slice in bottom of each mold.

Add remaining 1 pound carrots to same water and boil until tender. Drain well. Puree in processor or blender. Transfer to medium bowl and sprinkle with flour. *(Mixture can be prepared ahead to this point and refrigerated.)*

Beat eggs with cream in another bowl until thick and lemon colored. Add salt, pepper and nutmeg and mix well. Blend into pureed carrots.

Divide mixture evenly among prepared molds. Cover each mold with circle of buttered waxed paper. Arrange timbales in shallow baking dish and add enough boiling water to come halfway up sides of molds. Bake timbales until set, about 30 minutes.

Remove molds from water. Discard waxed paper. Let stand 5 minutes. Run tip of sharp knife around edge of timbales to loosen. Invert onto platter. Discard remaining waxed paper. Serve.

Zucchini with Pesto Sauce

6 servings

    Salt
  6 **small zucchini, cut julienne**

Pesto Sauce
  2 **cups chopped fresh basil**
  ½ **cup olive oil**
  3 **tablespoons pine nuts**
  2 **garlic cloves**
  1 **teaspoon salt**
  1 **cup freshly grated Parmesan cheese**
  2 **tablespoons (¼ stick) butter, room temperature**

    Unsalted butter

Lightly salt zucchini in colander and let drain for about 30 minutes.

Puree next 5 ingredients in processor or blender. Transfer to medium bowl. Add cheese and butter, mixing well.

Melt butter in large heavy skillet over medium-high heat. Add zucchini and sauté until heated through. Add sauce and toss, mixing well. Serve hot.

Warm Goat Cheese Salad

6 servings

  ¾ **cup walnut oil**
  ¼ **cup white wine vinegar (preferably tarragon)**
  2 **tablespoons prepared mustard (preferably stone-ground)**
    Salt and freshly ground pepper

  6 **2-ounce rounds of goat cheese, softened**
  1 **head red leaf lettuce, separated into leaves**
  2 **heads Belgian endive, separated into leaves (optional)**

Preheat oven to 350°F. Combine oil, vinegar, mustard, salt and pepper in small bowl and beat by hand until thickened.

Arrange cheese on baking sheet and warm in oven until slightly melted, about 5 minutes. Meanwhile, arrange lettuce leaves (and endive if desired) on 6 individual plates. Arrange round of cheese in center and spoon dressing over top. Serve immediately.

Lemon Tarts with Caramel

6 servings

Pâte Brisée
  1 egg
  1 egg yolk
  3 tablespoons water

  3 cups flour
 ½ cup sugar
     Pinch of salt
1¼ cups (2½ sticks) butter, cut into pieces (room temperature)

Caramel
 ⅓ cup sugar
  2 tablespoons water

Filling
  3 egg yolks
  1 cup sugar
  2 tablespoons (¼ stick) unsalted butter, melted
     Finely grated peel and juice of 1 lemon
  1 cup half and half

  2 tablespoons cornstarch

     Whipping cream (garnish)
     Candied violets and candied mimosa (decoration)

For pâte brisée: Whisk egg, egg yolk and water in small bowl until well blended.

Combine flour, sugar and salt in medium mixing bowl. Add butter, blending thoroughly. Stir in egg mixture, blending well. Cover with plastic wrap and refrigerate for 30 minutes.

Preheat oven to 400°F. Roll pastry out to thickness of ⅛ inch. Fit into six 2- to 3-inch tart pans. Cover pastry with waxed paper and fill with dried beans. Bake until pastry is lightly browned, 18 to 20 minutes. Remove beans and paper.

For caramel: Combine sugar and water in small saucepan. Place over medium-high heat and bring to boil. Let syrup cook until caramelized, about 10 to 15 minutes. Pour enough caramel into each tart just to cover bottom. Let cool.

For filling: Whisk egg yolks in top of double boiler set over simmering water until thick and lemon colored. Beat in sugar and butter. Add peel and lemon juice. Combine half and half and cornstarch in small bowl and stir until cornstarch is dissolved. Blend into yolk mixture. Cook until thick, about 30 minutes. Cool. Pour into tart shells and refrigerate until firm.

Just before serving, spoon whipped cream into pastry bag fitted with decorative tip and pipe swirl over top of each tart. Decorate tarts with candied violets and candied mimosa.

Lemon Tarts with Caramel decorated with whipped cream rosettes, candied violets and mimosa.

Rocky Mountain Buffet

THE MENU

Nat's Grog

Jalapeños en Escabeche
Stuffed with Peanut Butter

Gingered Tofu

Bowl of the Wife of Kit Carson

Swiss Enchiladas
with Lobster and Shrimp

Peaches Flambéed in Scotch

Serves 12

Nat's Grog (upper left) begins the buffet along with (clockwise from upper right) Gingered Tofu, Jalapeños en Escabeche Stuffed with Peanut Butter, and Monterey Jack cheese and avocado to be served with the Bowl of the Wife of Kit Carson.

THE STRATEGY

A collection of surprising ingredients—including tofu, peanut butter, pickled ginger, hot chilies and garbanzo beans—come together delightfully in this eclectic buffet. All the dishes are easy to prepare, with a minimum of last-minute fuss.

Shopping List

2 cups coarsely chopped cooked chicken
1 pound large shrimp
1 quart chicken stock or broth
1 lemon (for juice)
2 avocados plus additional avocado for garnish (optional)
2 medium-size white onions
6 to 8 peaches
1 pound shredded Monterey Jack cheese plus 2 cups cubed
1 pound longhorn cheddar cheese plus additional cheese for garnish (optional)
2 cups half and half
1 cup sour cream
1½ sticks butter
1½ cups cooked rice
12 to 16 corn tortillas
1 cup walnut halves
¼ cup pine nuts
1 cup firmly packed dark brown sugar
½ vanilla bean
 Allspice
 Sesame salt
 Dried oregano
 Garlic salt
 Salt
 Tofu
 Pickled ginger strips
1 12-ounce can medium or large pitted ripe olives
1 16-ounce can garbanzo beans
1 to 2 Mexican chipotles en adobado (canned)
1 7-ounce can whole green chilies
 Sliced black or green olives (optional garnish)
 Sliced red pimientos (optional garnish)
 Pickled jalapeño peppers
 Creamy peanut butter
1 6-ounce can frozen guava juice concentrate or one 12-ounce can guava nectar
1½ pounds frozen lobster tails
 Vanilla ice cream (or crepes; see recipe for Peaches Flambéed in Scotch)
1 cup Jamaica rum punch
¼ cup orange liqueur
¼ cup Scotch

Special Equipment

Large *cazuela* (Mexican casserole dish). This is optional, but lends an authentic touch to the presentation. A deep 4-quart baking dish can be substituted.

Tips

All the recipes can be doubled; the enchilada recipe can be tripled.
Tofu, sesame salt and pickled ginger strips are available in oriental markets.
Mexican chipotles in adobado are small smoked red chilies canned in brown pickling sauce. They are available in Mexican grocery stores.

Countdown

Morning of dinner
Shred and cube all cheese; transfer to plastic bags and refrigerate.

About 1½ hours before serving
Assemble Jalapeños en Escabeche Stuffed with Peanut Butter.
Begin preparation of Swiss enchiladas and sauce.

About 30 minutes before serving
Make Gingered Tofu.
Prepare Bowl of the Wife of Kit Carson.

Just before serving
Mix Nat's Grog.

Just before dessert
Prepare Peaches Flambéed in Scotch.

Wine Suggestions

With this hot and spicy food have plenty of chilled Chablis on hand as well as lots of beer.

The lavish ingredients for the Swiss Enchiladas with Lobster and Shrimp.

THE RECIPES

Nat's Grog

4 to 6 servings

1 6-ounce can frozen guava juice concentrate or
  1 12-ounce can guava nectar
2 cups crushed ice
1 cup Jamaica rum punch
2 ounces (¼ cup) orange liqueur
  Juice of 1 lemon
½ teaspoon allspice
  Ice cubes

Combine all ingredients except ice cubes in blender and mix until smooth. Pour over ice and serve.

Jalapeños en Escabeche Stuffed with Peanut Butter

Jalapeños en escabeche (pickled jalapeño peppers), preferably from Mexico
Creamy peanut butter

Cut peppers almost in half lengthwise from tip to stem and remove seeds. Using pastry tube or spoon, fill each chili with about 1 teaspoon peanut butter. Press halves of chili together gently and arrange on serving platter.

Avocado, pimiento and black olive slices top a bubbling casserole of Swiss Enchiladas.

Gingered Tofu

Tofu*
Sesame salt*
Pickled ginger strips*
Crushed ice

Cut tofu into 1-inch squares using waffled cutter or knife. Press between paper towels to remove as much moisture as possible. Sprinkle with sesame salt to taste and top each with thin slice of pickled ginger. Transfer to bed of crushed ice and serve immediately.

*Available in oriental markets.

Bowl of the Wife of Kit Carson

6 servings

1 quart chicken stock or broth
2 cups coarsely chopped cooked chicken
1½ cups cooked rice
1 16-ounce can garbanzo beans, drained

1 to 2 Mexican chipotles en adobado (canned), rinsed, seeded and chopped*
Pinch of leaf oregano

2 cups Monterey Jack cheese, cut into ½- to ¾-inch cubes
2 avocados, peeled and cubed

Combine stock, chicken, rice, garbanzos and peppers in large saucepan over medium heat. Bring to simmer, stirring occasionally. Add oregano.

Equally divide cheese and avocado among bowls and ladle small amount of soup into each *(there should be more solid than liquid ingredients).* Serve immediately.

*Chipotles are small smoked red chilies canned in brown pickling sauce (adobado) and are available in Mexican grocery stores. Rinse, drain and clean thoroughly, as the seeds are extremely hot.

Swiss Enchiladas with Lobster and Shrimp

12 servings

12 to 16 corn tortillas
2 medium white onions, coarsely chopped
1 7-ounce can green chilies, membranes discarded, coarsely chopped
1½ pounds frozen lobster tails, thawed and coarsely chopped
1 pound uncooked large shrimp, peeled and deveined, coarsely chopped
1 cup walnut halves, toasted
1 12-ounce can medium or large pitted ripe olives, well drained, halved
1 pound Monterey Jack cheese, shredded
1 pound longhorn cheddar cheese, shredded

2 cups half and half
1 cup sour cream
½ cup (1 stick) butter, melted
1½ teaspoons oregano leaves
1 teaspoon garlic salt

Shredded longhorn cheddar cheese (optional)
Sliced red pimientos, avocado slices, sliced black or green olives (optional garnish)

Preheat oven to 300°F. Generously butter large *cazuela* (Mexican casserole dish) or deep 4-quart baking dish.

Cover bottom with about ⅓ of tortillas. Sprinkle with half of onion and top with half of chilies. Add half of lobster and shrimp. Sprinkle with half of walnuts and half of olives. Combine Jack and cheddar cheeses; remove about 1½ cups and set aside. Sprinkle half of remaining cheese over olives.

Combine half and half, sour cream, butter, oregano and garlic salt in medium saucepan. Place over medium-low heat and stir frequently until lukewarm and well blended. Remove 1 cup and set aside. Pour half of remaining sauce over casserole. Repeat layering, covering top with remaining half of sauce. Add remaining tortillas, 1 cup reserved sauce and ¾ cup of the reserved cheese.

Bake 60 to 75 minutes, until casserole is bubbling hot. Remove from oven and increase temperature to 450°F. Sprinkle casserole with remaining cheese and return to oven for 5 to 7 minutes, until top is golden brown and cheese is bubbly. If using optional garnish add more cheddar and return to oven just until cheese is melted. Alternate pimientos, avocado slices and olives in wagon-wheel design and heat briefly until toppings begin to sink into cheese.

Other shellfish or cooked chicken may be substituted for lobster and shrimp.

Recipe can be doubled or tripled.

Swiss Enchiladas can be prepared several hours in advance and held in lukewarm (180°F) oven. They also freeze well. Defrost in refrigerator overnight before reheating.

Peaches Flambéed in Scotch

12 to 16 servings

¼ cup (½ stick) butter
¼ cup pine nuts
1 cup firmly packed dark brown sugar
Juice of 1 lemon
6 to 8 fresh peaches, peeled and halved
½ vanilla bean, halved, seeds scraped out and minced, or ½ teaspoon vanilla
½ teaspoon salt
¼ cup Scotch
Vanilla ice cream or crepes

Melt butter in chafing dish or large heavy skillet over medium flame or heat. Add nuts and stir until lightly toasted. Add sugar and stir constantly until sauce is syrupy. Blend in lemon juice. Add peach halves (if using chafing dish, add in batches), and coat well with sauce. Stir in vanilla and salt. Warm Scotch briefly, carefully ignite and add to pan, shaking constantly until flame dies. Serve over ice cream or crepes.

Peaches Flambéed in Scotch are spooned onto crepes.

In the Tex-Mex Style

THE MENU

Queso

Chile con Queso

Guacamole   Pico de Gallo

Tamales   Picadillo   Salsa

Texas-Style Barbecued Chicken

Texas Chili

Flour Tortillas   Corn Tortillas

Chicken Enchiladas

Refried Beans

Margarita Ice

Pralines   Buñuelos

Serves 8

On the sideboard, from left to right: Buñuelos, Pralines, Chicken Enchiladas and Queso. On the table, clockwise from top left: Pico de Gallo, Texas Chili, Tamales, Flour Tortillas, Guacamole, Chile con Queso on fried tortillas, Texas-Style Barbecued Chicken and Corn Tortillas.

THE STRATEGY

Here is a collection of terrific, easy-to-prepare dishes with the zesty flavors of Tex-Mex cooking. This party is perfect for casual entertaining. Use baskets, glazed Mexican pottery and brightly colored cloths to lend a festive touch to each dish.

Shopping List

1½ pounds lean ground beef
  2 3½-pound chickens plus 4 cups coarsely chopped cooked chicken
  2 pounds coarsely ground beef shoulder
  3 cups chicken broth
     Bacon drippings or lard (see recipe for Frijoles Refritos)
30 to 36 green or dried yellow corn husks
 ½ cup raisins
  1 pound mushrooms plus 2 cups sliced
12 garlic cloves
  2 to 4 serrano chilies
  2 jalapeño peppers (or more to taste) plus 2 to 3 more, plus 2 to 3 additional jalapeño peppers or serrano chilies
  5 medium-size white onions plus 1 cup and 2 tablespoons finely minced
  2 large yellow onions plus ¼ cup chopped and ¼ cup finely minced
  5 small fresh green chilies
  2 small fresh red chilies
  6 avocados
  3 limes (peel only) plus 2 cups fresh lime juice plus lime slices for garnish
  4 medium tomatoes
     Lettuce for garnish
     Radishes for garnish
     Green bell pepper (½ cup chopped)
     Fresh cilantro, also known as coriander or Chinese parsley
     Fresh lemon juice (3 tablespoons plus juice of 1 large)
     Fresh mint sprigs for garnish
  1 pound Monterey Jack, mozzarella or Havarti cheese plus additional Monterey Jack cheese (2 cups grated) plus additional grated or crumbled Monterey Jack, mozzarella or Havarti cheese for garnish

  1 pound processed American cheese
  1 cup sour cream
 ¼ stick unsalted butter
 ¼ stick butter
1½ cups whipping cream
  5 eggs
1½ cups buttermilk
     Milk (6 tablespoons)
 ½ pound dried small red pinto beans
     Commercial flour and corn tortillas (if not using homemade; but reduce amounts of flour, shortening and masa harina)
     Tortilla chips
 ½ cup chopped almonds
  2 cups pecan halves
  6 cups all purpose flour plus additional flour for rolling dough
  8 cups sugar
  1 cinnamon stick or additional ground cinnamon
 ½ cup vegetable shortening plus additional 2 cups plus 2 teaspoons vegetable shortening or lard
10 cups plus 2 tablespoons masa harina
     Baking powder
     Vanilla
     Baking soda
     Light corn syrup
     Vegetable oil
     Olive oil
     Vinegar
     Chili powder
     Salt
     Coarse salt
     Black pepper
     Cinnamon
     Ground cumin
     Ground cloves
     Sweet Hungarian paprika
     Ground red pepper
  1 10-ounce can tomatoes and green chilies or one 16-ounce can whole tomatoes mixed with ¼ cup diced green chilies
  3 16-ounce cans tomatoes
  1 6-ounce can tomato paste
  2 16- or 17-ounce cans kidney beans (optional)
  1 cup white tequila
 ½ cup Triple Sec

Guacamole is traditionally prepared and served in a Mexican lava mortar called a molcajete.

Special Equipment

Steamer
Charcoal grill
Tortilla press
Ice cream maker

Countdown

2 weeks ahead
Prepare Tamales (with Picadillo filling) and freeze.
Make Chile con Queso; let cool, then freeze in airtight container.

2 days ahead
Prepare Crema Fresca for enchiladas.
Make Margarita Ice; freeze.
Prepare and fry Buñuelos and prepare Cinnamon Sugar Syrup; let cool and store in airtight container.
Make Pralines and store in airtight container.
Prepare dough for Flour Tortillas and refrigerate.

1 day ahead
Prepare chicken for Texas-Style Barbecued Chicken to point noted in recipe and refrigerate overnight.
Cook Flour Tortillas; wrap tightly and refrigerate.
Make Corn Tortillas; wrap tightly and refrigerate.
Remove Chile con Queso from freezer and let thaw in refrigerator overnight.

Morning of dinner
Let Tamales stand at room temperature.

About 3 hours before serving
Prepare Frijoles Refritos.

About 2 hours before serving
Make Pico de Gallo and refrigerate.
Fill Chicken Enchiladas and refrigerate.
Prepare Texas Chili.

About 1 hour before serving
Finish Texas-Style Barbecued Chicken.

About 30 minutes before serving
Make Guacamole.
Resteam Tamales until heated through.
Reheat Chile con Queso over very low heat, stirring occasionally.

Just before serving
Prepare Queso.
Make Salsa if using.
Rewarm Corn Tortillas and Flour Tortillas in low oven or steamer.

Wine Suggestions

This highly flavored food requires fresh and simple wine—well-chilled Chablis or Soave, well-chilled rosé or lightly chilled Burgundy—and a large quantity of icy beer.

THE RECIPES

Queso

Based on a recipe from Armando's, one of Houston's most popular Mexican restaurants, this is delicious served either as an appetizer or a main dish.

9 to 10 main-course servings or 18 to 20 appetizer servings

   1 pound Monterey Jack, mozzarella or Havarti cheese, grated

   3 tablespoons vegetable oil
   1 large yellow onion, chopped
   ½ cup chopped green bell pepper
   1 pound mushrooms, sliced

   ½ cup whipping cream
   18 to 20 flour tortillas, warmed (see recipe on page 159)

Preheat oven to 200°F. Spread cheese evenly in shallow glass baking dish or casserole and place in oven until partially melted, about 10 minutes.

Meanwhile, heat oil in large skillet over medium-high heat. Add onion and pepper and sauté 3 to 4 minutes. Add mushrooms and cook, stirring frequently, until mushrooms are moist and slightly darkened, 4 to 5 minutes.

Remove cheese from oven and gradually blend in cream, stirring until well mixed. Add mushroom mixture and any liquid in pan a little at a time, blending thoroughly. Bring immediately to table and spoon over tortillas.

Chile con Queso

Ladle over crisp tortillas or serve from a chafing dish as a dip for tortilla chips.

Makes about 4 cups

   1 tablespoon vegetable oil
   1 large onion, chopped
   1 garlic clove, minced
   1 tablespoon all purpose flour
   1 tablespoon chili powder or to taste
   1 10-ounce can tomatoes and green chilies or 1 16-ounce can whole tomatoes mixed with ¼ cup diced green chilies
   1 pound processed American cheese, cut into 1-inch cubes

   2 jalapeño peppers (or to taste), seeded and chopped

Heat oil in 3-quart saucepan over medium heat. Add onion and garlic and sauté until onion is translucent, about 5 minutes. Stir in flour and chili powder and cook, stirring constantly, 1 minute. Add tomatoes (and chilies if necessary) and continue cooking until thickened, about 5 to 6 minutes. Reduce heat to low and gradually add cheese, stirring constantly until cheese is completely melted. Stir in peppers. Taste and adjust seasoning. Serve hot.

Guacamole

Makes about 2 cups

   2 tablespoons finely minced white onion
   1 to 2 serrano chilies, seeded and coarsely chopped
   1 teaspoon chopped fresh cilantro
      Salt
   2 medium avocados
   1 medium tomato, peeled, seeded and chopped
   2 tablespoons finely minced white onion
   1 teaspoon chopped fresh cilantro
   1 garlic clove, minced

Combine first 3 ingredients with salt in blender or *molcajete* (mortar and pestle) and mix to smooth paste. Transfer to serving bowl. Peel and seed avocados. Add to chili paste, mashing coarsely with fork. Blend in remaining ingredients.

Garnish with additional chopped tomato and onion if using as dip.

Pico de Gallo (Rooster's Beak)

This subtle accompaniment to spicy food can be served as a salad.

8 servings

   4 ripe avocados, peeled and cubed
   2 medium tomatoes, peeled and cut same size as avocado cubes
   1 medium-size white onion, finely minced

2 garlic cloves, minced
2 tablespoons chopped fresh cilantro
1 or 2 serrano chilies, finely chopped
3 tablespoons fresh lemon juice
2 tablespoons olive oil
  Salt and freshly ground pepper

Combine all ingredients and mix well. Cover and refrigerate 1 to 2 hours.

Tamales

Makes 2½ to 3 dozen Tamales

30 to 36 green or dried yellow corn husks

2 cups shortening or lard
8 cups masa harina
3 cups chicken broth or water, heated to *lukewarm* (95°F)
2 tablespoons baking powder
1 tablespoon salt

  Picadillo (see following recipe)

Salsa (optional) (see recipe)

If using dried corn husks, soak overnight in enough cold water to cover.

Beat shortening in large bowl of electric mixer until light and fluffy, about 5 minutes. Gradually add masa harina alternately with chicken broth, adding the broth in slow, steady stream. (*If broth is too warm, dough will separate. If dough does separate, or is too thin, refrigerate before adding remaining masa and broth.*) Stir in baking powder and salt.

Drain corn husks and dry between 2 dish towels. Place in single layer on work surface. Divide dough among husks, spreading on wider half of each and leaving 1-inch border on one long side. Spoon 1 to 2 tablespoons Picadillo down center of dough. Fold in long sides of husk, then fold narrow half over to make packets open at one end.

Arrange Tamales upright in steamer. Cover with dish towel, then steamer lid, and steam over gently boiling water until done, 1½ to 2 hours. Transfer to platter and serve with bowl of Salsa.

Cooked Tamales can be wrapped tightly and refrigerated or frozen. Reheat in steamer.

1

2

1. *Corn husks are spread with dough,*
(**2**) *topped with Picadillo and rolled.*
3. *Tamales steam for two hours.*

3

Picadillo

This spiced meat mixture is also a good filling for tacos and chiles rellenos.

   2 tablespoons vegetable oil
   1 medium onion, chopped
1½ pounds lean ground beef
   1 16-ounce can tomatoes, undrained
   1 6-ounce can tomato paste
 ½ cup raisins
   2 tablespoons vinegar
   2 tablespoons chili powder or to taste
   1 teaspoon cinnamon
   1 teaspoon ground cumin
   1 teaspoon sugar
     Pinch of ground cloves
   2 cups sliced mushrooms
 ½ cup toasted chopped almonds
   2 to 3 jalapeño peppers, seeded and finely
     chopped

Heat oil in Dutch oven or large saucepan over medium heat. Add onion and sauté until softened, about 5 minutes. Increase heat, add beef and brown well. Add remaining ingredients except mushrooms, almonds and jalapeños; cover and simmer 1 hour. Stir in mushrooms and simmer another 30 minutes. Blend in almonds and peppers.

Salsa

Best made just before serving.

Makes about 1½ cups

 ½ cup cold water
   5 small fresh green chilies, finely chopped
   2 small fresh red chilies, finely chopped
   2 garlic cloves, minced
   1 medium tomato, finely chopped
   1 medium onion, finely chopped
   1 teaspoon salt

Combine all ingredients and mix well.

Texas-Style Barbecued Chicken

8 servings

   2 3½-pound chickens, split
     Juice of 1 large lemon
   4 garlic cloves, minced

 ¼ cup coarse salt
   2 tablespoons sweet Hungarian paprika
   2 teaspoons ground red pepper

Rub chicken with lemon juice and garlic. Mix together salt, paprika and pepper and sprinkle over skin. Place skin side up on wire rack(s) set over baking sheet(s) and refrigerate uncovered at least 8 hours or, preferably, overnight.

Preheat oven to 300°F. Bake chicken 1 hour. Meanwhile, prepare charcoal. Transfer chicken to barbecue and grill, turning occasionally, until meat is done and skin is crisp, about 15 minutes per side. Cut in half and arrange on platter.

Corn Tortillas

Makes about 16 tortillas

   2 cups masa harina
1½ cups warm water (115°F)

Measure masa harina into large mixing bowl. Using hands, gradually work in water until mixture forms solid mass. (Adjust water to achieve a workable dough; it should be firm but not dry or crumbly.)

To test: Pinch off enough dough to roll between palms into 1½-inch ball. Cut open 2 long sides of plastic sandwich bag. Lay one half on bottom of tortilla press. Place ball of dough in center of press and fold other half of bag over top. Close press to flatten.

Remove tortilla and plastic. Hold tortilla in your hand and peel off one side of plastic; turn and peel off other half of bag. *If dough is too dry, cracks will form around edges of tortilla; if it is too moist, plastic will not peel off without tearing the tortilla. Adjust consistency of remaining dough as necessary, adding more masa harina or warm water, and test again.*

Roll remaining dough into 1½-inch balls. Press 5 or 6 into tortilla shape and line up on work surface.

Lightly oil electric skillet or griddle and preheat to 375°F (or lightly oil 10-inch skillet and place over medium-high heat). Cook tortilla 1 minute; turn and cook 30 seconds on other side. Transfer to towel-lined basket, cover lightly and keep warm. If necessary, wrap tortillas in foil and reheat in oven or steamer 5 minutes before serving.

Chicken Enchiladas

If using commercial tortillas, just before filling, dip each into boiling water for about 1 second. This will soften them and prevent cracking or unrolling.

8 to 10 servings

  4 cups coarsely chopped cooked chicken
16 to 20 corn or flour tortillas (see recipes on this and preceding page)
  2 cups grated Monterey Jack cheese
  1 cup finely minced white onion
  2 cups Crema Fresca (see following recipe)
    Guacamole (see recipe on page 156)

Preheat oven to 375°F and generously butter baking dishes. Place about ¼ cup chicken down center of each tortilla. Sprinkle with about 2 tablespoons cheese and 1 tablespoon onion. Roll up carefully and place seam side down in baking dishes. Cover with foil and bake until heated through, about 25 to 30 minutes. Spread Crema Fresca over enchiladas and top with a generous dollop of Guacamole.

Tortillas can be filled several hours ahead and refrigerated before baking.

Crema Fresca

Makes 2 cups

  1 cup sour cream
  1 cup whipping cream

Combine sour cream and whipping cream in small bowl and blend well. Cover surface with plastic and let stand at room temperature about 8 hours, then chill until thick, about 24 hours.

Texas Chili

10 to 12 servings

  ¼ cup vegetable oil
  2 medium onions, chopped
  2 garlic cloves, minced
  2 pounds coarsely ground beef shoulder
  2 16-ounce cans tomatoes, undrained
  1 cup water
  ½ cup chili powder or to taste
  2 tablespoons masa harina
  1 tablespoon sugar
  2 teaspoons ground cumin

  2 teaspoons salt
  ½ to 1 teaspoon ground red pepper or to taste
  ¼ teaspoon freshly ground pepper
  2 16- or 17-ounce cans kidney beans (optional), drained
  2 to 3 jalapeño peppers or serrano chilies, seeded and finely chopped

Heat oil in Dutch oven or other large pot over medium heat. Add onion and garlic and sauté until softened, about 5 minutes. Increase heat, add beef and cook until meat and onions are well browned. Spoon off any excess fat. Add remaining ingredients except beans and peppers or chilies and bring to boil over high heat. Reduce heat and simmer 2 hours, adding water if chili becomes too thick; stir in beans during last 30 minutes of cooking time if desired. Blend in peppers or chilies just before serving.

Flour Tortillas

While experienced cooks can turn these out with no problem using a large skillet over medium-high heat, the first-time tortilla maker would do well to use an electric frypan or griddle.

Makes about 20 tortillas

  4 cups all purpose flour
  ½ cup shortening
  2 teaspoons salt
1¼ cups warm water (115°F)

Sift flour into large bowl. Add shortening and rub with fingertips until consistency of coarse meal. Dissolve salt in warm water and add to flour in steady stream, using fingertips to blend. Knead in bowl until dough forms ball. Turn out onto lightly floured surface and knead about 3 minutes *(dough will not be smooth)*. Cover with towel and let rest at room temperature for 1 hour (or overnight in refrigerator).

    Knead dough on work surface about 1 minute. Cover and let rest at room temperature 10 minutes.

    Pinch off dough in 1½-inch pieces. Roll on lightly floured surface into 7-inch circles (roll outward from center but do not get edges too thin). Stack between pieces of waxed paper.

    Heat electric skillet or griddle to 375°F, or place 10-inch skillet over medium-high heat. Cook tortilla, turning occasionally and pushing edges down with folded pot holder or small towel so edges brown evenly and light brown spots appear on surface, about 2 to 3 minutes (*if using skillet over direct heat, cooking time will be less*). Transfer tortilla to plate and cover with cloth napkin or towel to keep warm. Repeat with remaining dough, wiping out any flour in skillet as necessary. Just before serving, wrap tortillas in foil and reheat in 250°F oven or steamer about 5 minutes.

Refried Beans (Frijoles Refritos)

6 servings

   5 **cups water**
  ½ **pound dried small red pinto beans**
  ¼ **cup chopped onion**
   1 **tablespoon lard or bacon drippings**
 1½ **teaspoons salt**

   5 **to 6 tablespoons lard or bacon drippings**
  ¼ **cup finely minced onion**
      Tortilla chips, shredded lettuce, sliced radishes and grated or crumbled Monterey Jack, mozzarella or Havarti cheese (garnish)

Combine first 4 ingredients in large saucepan and bring to boil over medium-high heat. Reduce heat, cover and simmer *without stirring* until beans are tender but not completely soft, about 1½ to 2 hours. Add salt and simmer for another 30 minutes.

Melt lard in heavy large skillet over medium heat. Add onion and cook until soft but not brown. Increase heat to high, add 1 cup beans with some of cooking liquid and mash well (a large wooden mallet is best). Add remaining beans and some of liquid 1 cup at a time and continue mashing until mixture becomes a coarse paste. Continue cooking, swirling mixture with mallet, until beans begin to dry out and start coming away from skillet, about 15 to 20 minutes. Turn onto platter and garnish.

Margarita Ice

10 to 12 servings

   2 **cups fresh lime juice (reserve shells)**
   3 **cups sugar**

   2 **cups water**
      Finely grated peel of 3 limes

   3 **egg whites**

   1 **cup white tequila**
  ½ **cup Triple Sec**
      Lime slices and mint sprigs (garnish)

Pour lime juice into ice cream maker. Combine sugar, water and lime peel in heavy 3-quart saucepan. Bring to boil and cook without stirring until syrup reaches 234°F (thread stage) on candy thermometer, about 5 to 7 minutes. Set pan in large bowl of ice water and stir syrup with wooden spoon until cooled to lukewarm. Blend into lime juice.

Fill ice cream freezer with mixture of 8 parts ice to 1 part rock salt. Freeze lime mixture according to manufacturer's instructions until just partially frozen (this should take about 20 minutes).

Meanwhile, beat egg whites in mixing bowl until stiff peaks form. Spoon over lime mixture and continue churning until firm, about 10 minutes. Remove container and transfer to freezer.

To serve: Scoop Margarita Ice into glasses and top with small amount of tequila and Triple Sec. Garnish with lime slices and mint sprigs.

Pralines

Makes about 3 dozen

   3 **cups sugar**
 1½ **cups buttermilk**
  ½ **teaspoon baking soda**
   2 **tablespoons (¼ stick) unsalted butter**
   2 **cups pecan halves**
   2 **teaspoons vanilla**

Line 2 baking sheets with waxed paper or buttered foil. Combine sugar, buttermilk and baking soda in heavy large saucepan and stir *once*. Bring to boil over medium-high heat; reduce heat and boil gently *without stirring* until syrup registers 238°F (soft-ball stage) on candy thermometer, about 20 minutes. Remove from heat and add butter, beating with wooden spoon until mixture begins to lose its shine and thickens slightly, about 5 to 7 minutes. Quickly stir in nuts and vanilla (mixture will firm almost immediately). Drop by spoonfuls onto baking sheets. Let stand until completely cool.

1. *Boiled sugar-buttermilk syrup should be beaten for five minutes.* 2. *Candy firms up once pecans are added.*
3. *Pralines cool on sheets of waxed paper.*

Buñuelos

Drizzled with a homemade syrup or sprinkled with cinnamon sugar, they are a delightful treat. Roll them out using as little flour as possible or they will be tough. Since Buñuelos tend to become soggy quickly once syrup is drizzled over the top, it is best to make them right when you serve them, although they can be held up to 2 hours. Sprinkled with cinnamon sugar, they will remain crisp for 2 or 3 days stored in an airtight container.

Makes 18 to 20

   2 **cups all purpose flour**
   2 **tablespoons sugar**
   ¼ **teaspoon salt**
   2 **eggs**
   6 **tablespoons milk**
   2 **tablespoons (¼ stick) butter, melted**

   Flour
   Oil for deep frying
   Cinnamon Sugar Syrup (see following recipe)
   or cinnamon sugar

Blend flour, sugar and salt in medium bowl; set aside. Combine eggs and milk in small bowl and mix lightly with whisk. Gradually add butter and whisk until thick but still sticky. Using fork, blend egg mixture into flour and stir until dough barely holds together.

Turn dough out onto *very lightly floured* surface and knead 3 to 5 minutes. Divide into 18 to 20 pieces. Heat about 1 inch oil in electric frypan or 10-inch skillet to 375°F. Roll 1 piece dough into *very thin 6-inch circle* (keep remaining pieces covered with towel to prevent drying). Immerse Buñuelo in hot oil and fry until golden on both sides, about 2 to 3 minutes. Drain well on paper towels. Repeat, adding oil as necessary. Drizzle Buñuelos lightly with syrup or sprinkle with cinnamon sugar and serve immediately.

Cinnamon Sugar Syrup

1½ **cups sugar**
 ½ **cup water**
  2 **tablespoons light corn syrup**
  1 **cinnamon stick or pinch of ground cinnamon**

Combine ingredients in 1-quart saucepan. Bring to boil, shaking pan gently until sugar dissolves, then boil *without stirring* until thick and syrupy, 8 to 10 minutes. Discard cinnamon stick.

International Menus

THE LATE A. J. LIEBLING, peerless journalist and gourmand *extraordinaire,* once noted that people travel for just three reasons: to pursue business affairs, to see the sights, and to eat. He went on to say that while conducting business is tiresome enough at home, and while sightseeing is greatly overrated, a chance to sample the cuisines of the world is good and sufficient reason to pack the bags, call the travel agent and get the passport renewed.

Had Liebling lived to see the great growth of international cooking classes in this country, as well as the increase of both exotic food markets and restaurants of all nationalities, he might have added that it isn't actually necessary to go abroad in order to enjoy the best of foreign cuisines. Yesterday's "armchair traveler" has become today's "kitchen traveler": armed with good recipes, a few specialty ingredients and a well-rounded *batterie de cuisine,* modern American cooks can treat guests to an exciting array of menus from all over the globe—even if they themselves have never been farther afield than the next county.

The international menus in this chapter span many thousands of miles and a quintet of fascinating cultures. From the Far East there is a Chinese dinner (page 165) and one from Japan (page 173)—menus that express both the geographic proximity and the extreme cultural differences of the two countries. Then there is a buffet with the seductive aromas of Northern India (page 181), and, a bit closer to home, there are samplings of the two great European cuisines: a lavish affair representing *la cucina nuova,* the "new Italian cooking," (page 191) and a lighter but no less satisfying French dinner from sunny Provence (page 199).

Complement any of these menus with wines, spirits and other beverages appropriate to the country, and—without giving a thought to passports, airline reservations or jet lag—you will transport your dining table to a wonderful faraway place.

Easy Chinese Cuisine

THE MENU

Open-Face Dumplings

Pot Stickers

Paper-Wrapped Chicken and Ham

Steamed Salmon with Black Beans

Hot Garlic Eggplant

Almond Cookies

*Homemade Ice Cream
or Fresh Fruit Sorbet*

Serves 4

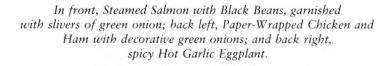

*In front, Steamed Salmon with Black Beans, garnished
with slivers of green onion; back left, Paper-Wrapped Chicken and
Ham with decorative green onions; and back right,
spicy Hot Garlic Eggplant.*

THE STRATEGY

Here is an easy-to-prepare menu just perfect for a small dinner party. Begin with two do-ahead hors d'oeuvres: won ton–wrapped Shrimp Shiu Mai and whimsical Pot Stickers. Individual packages of succulent chicken and Black Forest ham are the first course served at table. A subtly flavored Steamed Salmon with Black Beans and a delicious, spicy eggplant dish round out the menu. Offer almond cookies and homemade ice cream or a smooth fruit sorbet for a refreshing dessert.

Shopping List

  1 pound uncooked shrimp
  1 pound ground pork
  1 whole chicken breast
 16 very thin slices Black Forest or Smithfield ham
  4 salmon steaks (of equal thickness; about 1¾ to 2 pounds total)
    Chicken stock (optional)

 70 won ton skins
  8 green onions (1 finely minced, 2 minced, 5 whole)
  8 water chestnuts (preferably fresh; canned can be substituted)*
  1 orange (optional; only peel will be used)
 11 garlic cloves
 1½ pounds eggplant (preferably oriental)
  1 large yellow onion
    Fresh ginger (about 2 teaspoons minced total)
    Cabbage (1 cup minced)
    Carrots (¼ cup finely slivered)
  2 eggs
    Salted black beans (1 tablespoon)*
    Heavy soy sauce
    Light soy sauce
    Regular soy sauce
    Sesame oil
    Salt
    Black pepper
    White pepper

The more exotic ingredients for this dinner can be found in oriental markets.

Hot chili oil
White wine vinegar, red wine vinegar
or Chinese vinegar
Hot Chinese mustard
Peanut oil plus additional peanut oil (or corn
oil) for deep frying
Oyster sauce
Chili paste with garlic*
Sugar
Cornstarch
Dry Sherry

*Available in oriental markets.

Special Equipment

Wok
Chinese or other large steamer
Parchment paper

Tips

All of the recipes can be doubled.

Countdown

1 month ahead
Prepare Open-Face Dumplings and freeze.
Prepare Pot Stickers and freeze.

Morning of dinner
Remove Pot Stickers from freezer and let stand at
    room temperature to thaw.

2 hours before serving
Assemble packages of Paper-Wrapped Chicken and
    Ham and set aside.
Prepare marinade for fish; add salmon and set
    aside.

About 30 minutes before serving
Arrange condiments for Open-Face Dumplings and
    Pot Stickers on tray and bring to serving area.
Assemble ingredients for Hot Garlic Eggplant to
    point of cooking.
Place Open-Face Dumplings on aluminum foil to
    ready for cooking.

As guests arrive
Steam Open-Face Dumplings.
Fry Pot Stickers.

Just before first course
Sauté Paper-Wrapped Chicken and Ham quickly.
Bring water to boil in steamer for salmon.

Just before main course
Cook salmon in steamer.
Finish Hot Garlic Eggplant in wok.

Wine Suggestions

Chinese food with all its diverse flavors and textures
is difficult to team with wine. The easy way out is to
serve a selection of well-chilled imported beers. More
adventuresome souls should try a dry or slightly off-
dry Gewurztraminer from California or Alsace. This
aromatic, spicy wine will blend well with the many
flavors offered by this menu.

Basics for Stocking the Pantry

Ingredients
    Light soy sauce
    Heavy soy sauce
    Oyster sauce
    Sesame oil
    Hoisin sauce
    Chili paste with garlic
    Salted black beans
    Szechwan peppers
    Fresh ginger
    Plum sauce (also called duck sauce)
    Hot chili oil
    Dried black mushrooms
    Cloud ears (also known as black fungus)
    Golden needles (also known as tiger lilies)

Equipment
14-inch round-bottomed wok with lid (for gas
    stoves)
14-inch flat-bottomed wok with lid (for electric
    stoves)
Aluminum steamer (10- or 12-inch diameter is
    most practical)
No. 3 carbon steel Chinese cleaver (blade is half
    black and half shiny)

THE RECIPES

Open-Face Dumplings (Shrimp Shiu Mai)

Makes 30 dumplings

30 won ton skins
 1 pound uncooked shrimp, shelled, deveined and minced
 ¼ cup finely slivered carrot
 1 green onion, finely minced
 8 water chestnuts, finely minced
 1 tablespoon light soy sauce
 1 egg white, lightly beaten
 2 to 3 teaspoons cornstarch
 1 teaspoon dry Sherry
 1 teaspoon sesame oil
 ⅓ to ½ teaspoon finely minced fresh ginger
 ½ teaspoon salt
 ¼ teaspoon freshly ground pepper
 ¼ teaspoon sugar

   Additional cornstarch

   Soy sauce
   Hot chili oil
   Vinegar
   Hot Chinese mustard

Make 3-inch round indentation on won ton skins using jar, can or beverage glass. Using indentation as guide, cut won ton skins into circles with scissors (you can do as many as 6 at a time; do not worry about ragged edges).

Combine all remaining ingredients except additional cornstarch and condiments in large bowl and blend.

Dust waxed paper or parchment with cornstarch. Moisten top of won ton with water. Place 2 level teaspoons of filling in center. Draw edges up around filling. Set dumpling in hollow between thumb and index finger. Gently squeeze dumpling while pressing top and bottom simultaneously. Pleat top edge to form narrow column with filling showing at top. Set on cornstarch-dusted paper. Cover with dry kitchen towel. Repeat with remaining won ton.

Bring water to rapid boil in steamer (preferably Chinese). Arrange dumplings on layer of aluminum foil. Transfer to steamer tray. Cover and steam until shrimp has lost raw color in center, about 8 minutes. Serve immediately with soy sauce, hot chili oil, vinegar and hot Chinese mustard.

Can be assembled ahead and frozen. Do not dust waxed or parchment paper with cornstarch before shaping. Do not thaw before steaming and double the cooking time.

Pot Stickers

Makes 40 dumplings

 ⅔ pound ground pork
 1 cup minced cabbage
 2 green onions, minced
 1 egg
 1 tablespoon light soy sauce
 ½ teaspoon salt
 ½ teaspoon grated orange peel (optional)
 ½ teaspoon hot chili oil (optional)

   Cornstarch
40 won ton skins, each cut into largest circle possible

 ½ cup peanut oil

 1 cup water
   Hot chili oil
   White wine vinegar, red wine vinegar, or Chinese vinegar

Combine pork, cabbage, onion, egg, soy sauce, salt, orange peel and hot chili oil in large bowl; mix well.

To assemble: Dust waxed or parchment paper with cornstarch. Set 1 rounded teaspoon filling in center of won ton skin, pressing lightly so filling forms narrow band across middle. Moisten rim of skin. Bring opposite sides together to form semicircle. Pinch corners together. Seal remainder by pleating one side 3 to 4 times and pressing against opposite (unpleated) side. Tap lightly on bottom if necessary so dumpling stands upright. Transfer to cornstarch-dusted paper. Cover with dry kitchen towel. Repeat with remaining won ton and filling.

Place 2 heavy 12-inch skillets over low heat. Add ¼ cup oil to each. Arrange dumplings in skillets in rows, fitting closely together. Increase heat to medium-high and cook uncovered until bottoms are deeply golden, about 2 minutes, checking occasionally.

Add ½ cup water to each pan and cover immediately. Let steam until skins are translucent, about 3 minutes. Remove cover and continue cooking over medium to medium-high heat until bottoms are very crisp and well browned. Drain off excess oil if necessary. Loosen with spatula and transfer to serving dish. Serve immediately with chili oil and vinegar.

Pot stickers can be assembled ahead and frozen. Do not dust waxed or parchment paper with cornstarch before shaping. Allow to defrost before frying and steaming.

Paper-Wrapped Chicken and Ham

Top sirloin, shrimp and scallops are also excellent when paper-wrapped.

Makes 16 packages

  2 tablespoons dry Sherry
  2 tablespoons oyster sauce
  1 tablespoon light soy sauce
  ½ teaspoon sesame oil
  ¼ teaspoon freshly ground white pepper
  ¼ teaspoon sugar
  1 small garlic clove, finely minced

  ⅓ to ½ teaspoon finely minced fresh ginger
  1 whole chicken breast, halved, skinned and boned
 16 6-inch squares parchment paper
 16 very thin slices Black Forest or Smithfield ham, cut into 1½ × 3-inch rectangles
  4 green onions, green stalks cut into 3-inch pieces, white part cut in half lengthwise

   Peanut or corn oil for deep frying

Mix first 8 ingredients in small bowl and set aside. Holding knife against grain and at sharp angle, cut chicken into 1½ × 3-inch rectangles. Add to sauce and marinate at least 15 minutes.

To assemble: Point corner of parchment toward you. Set 1 piece of chicken horizontally in center. Cover with 1 piece of ham. Top with 2 to 3 pieces of onion. Turn bottom corner over ingredients. Fold sides over, creasing well. Bring bottom portion (containing filling) up and fold over, creasing well. Bring remaining top corner down and tuck inside flap, creasing well. Repeat with remaining ingredients. *(Wrapping can be done up to 2 hours ahead.)*

Heat about ¼ inch oil in heavy large skillet to 365°F. Add half of packages, filling side down, and cook 1 to 1½ minutes. Drain on paper towels, pressing gently to remove excess oil. Repeat with remaining packages. Serve hot.

  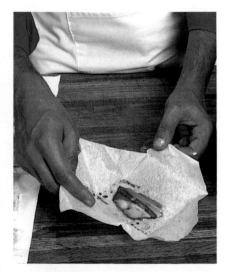

1. *Chicken, ham and green onion are layered in paper and securely folded, then* (**2**) *deep-fried in peanut oil.*
3. *Opened package reveals oil-free ingredients perfectly cooked.*

Hot peanut oil is the finishing touch for the salmon.

Steamed Salmon with Black Beans

Adding fresh banana chilies to the marinade will make this dish spicy-hot.

4 servings

   2 tablespoons light soy sauce
   1 to 2 tablespoons dry Sherry
   1 teaspoon sesame oil
   ¼ teaspoon salt (or more to taste)
   ¼ teaspoon freshly ground pepper
   ¼ teaspoon sugar
   1 tablespoon salted black beans, rinsed, drained and squeezed dry with fingertips
   ½ teaspoon chopped fresh ginger
   2 to 3 salmon steaks of equal thickness (about 1¾ pounds total)

   2 green onions, cut into 2-inch slivers
   3 tablespoons peanut oil

Combine soy sauce, Sherry, sesame oil, salt, pepper and sugar in measuring cup and mix well. Mince beans very finely with ginger. Arrange fish on flame-proof plate. Rub bean mixture over both sides of fish. Pour soy sauce mixture over. Marinate 2 hours.

Bring water to rapid boil in steamer (preferably Chinese). Set plate with fish in steamer. Cover and steam until fish tests done, about 9 minutes for every inch of thickness.

Transfer fish to serving dish. Sprinkle with green onion. Warm small saucepan over medium heat. Add oil and heat until it just begins to smoke. Drizzle over fish. Serve immediately.

Seven Steps to the Perfect Stir-Fry

Stir-frying is one of the most frequently used Chinese cooking methods, perfect for the busy cook. Leftover meat, seafood and vegetables can easily make a meal. But remember not to overdo the soy sauce at the table, since all the seasoning is done beforehand by the cook.

All ingredients should be as uniform as possible in shape and size.

If food is cut into small pieces, it will cook more quickly and will retain its fresh natural flavor and texture.

Never cook more than 1 pound of meat or shellfish at a time or it will end up boiling in its own juices.

All stir-frying should be done over the highest possible heat.

Read the recipe instructions carefully before you begin and line the ingredients up on the counter in the order they are to be added to the wok; the most dense ingredients will go in first, the least dense last.

Undercook everything—the wok is very hot and the degree of doneness of ingredients can be deceptive.

Serve the finished dish *immediately.*

Hot Garlic Eggplant

For variation, use shrimp instead of pork. Add to wok just before serving.

4 to 8 servings

⅓ **pound ground pork**
 2 **teaspoons heavy soy sauce**

1½ **pounds eggplant (preferably oriental), trimmed**
 1 **large yellow onion, cut into ½-inch cubes**

¼ **cup (or more) dry Sherry**
 3 **tablespoons oyster sauce**
 1 **tablespoon heavy soy sauce**
 2 **teaspoons sesame oil**
 1 **teaspoon sugar**

 3 **tablespoons peanut oil**
10 **garlic cloves, finely minced**
 1 **tablespoon chili paste with garlic**
⅓ **to ½ teaspoon finely minced ginger**

　　Chicken stock (optional)

Mix pork and 2 teaspoons soy sauce in small bowl and set aside.

Quarter each unpeeled oriental eggplant lengthwise. Place strips together and cut crosswise into ½-inch pieces. (If using large globe eggplant, peel and cut into ½-inch squares.) Transfer to medium bowl. Blend in onion.

Combine ¼ cup Sherry with oyster sauce, soy sauce, sesame oil and sugar in another small bowl. Set sauce aside.

Heat wok until very hot. Pour in peanut oil; add garlic, chili paste and ginger and cook several seconds; do not allow garlic and ginger to brown.

Add pork mixture and stir-fry, pressing pork against sides of wok until meat loses raw color. Add eggplant mixture. Stir in sauce, adding more Sherry if necessary so that liquid covers about half of the stir-fry mixture.

Cover and cook over high heat until eggplant softens and is no longer raw tasting, about 3 minutes for oriental eggplant or 5 minutes for large globe type. If wok becomes dry during cooking, add small amount of Sherry or chicken stock. Continue cooking, uncovered, until most of sauce evaporates. Adjust seasoning. Turn into dish and serve immediately.

A Taste of Japan

THE MENU

Year-Passing Noodles

White Rice, Decoratively Shaped

Misty Fried Shrimp

Simmered Vegetables

*Radish and Carrot Salad
in Lemon Cups*

Serves 8

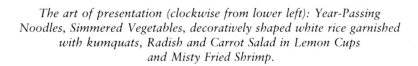

*The art of presentation (clockwise from lower left): Year-Passing
Noodles, Simmered Vegetables, decoratively shaped white rice garnished
with kumquats, Radish and Carrot Salad in Lemon Cups
and Misty Fried Shrimp.*

THE STRATEGY

Here is a delightful dinner that will introduce your guests to the appealing flavors of Japanese cuisine. The selection also focuses on the simple, colorful presentation that is evocative of Japanese dining. Offer homemade ice cream, or a delicate sponge cake topped with preserved kumquats or lychee, for a sweet finish.

Shopping List

The following ingredients are available in oriental markets and some specialty food stores.

- 10 to 12 inches dashi-konbu (dried kelp)
  Katsuo bushi (dried bonito flakes; you will need about 1¼ cups)
- 3 to 4 ounces dried soba (buckwheat noodles)
- 2 to 3 ounces harusame or saifon (dried soy flour noodles)
  Shichimi tōgarashi (dried blend of hot spices)
  Goma shio (black sesame seed and salt mixture), for garnish
  Sansho (Japanese fragrant pepper)
- 12 dried shiitaké (oriental black mushrooms)
- 1 konnyaku cake (gelatinous loaf made from tuber vegetable)
  Usu kuchi shōyu (light soy sauce)
  Rice vinegar
  Daikon (Japanese white radish; also available at major supermarkets in many areas of the country) (you will need 1½ cups cut julienne)
  Saké (rice wine)
  Mirin (syrupy rice wine)

From regular supermarket

- 30 large shrimp
- 6 small lemons, plus additional lemons for lemon peel twists (optional)
- 1 to 2 green onions
- 12 snow peas
- 2 large carrots plus ¼ cup cut julienne
  Fresh ginger
  Lemon or lime wedges
- 2 eggs
- 2 cups white rice
  Vegetable oil (for deep frying)

Salt
Soy sauce
All purpose flour
Sugar

Special Equipment

Decorative rice molds (optional; see recipe for White Rice, Decoratively Shaped)
Wok

Tips

You will need to prepare a double recipe of Dashi to have enough for the entire menu.

An inspiring array of ingredients.

All the other recipes can be doubled if desired.
The recipe for White Rice, Decoratively Shaped can be decreased as indicated.

Countdown

5 days ahead
Prepare Radish and Carrot Salad to point noted in recipe and refrigerate.

4 days ahead
Prepare Dashi for Year-Passing Noodles and Simmered Vegetables and refrigerate (do not freeze).

Morning of dinner
Make White Rice and shape; set aside at room temperature.
Prepare Simmered Vegetables to point of final cooking and set aside at room temperature.

About 1 hour before serving
Remove Radish and Carrot Salad from refrigerator and drain well. Mound into lemon cups; re-

turn to refrigerator if serving chilled (or let stand at room temperature).

About 30 minutes before serving
Ready shrimp for Misty Fried Shrimp to point of cooking.
Prepare Year-Passing Noodles.

Just before serving
Finish Simmered Vegetables.
Cook shrimp for Misty Fried Shrimp.

Wine Suggestions

This exquisitely delicate food requires a wine that is equally delicate and refined. A very good French white Burgundy or one of the lighter California Chardonnays (Trefethen, Vichon or Wente, for example) should be just right. As an alternative, a good Champagne or sparkling wine would add a festive note to this elegant menu.

The Japanese Way

Use corn oil or peanut oil or a combination of vegetable oils when frying. The Japanese use vegetable oils almost exclusively. Dark sesame oil is sometimes used sparingly as a flavoring in the vegetable oil.

The temperature of the oil is most important. It is ready when it bubbles around the chopsticks.

Used oil may be cooled, strained and refrigerated for further use.

Although a wok is not traditional, using it conserves oil, since you can use much less oil than in a flat pan.

Drain fried foods, such as shrimp, on a rack covered with paper towels.

When beating eggs with chopsticks, use four chopsticks to speed the work. And use chopsticks when cooking in deep oil; they help keep you from being spattered.

To make decorative vegetable flowers and leaves easily, always use a razor-sharp knife.

When cutting dried noodles for the shrimp dish, put noodles in a paper bag and cut with scis-

sors to avoid scattering pieces; or chop in a processor fitted with Steel Knife.

In Japan there is a right and a wrong side to food. For instance, when a whole fish is presented on a platter, the "right" side is with the head to the left and the belly toward you, the tail to the right. With fish steaks and chicken breasts, skin side up is the "right" side. When broiling, broil the "wrong" side first, turn and finish on the right side.

In setting forth a Japanese meal, the following order is prescribed: rice bowl to the left, soup to the right, featured dish in center just behind these, and side dishes and pickles to the right and left behind the main dish. Sauces and condiments are placed close to the dishes with which they belong, and the chopsticks are directly in front of the diner, always pointing to the left and frequently resting on a small "pillow" of porcelain to keep tips off the table.

As in present-day nouvelle cuisine, most Japanese dishes are served at room temperature or lukewarm for the best flavor emphasis.

THE RECIPES

Year-Passing Noodles (Toshi Koshi Soba)

These noodles are traditionally served by the Japanese on New Year's Eve to symbolize a long and happy life.

6 to 8 servings

1½ quarts (6 cups) Dashi (basic stock; see
  following recipe)
⅓ cup usu kuchi shōyu (light soy sauce)
⅓ cup mirin (syrupy rice wine)
½ cup loosely packed katsuo bushi (dried bonito
  flakes)

3 to 4 ounces dried soba (buckwheat noodles)

Garnishes
1 to 2 green onions, chopped
Grated fresh ginger
Shichimi tōgarashi (dried blend of hot spices)
Lemon peel twists (optional)

Combine stock, soy sauce and syrupy wine in large saucepan and bring just to boil over medium-high heat. Sprinkle with dried bonito flakes. Remove from heat. Let stand 2 to 3 minutes. Strain through cheese-cloth-lined colander set over bowl. Return broth to saucepan and keep warm.

Bring large pot of water to rolling boil. Add noodles and return to boil. Add 1 cup cold water. Return to boil. Let boil until noodles are tender (but not soggy), about 5 to 6 minutes. Drain well. Rinse in cold water and drain.

To serve, rinse noodles quickly in boiling water and drain well. Rinse soup bowls in boiling water. Divide noodles among bowls and ladle hot broth over top. Pass garnishes separately.

Dashi (Basic Stock)

Makes about 1 quart

5 to 6 inches dashi-konbu (dried kelp)
4½ cups cold water
⅓ cup loosely packed katsuo bushi (dried bonito
  flakes)

Bring kelp and water to boil in large saucepan over high heat. Immediately remove from heat and sprinkle with dried bonito flakes. Let flakes settle to bottom of saucepan (stir if they do not readily settle). Line colander with linen napkin, towel or handkerchief and set over bowl. Strain stock through cloth, twisting and squeezing to release all liquid. *(Dashi can be prepared ahead and refrigerated up to 4 days. It should not be frozen.)*

White Rice, Decoratively Shaped (Gohan)

You can use specially designed molds to shape rice, but a tuna fish can works well also (see directions).

8 servings (makes about 4 cups cooked rice)

2 cups uncooked white rice
2⅓ cups water

Goma shio (black sesame seed and salt
  mixture) (garnish)

Wash rice in colander under cold running water, draining until water runs clear. Transfer to saucepan. Add 2⅓ cups water. Let stand until rice is opaque, about 15 minutes. Cover pan tightly, place over high heat and cook until water bubbles and foams, about 5 minutes (do not uncover during cooking period). Reduce heat and continue cooking until water is absorbed, about 5 more minutes. Increase heat to high and cook 30 seconds to dry slightly. Remove from heat and let stand, covered, at least 10 minutes before serving.

To shape rice decoratively: Remove top and bottom of thoroughly clean tuna fish can (reserve top). Cover edges with masking tape to smooth any rough surfaces (cover reserved top with tape also). Dip can in cold water. Place on serving plate or platter in position desired. Pack with rice. Dip reserved top in water and press down firmly over rice. Push rice all the way through to remove can. Sprinkle top of rice with black sesame seed and salt mixture.

For 4 servings, use 1 cup rice and 1 cup plus 2 tablespoons water; for 6 servings, use 1½ cups rice and 1¾ cups water.

Misty Fried Shrimp (Ebi No Kasumi Age)

An appealing texture and taste: moist, succulent shrimp covered with delicate, transparent noodles.
8 to 10 servings

  2 to 3 ounces harusame or saifon (dried soy flour noodles)

30 large shrimp, peeled and deveined (tails intact)
⅓ cup flour seasoned with ½ teaspoon salt and ¼ teaspoon sansho (Japanese fragrant pepper)

  2 egg whites

   Vegetable oil for deep frying
   Lemon or lime wedges and soy sauce

Hold noodles over large paper bag and cut with scissors into ¼- to ½-inch pieces (or chop in batches in food processor fitted with Steel Knife). Transfer to large bowl (you should have ⅔ to ¾ cup noodles).

Score underbelly of shrimp to prevent curling. Pat dry with paper towels. Pour seasoned flour into plastic bag. Add shrimp in batches and shake to coat lightly. Set aside.

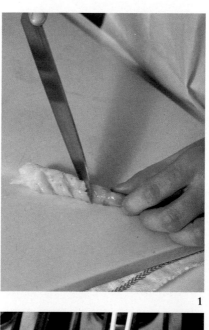

1. *Score the underside of the shrimp to prevent curling.* 2. *Coat shrimp lightly with flour, dip into egg whites and (3) cover with dried soy flour noodles.* 4. *Fry quickly in hot vegetable oil.* 5. *Drain on paper towels.*

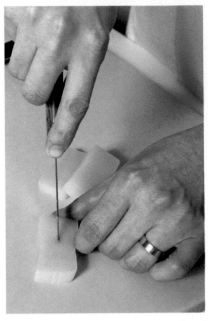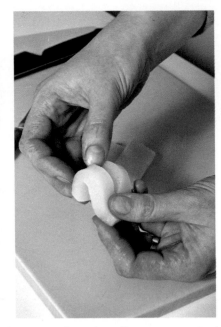

To braid konnyaku, slit center of each slice (1) and gently pull open (2). 3. End is pulled through and twisted.

Beat egg whites in medium bowl just until foamy. Dip shrimp into white; pat noodles onto shrimp, covering completely.

Heat oil in deep-fat fryer or wok to 325°F. (Add piece of noodle to test. Temperature is correct if noodle sinks slightly, rises to the surface and puffs.) Add shrimp in batches (do not crowd) and fry until opaque, about 2 minutes (noodles should remain pale). Transfer to paper towels and let drain. Serve hot or at room temperature with lemon or lime wedges and soy sauce.

Simmered Vegetables (Yasai No Uma Ni)

Celebrate the Japanese New Year in traditional fashion with sculptured vegetables in a flavorful soy broth.

6 to 8 servings

- **12 dried shiitaké (dried black oriental mushrooms)**
  Pinch of sugar

- **1 konnyaku cake* (gelatinous loaf made from a tuber vegetable)**

- **12 snow peas, strings removed**

- **2 large carrots, cut into ¼-inch rounds**

- **1½ cups Dashi (basic stock; see recipe with Toshi Koshi Soba)**
- **2 teaspoons saké (rice wine)**
- **2 to 3 tablespoons sugar**
- **3 to 4 tablespoons soy sauce**
- **3 tablespoons mirin (syrupy rice wine)**

Combine mushrooms and sugar in bowl with enough warm water to cover (at least 2 cups) and let soak 15 to 20 minutes. Drain mushrooms, reserving 1½ cups soaking liquid. (If gritty, drain through strainer lined with dampened paper towel.) Remove mushroom stems and discard. Rinse caps under cold water and squeeze dry.

Cut konnyaku into ¼-inch slices. Using sharp knife, slit center and pull one end of konnyaku through slit, twisting gently as you pull. Bring large saucepan of water to boil over high heat. Carefully add konnyaku braids and blanch 1 minute. Drain well; let cool to room temperature.

Cut ¾-inch wedge at top of each snow pea. Bring large saucepan of water to boil over high heat. Add snow peas and blanch about 30 seconds. Drain well; let cool to room temperature.

Cut each carrot round with small flower-shaped cutter. Make 5 shallow slits with sharp, thin knife between each petal to center of "flower." Holding knife at angle, slice thin wedge from middle of each petal up to slits.

Bring stock, 1 cup reserved mushroom soaking liquid and rice wine to boil in saucepan over medium-high heat. Reduce heat, add mushrooms and konnyaku and simmer 5 minutes. Add carrot and sugar and cook 5 minutes. Stir in soy sauce; add more stock or mushroom liquid if vegetables appear too dry. Cook another 5 minutes. Remove mushrooms, konnyaku and carrot from pan using slotted spoon. Add syrupy rice wine and cook 20 to 30 seconds. Return konnyaku and vegetables to pan and cook until glazed, about 30 to 40 seconds. Let cool to room temperature. Arrange on serving platter with snow peas.

*Also called yam cakes.

Radish and Carrot Salad in Lemon Cups (Kohaku Namasu)

Use as a first course or garnish.
Makes 12 salad cups

6 small lemons
  Rice vinegar
¼ cup sugar
¼ teaspoon salt
1½ cups julienne of peeled daikon (Japanese white radish)
  Salt
¼ cup julienne of peeled carrot

Cut lemons in half. Squeeze juice into measuring cup. Scoop out pulp and discard, reserving lemon shells. Trim bottoms so halves stand upright. If using within 2 hours, stuff each with damp paper towels. (Cover with plastic and freeze if preparing ahead.)

Add enough vinegar to lemon juice to equal ½ cup. Transfer mixture to small saucepan. Add sugar and ¼ teaspoon salt and cook over low heat just until sugar and salt dissolve. Remove sauce from heat, cover and refrigerate.

Place radish julienne in medium bowl. Sprinkle lightly with salt. Let stand 2 to 3 minutes. Squeeze to wilt slightly; drain well. (If radish is strongly flavored, soak in cold water 5 minutes and squeeze dry.) Repeat for carrot.

Combine carrot and radish in large bowl. Pour chilled lemon sauce over vegetables. *(Can be made 5 days ahead to this point, covered and refrigerated.)* Let stand at room temperature at least 30 minutes. To serve, drain vegetables well. Mound into lemon shells. Serve chilled or at room temperature.

Remaining salad can be removed from lemon shells and refrigerated overnight.

Buffet from Northern India

THE MENU

Chicken Tandoori   Lamb Korma

Curried Cauliflower and Potatoes

Curried Lentils

Saffron Vegetable Rice Medley

Yogurt and Fresh Vegetables

Parathas   Chapatis

Mint Chutney

Hot Pepper Chutney

Pineapple-Papaya Chutney

Pretzels Dipped in Sweet Syrup

Rice Pudding   Yogurt Drink

Serves 8

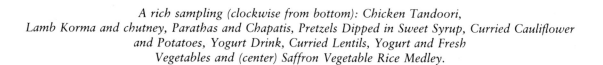

*A rich sampling (clockwise from bottom): Chicken Tandoori,
Lamb Korma and chutney, Parathas and Chapatis, Pretzels Dipped in Sweet Syrup, Curried Cauliflower
and Potatoes, Yogurt Drink, Curried Lentils, Yogurt and Fresh
Vegetables and (center) Saffron Vegetable Rice Medley.*

THE STRATEGY

Introduce your friends to the varied flavors of India with this lavish dinner. Two delicious main dishes— Chicken Tandoori and Lamb Korma—are the centerpiece of this delicious menu. They are accompanied by a number of traditional vegetable dishes, breads, chutneys and sweets. The intriguing spices are easily obtained at Indian specialty food stores.

Shopping List

2 chickens
2 pounds lean lamb
1 large or 2 to 3 small fresh beets
1 lime (only ½ will be used)
1½ pounds onions plus 2¼ cups chopped plus 1 medium onion
½ pound tomatoes plus 4 whole, ½ cup coarsely chopped and 1 cup chopped plus additional chopped tomato for garnish
1 pound potatoes
3 pounds cauliflower
1 cup fresh peas (shelled)
1 bunch fresh mint
2 jalapeño peppers (optional)
1 serrano chili plus additional 1 cup serrano chilies or jalapeño peppers
2 additional hot green chilies
3 cups pineapple chunks
　Garlic
　Fresh ginger
　Fresh lemon juice
　Lemon or lime wedges for garnish
　Lettuce
　Radishes for garnish
　Green chilies for garnish
　Fresh cilantro for garnish plus additional cilantro, also known as coriander or Chinese parsley
　Green onion for garnish
　Carrots (1 cup sliced)
　Cucumber (1 cup grated)
　Fresh parsley for garnish
　Papaya (½ cup chopped)
　Preserved ginger (½ cup chopped)
　Seedless raisins (½ cup)
　Pitted dates (¼ cup chopped)
1 stick margarine
3½ sticks plus ⅔ cup butter

9½ cups plain yogurt (about 2½ quarts)
3½ quarts milk
　Half and half (¼ cup)
4½ cups long-grain rice
2 cups dried lentils
2 ounces raw cashews
2 tablespoons whole almonds plus ½ cup chopped almonds plus additional whole almonds and chopped almonds for garnish
2½ pounds plus ½ cup whole wheat flour
1¾ cups all purpose flour
2¾ cups sugar plus additional 2 tablespoons sugar *or* 2 tablespoons honey (or to taste)
1 cup firmly packed brown sugar
　Active dry yeast
　Baking soda
1¼ cups white vinegar
　Mustard oil* or vegetable oil
　Vegetable oil for deep frying
　Saffron threads (1½ teaspoons)
　Ground coriander
　Ground cumin
　Whole cumin seed
　Paprika
　Salt
　Black pepper
　Ground red pepper
　Poppy seed
　Curry powder
　Ground turmeric
　Ground cardamom
　Ground cinnamon
　Cinnamon sticks
　Black or white mustard seed
　Mango powder (amchoor)*
　Asafetida (dried gum resin)* (optional)
　Bay leaves
　Whole cloves
　Ground cloves
　Edible silver leaf* for garnish
　Garam masala*
　Anardana* (dried pomegranate seeds)
　Ground allspice
　Orange or yellow food coloring (optional; see note with Jalabis)
　Rose water*

*Available at Indian specialty food stores.

Tips

All the recipes can be doubled.

Countdown

3 months ahead
Prepare Parathas; wrap tightly and freeze.
Make Chapatis; wrap tightly and freeze.

2 to 3 weeks ahead
Prepare Mint Chutney and refrigerate.
Make Hot Pepper Chutney and refrigerate.
Prepare Pineapple-Papaya Chutney and refrigerate.

2 to 3 days ahead
Prepare Pretzels Dipped in Sweet Syrup and store at room temperature.

1 day ahead
Make Lamb Korma. Let cool, cover and refrigerate.
Prepare chicken as directed to point of cooking and let stand at room temperature 12 hours.
Prepare Rice Pudding. Let cool, cover and refrigerate.
Remove Chapatis from freezer and let thaw in refrigerator overnight.
Remove Parathas from freezer and let thaw in refrigerator overnight.

2 hours ahead
Mix Yogurt and Fresh Vegetables and refrigerate.

Remove chutneys from refrigerator to bring to room temperature.

About 1 hour before serving
Prepare Saffron Vegetable Rice Medley.

About 45 minutes before serving
Finish Chicken Tandoori.

About 30 minutes before serving
Make Curried Cauliflower and Potatoes.
Prepare Curried Lentils.

About 20 minutes before serving
Rewarm Lamb Korma over low heat.
Warm Chapatis and Parathas in very low oven.

As guests arrive
Prepare Yogurt Drink.

During dinner
If desired, rewarm Rice Pudding in low oven.

Wine Suggestions

The spicy foods of India present a major challenge to the wine lover. The simple solution is to serve chilled beer, preferably of the dark variety. A bit more interesting solution would be to serve a crisp Sauvignon Blanc or white French Bordeaux, which would work with the chicken dish, and a big California Zinfandel or Petite Sirah to balance the Lamb Korma.

THE RECIPES

Chicken Tandoori

6 to 8 servings

   2 chickens, halved and skinned
   1 teaspoon saffron threads
   2 tablespoons boiling water

   2 ounces garlic cloves (about 8 large)
   2 ounces fresh ginger, cut into small pieces
   1 cup plain yogurt
   ½ cup beetroot color extract*
   2 tablespoons fresh lemon juice
   1 heaping tablespoon ground coriander
   2 heaping teaspoons ground cumin

   1 teaspoon paprika
   1 teaspoon salt
   ½ teaspoon ground red pepper
   ½ teaspoon whole cumin seed

   ½ cup (1 stick) butter, melted
     Lettuce
     Lemon or lime wedges, radishes and green chilies (garnish)

Cut 4 to 5 slits (almost to bone) in legs and breasts of each chicken. Soak saffron in boiling water for about 5 minutes. Brush generously over chickens and into slits. Cover and let stand at room temperature for 20 minutes.

Puree garlic and ginger in processor or blender. Transfer to bowl and add next 9 ingredients, blending thoroughly. Using pastry brush, generously paint chickens with spice mixture, making sure it reaches into slits. Cover chickens and let stand at room temperature 12 hours.

Preheat oven to 500°F. Butter shallow roasting pan. Add chickens and drizzle with melted butter. Roast 10 to 12 minutes. Reduce oven temperature to 350°F and continue roasting until chickens test done and are a poppy red color, about 25 to 30 minutes. Arrange chickens on lettuce leaves and garnish with citrus wedges, radishes and chilies.

*Slice 1 large or 2 to 3 small beets. Combine in saucepan with ½ cup water. Cover and boil until fork tender, about 15 to 20 minutes. Drain well, reserving liquid.

Lamb Korma

8 servings

  2 ounces garlic cloves (about 8 large)
  2 ounces fresh ginger, cut into small pieces

  ½ cup milk
  2 ounces raw cashews
  2 teaspoons poppy seed

  ¾ cup (1½ sticks) butter
  1 pound onions, finely chopped
  2 pounds lean lamb, cut into 1½-inch cubes
  2 teaspoons ground coriander (also known as Chinese parsley or cilantro)
1½ teaspoons curry powder
  1 teaspoon ground cumin
  1 teaspoon salt
  ½ teaspoon ground red pepper
  ½ teaspoon ground turmeric
  ¼ teaspoon ground cardamom
  ¼ teaspoon cinnamon

  ½ pound tomatoes, cut into ½-inch pieces
  ½ cup plain yogurt, beaten
    Chopped fresh cilantro (garnish)

Puree garlic and ginger in processor or blender. Remove and set aside.

Mix milk, cashews and poppy seed in processor or blender until smooth.

Melt butter in heavy large skillet over medium-high heat. Add onion and sauté until lightly browned. Increase heat to high, blend in garlic puree and brown lightly. Reduce heat to medium, add lamb and sauté until browned on all sides, scraping skillet constantly

to prevent sticking (if mixture seems too dry, reduce heat and add several drops of water to loosen from skillet). Add spices, mixing constantly. Reduce heat to low and cook until lamb is nicely glazed, about 10 minutes.

Add tomatoes, yogurt and cashew–poppy seed mixture to lamb, stirring well. Cover and simmer about 20 to 25 minutes. Turn into serving bowl and garnish with chopped cilantro.

Curried Cauliflower and Potatoes (Alu Gobi)

8 to 10 servings

  ½ cup (1 stick) margarine
  1 pound potatoes, peeled and cut into 1½-inch cubes

  ½ cup mustard oil or vegetable oil
  1 teaspoon black or white mustard seeds
  ½ cup chopped onion
  1 teaspoon mango powder (amchoor)* or fresh lemon juice
  ¾ to 1 teaspoon ground coriander
  ¾ to 1 teaspoon ground cumin
  ¾ teaspoon ground turmeric
  ½ teaspoon ground red pepper
  ½ teaspoon paprika
    Pinch of asafetida (dried gum resin)* (optional)

  2 tomatoes, cut into 1½-inch cubes
  2 tablespoons chopped fresh cilantro (optional)
  2 teaspoons slivered fresh ginger
  2 jalapeño peppers (optional), seeded and chopped
  1 teaspoon salt
  3 pounds cauliflower, broken into florets (and some tender green leaves from base)
    Chopped green onion and lemon wedges (garnish)

Melt margarine in skillet over medium heat. Add potatoes and sauté until lightly browned. Remove from heat.

Heat oil in heavy saucepan over high heat. When hot but not smoking, add mustard seeds, shaking pan constantly until they pop. Add onion and brown lightly. Reduce heat, add next 7 ingredients and blend thoroughly.

Curried Cauliflower and Potatoes.

Add tomatoes, cilantro, ginger, peppers and salt. If mixture seems too dry, sprinkle small amount of water in pan. Add cauliflower and potatoes, turning to coat with spices. Reduce heat to low, cover tightly. Cook 15 minutes (cauliflower and potatoes should stay firm). Turn onto serving platter; garnish with chopped green onion and lemon wedges.

Note: If fresh cilantro is not available, omit entirely; do not use dried.

*Available at Indian specialty food stores.

Curried Lentils (Dal)

6 to 8 servings

  4 cups (1 quart) water
  2 cups dried lentils
  1 teaspoon curry powder
  ½ teaspoon salt

⅔ cup butter
¾ cup chopped onion
  1 teaspoon cumin seed
½ cup coarsely chopped tomatoes
¼ cup half and half

  1 tablespoon chopped fresh cilantro (garnish)
  1 teaspoon paprika (garnish)
    Chopped tomato (garnish)

Bring water to boil in large saucepan. Add lentils, curry powder and salt and blend well. Cover and let simmer until lentils are tender and have absorbed most of water, about 20 to 30 minutes.

Meanwhile, melt butter in medium skillet over medium heat. Add onion and sauté until golden. Add cumin, increase heat to high and cook 30 seconds, stirring constantly. Reduce heat and stir in tomatoes and half and half.

Transfer lentils to serving bowl and pour onion mixture over top. For garnish, sprinkle with cilantro, paprika and tomato.

Saffron Vegetable Rice Medley

The fragrance and flavor of saffron, released only by cooking the spice in hot liquid (cooking saffron in oil will destroy it), adds an exotic touch.

8 to 10 servings

¼ cup (½ stick) butter
3 cinnamon sticks, broken
6 bay leaves, broken
½ teaspoon whole cumin
1 cup chopped onion
8 whole cloves
½ teaspoon ground turmeric
1 cup peas
1 cup sliced carrots
4 cups long-grain rice
4 cups (1 quart) boiling water
2 teaspoons salt
½ teaspoon saffron threads
Almonds and silver leaf* (garnish)

Melt butter in large saucepan over medium-high heat. Add cinnamon, bay leaves and cumin and sauté. Add onion, cloves and turmeric and continue sautéing until onion is golden and coated with spices. Stir in peas and carrots. Blend in rice, water, salt and saffron and bring to boil. Stir through several times, then cover and reduce heat to lowest setting. Cook until water is evaporated (check after 30 minutes), about 35 to 45 minutes. Turn onto shallow platter and garnish with almonds and silver leaf.

*Available at Middle Eastern and Indian specialty stores.

Yogurt and Fresh Vegetables (Raita)

8 to 10 servings

1 quart (4 cups) plain yogurt
1 cup chopped tomatoes
1 cup grated cucumber, lightly squeezed to remove some of excess water
1 tablespoon finely chopped fresh cilantro
1 teaspoon sugar
½ teaspoon garam masala*
½ teaspoon salt
Paprika and minced fresh parsley (garnish)

Using whisk or spatula, stir yogurt gently in medium bowl until smooth. Add remaining ingredients except garnish and blend well. Sprinkle generously with paprika and parsley.

*Available at Indian specialty food stores.

Parathas

Parathas could be made 1 day ahead and reheated in a 350°F oven for about 1 minute just before serving.

Makes about 14 to 16

1½ pounds whole wheat flour
¼ teaspoon salt
½ to ¾ cup milk

¼ cup (½ stick) butter, melted

Fill small bowl with 2 cups cold water and keep next to you as you work. Combine flour and salt in large bowl. Add ½ cup milk and stir with spatula or hands, adding milk as necessary to make dough semifirm and come clean from sides of bowl (*dough should not be too hard or too soft*). Sprinkle dough with a few drops of water, cover with damp cloth and let rest 15 minutes.

Brush working surface with some of melted butter. Knead dough until smooth, dampening hands with reserved water to prevent sticking as you work. Cover dough with damp cloth; let rest for 5 minutes.

Divide dough into 14 to 16 balls. Roll each ⅛ inch thick. Brush with some of melted butter and roll into cylinders about 9 inches long. Coil into ball shape. Roll each coil into circle about ⅛ inch thick. Brush each side with melted butter and cook on ungreased griddle or nonstick skillet until lightly browned, about 5 minutes, turning once. Transfer to plate, stacking between sheets of paper towels to absorb excess butter. Serve warm.

Chapatis

Both Parathas and Chapatis are frequently used as tools for eating. Chapatis are best if made about 1 hour before serving. They can be fully cooked 1 day ahead and stored in the refrigerator, but do not refrigerate the dough, as it becomes difficult to work with when chilled.

Makes about 24

1 **pound whole wheat flour**
¼ **teaspoon salt**
½ **to ¾ cup water**

½ **cup whole wheat flour**

Fill small bowl with 2 cups cold water and keep next to you as you work. Combine 1 pound flour and salt in large bowl. Add ½ cup water and stir with spatula or hands, adding water as necessary to make dough semifirm and come clean from sides of bowl *(dough should not to be too hard or too soft)*. Sprinkle with a few drops of water, cover with damp cloth and let rest 15 minutes.

Knead dough until smooth, dampening hands with reserved water as you work to prevent sticking. Cover dough and let rest for another 5 minutes.

Lightly flour working surface, placing remaining ½ cup whole wheat flour in pile alongside. Divide dough into about 24 golf ball–size portions. Flatten each ball into discs ½ to ¾ inch thick. Dip both sides into flour and roll out ⅛ inch thick. Place one at a time on ungreased griddle or small nonstick skillet and cook 30 seconds; turn and cook another 30 seconds. Turn again; pat surface of Chapatis with dry towel, rotating them in pan while doing so, about 1 minute (steam will make Chapatis puff); *do not turn; pat only on one side.* Slide Chapatis out onto plate (they will deflate when taken out of pan) and repeat with remaining dough.

Both Parathas and Chapatis can be stored in refrigerator up to 1 week and can be frozen up to 3 months. However, Chapatis are more fragile and have a tendency to dry out. They will not hold up as well as Parathas.

Rice Pudding (Kheer)

8 servings

¾ **gallon (3 quarts) milk**
½ **cup long-grain rice**

¾ **cup sugar**
½ **cup chopped almonds**
¼ **teaspoon ground cardamom seed**
   Toasted chopped almonds (garnish)

Bring milk to boil in large saucepan (a wide, shallow pan will work better than a deep one). Add rice and cook over medium-low heat, stirring frequently and watching carefully to prevent milk from boiling over, until mixture is consistency of heavy cream and begins sticking to bottom of pan, about 2¼ hours.

Stir in remaining ingredients except garnish. Continue cooking 3 to 4 minutes, stirring constantly. Serve warm or chilled, sprinkled with almonds.

Yogurt Drink (Lassi)

6 to 8 servings

1 **quart (4 cups) plain yogurt**
2 **tablespoons almonds**
2 **tablespoons sugar or honey or to taste**
1 **cup ice cubes**
   Rose water

Combine 1 cup yogurt with nuts and sugar in blender and mix at high speed until nuts are pulverized. Add ice cubes and remaining yogurt and blend again at high speed. Pour into glasses and sprinkle with a few drops of rose water.

Mint Chutney

Refreshing with Chicken Tandoori.
Makes about 2 cups

1 **bunch fresh mint (leaves only)**
¼ **bunch fresh cilantro (leaves only)**
1½ **teaspoons anardana* (dried pomegranate seeds)**
½ **pound onions, chopped**
1 **serrano chili, seeds removed**
½ **teaspoon salt**

Combine mint and cilantro in processor or blender and puree until completely smooth. Add anardana and mix until smooth. Add remaining ingredients and mix again until smooth.

*Available at Indian specialty food stores.

Hot Pepper Chutney

Makes about 2 cups

1 **cup fresh serrano or jalapeño peppers**
2 **medium tomatoes, coarsely chopped**
1 **teaspoon salt**
1 **teaspoon beetroot color extract (see Chicken Tandoori)**

Puree ingredients in processor or blender. Serve at room temperature.

Pineapple-Papaya Chutney

Any fruit that is not fully ripened, such as peaches, apricots, plums, mangoes or apples, can be substituted for the pineapple and/or the papaya.

Makes 4 cups

  3 cups pineapple chunks (½-inch chunks)
1¼ cups white vinegar
  1 cup firmly packed brown sugar
  1 medium onion, finely chopped
  2 hot green peppers, finely chopped
  2 garlic cloves, minced or pressed
 ½ cup chopped preserved ginger
 ½ cup seedless raisins
 ½ cup chopped papaya
 ½ fresh lime, peeled, seeded and chopped
 ¼ cup chopped pitted dates
  1 teaspoon cinnamon
 ½ teaspoon salt
 ¼ teaspoon ground cloves
 ¼ teaspoon ground allspice
 ¼ teaspoon ground red pepper
 ¼ cup fresh lemon juice

Combine all ingredients except lemon juice in heavy large saucepan and bring to boil. Reduce heat and simmer 1 hour, stirring frequently. Stir in lemon juice and simmer an additional 5 minutes. Cool completely before serving.

Crisp Jalebis are thoroughly drained after frying, before being dipped into sweet syrup.

Pretzels Dipped in Sweet Syrup (Jalebis)

Jalebis ("multiple coils") should always be vividly colored—either red, orange or yellow. They can be made any size, from an 8-inch length to be shared or individual 2-inch coils. They will keep 2 to 3 days at room temperature. Do not refrigerate or they will get soggy.

Makes about 8 to 10 servings

2 cups sugar
1 cup water

1½ cups warm water (105°F to 115°F)
½ teaspoon active dry yeast
Orange or yellow food coloring or beetroot color extract (see Chicken Tandoori)

1¾ cups all purpose flour
Pinch of baking soda

Vegetable oil (for deep frying)

Combine sugar and 1 cup water in small saucepan and stir until sugar is dissolved. Boil over medium-high heat without stirring until mixture becomes a medium-thick syrup. Remove from heat, cover partially and keep warm.

Combine warm water, yeast and coloring in bowl and let stand for 5 minutes. Stir mixture until completely blended.

Combine flour and baking soda in large bowl. Gradually whisk in 1 cup of yeast mixture. Continue adding, whisking constantly until mixture is consistency of pancake batter. Let stand 10 minutes. Adjust consistency by adding additional flour or lukewarm water as necessary.

Heat ¾ inch oil in heavy large skillet over medium heat. Pour 1 cup batter into pastry bag fitted with ¼- to ⅛-inch tip. Carefully pipe into hot oil, making overlapping coils of desired lengths. Fry 10 seconds on first side; turn with tongs and fry 15 seconds on other side. Remove from skillet, letting excess oil drip back into skillet. Dip into syrup for 15 seconds. Repeat with remaining batter. Serve hot or at room temperature.

La Cucina Nuova from Italy

THE MENU

Chicken Liver Toasts

Italian Beef Appetizer

Mushrooms with Pearl Onions

Red, White and Green Lasagne

Lamb with Sweet-Sour Sauce

Rice with Artichokes and Olives

Genoa-Style Spinach

Fantasy Salad

Piedmont-Style Almond Cake

Serves 8

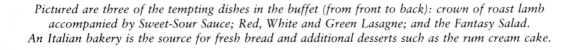

Pictured are three of the tempting dishes in the buffet (from front to back): crown of roast lamb accompanied by Sweet-Sour Sauce; Red, White and Green Lasagne; and the Fantasy Salad. An Italian bakery is the source for fresh bread and additional desserts such as the rum cream cake.

THE STRATEGY

Here is a festive buffet celebrating *La Cucina Nuova,* "the New Italian Cooking," which caters to today's taste for lighter fare. New approaches to old favorites include beef, lamb and chicken dishes, but vegetables are foremost. And their visual artistry complements their gustatory delights.

Shopping List

  3 cups chicken broth
  2 cups beef broth
½ pound chicken livers plus additional chicken livers (½ cup coarsely chopped)
  2 pounds prime beef top round
  1 pound ground veal
  1 6-pound crown roast of lamb *or* 3 2-pound racks of lamb
    Chicken hearts (½ cup coarsely chopped)
    Chicken giblets (½ cup coarsely chopped)
  4 fresh sage leaves
  3 to 4 mushrooms plus 1⅓ cups plus 6 large mushrooms (optional)
  4 to 5 dried Italian mushrooms
  1 large carrot plus 2 additional carrots
  1 large onion plus 1 medium onion
  2 garlic cloves

  1 orange (for 2 to 3 strips orange peel)
  2 artichokes
  3 lemons
12 green Sicilian olives
  2 pounds fresh spinach
  1 head lettuce
  1 red bell pepper
  1 green bell pepper
  1 yellow bell pepper
  1 large red onion
  2 small cucumbers
  3 to 4 ounces rughetta*
  3 to 4 ounces chicory
  3 to 4 ounces red-leaf lettuce
    Pitted prunes (2 tablespoons minced)
    Golden raisins (⅓ cup plus ½ cup and 2 tablespoons minced)
    Parsley (2 tablespoons chopped)
    Italian parsley (10 sprigs plus 3 to 4 tablespoons minced)
  6 eggs
  3 cups milk (about)
1¼ sticks unsalted butter
1½ sticks butter
    Parmesan cheese

Ingredients for the Fantasy Salad.

6 13 × 3-inch fresh egg pasta rectangles
   (homemade or commercial)
3 13 × 3-inch fresh spinach pasta rectangles
   (homemade or commercial)
1½ cups arborio rice** *or* long-grain rice
1 loaf Italian or French bread
   Pine nuts (2 tablespoons minced plus ¼ cup
   whole)
   Whole almonds (⅓ cup)
1 cup red wine vinegar plus 1½ tablespoons
1¼ cups red or white wine vinegar
3 cups olive oil
1¼ cup sugar (about)
   Capers (2 to 3 tablespoons plus ¼ cup)
   Salt
   Black pepper
   Whole white peppercorns
   Beef bouillon cube *or* meat extract
   Whole nutmeg
   Dried rosemary
   Juniper berries
   Whole clove
   Dijon mustard
   All purpose flour
   Corn flour
   Cake flour
   Potato flour
   Baking powder
   Almond extract
   Unsweetened cocoa
   Tomato paste
   Tomato sauce
4 2-ounce cans anchovy fillets plus 6 additional
   fillets
1 7½-ounce jar cocktail onions
   Pitted black olives (1 cup halved)
1 10-ounce package frozen pearl onions (1⅓ cups)
3 cups red wine
   Cognac or brandy
   Dry Marsala
   Dry white wine

*Available in specialty produce markets.
**Available at Italian markets.

Tips

Salad ingredients and dressing for Fantasy Salad
   can be halved. The following recipes can be
   doubled: Chicken Liver Toasts, Italian Beef
   Appetizer, Mushrooms with Pearl Onions,
   Rice with Artichokes and Olives, and Genoa-
   Style Spinach.
Recipes for Red, White and Green Lasagne and
   Lamb with Sweet-Sour Sauce can be doubled
   but are best prepared in two batches.

Countdown

1 week ahead
Prepare Red, White and Green Lasagne to point of
   baking; let cool, cover and freeze.

1 day ahead
Remove Red, White and Green Lasagne from
   freezer and let thaw in refrigerator overnight.
Prepare lamb with marinade mixture and refrigerate overnight.
Bake Piedmont-Style Almond Cake; let cool, wrap
   in plastic and store at room temperature.

Morning of buffet
Assemble salad ingredients for Fantasy Salad in
   salad bowl and refrigerate.
Prepare dressing for Fantasy Salad. Transfer to jar
   and refrigerate.
If desired, finish Almond Cake with frosting and
   sprinkle with toasted slivered almonds (cake
   can also be served plain).

About 3 hours before serving
Prepare artichokes for Rice with Artichokes and
   Olives and set aside in acidulated water.
Toast bread rounds for Chicken Liver Toasts; let
   cool, wrap tightly and set aside at room
   temperature.

About 1 hour before serving
Finish Rice with Artichokes and Olives.
Soak mushrooms for Mushrooms with Pearl
   Onions.

Just before serving appetizers
Sauté chicken liver mixture for Chicken Liver
   Toasts.

Assemble individual plates of the Italian Beef
    Appetizer.
Prepare Mushrooms with Pearl Onions.
About 45 minutes before serving main course
Begin baking Red, White and Green Lasagne.
Drain marinade; put lamb in oven to roast and
    begin sauce.
Just before serving main course
Toss salad with dressing.
Prepare Genoa-Style Spinach.

Wine Suggestions

Italian wines should be served to complement this
menu. A crisp Vernaccia di San Gimignagno, a Soave
or a Verdicchio will go well with the pasta course,
and a full-bodied red such as a Barolo, a Brunello di
Montalcino or an Amarone will blend nicely with the
main course. Finish the meal with a lovely sparkling
Asti Spumante.

THE RECIPES

Chicken Liver Toasts (Crostini di Fegatini di Pollo)

Makes about 24 appetizers

    2 tablespoons (¼ stick) unsalted butter
    ½ pound chicken livers, coarsely chopped
    10 sprigs parsley (preferably Italian), finely
       chopped
    4 fresh sage leaves, chopped
    ¼ cup capers, rinsed, drained and finely chopped
    2 anchovy fillets, mashed with fork
    1½ tablespoons red wine vinegar
    1 loaf Italian or French bread, cut into 2- to 3-
       inch squares or rounds and toasted

Melt butter in medium saucepan over medium heat.
Add livers, parsley, sage and capers. Cook just until
livers are no longer pink. Add anchovies and vinegar
and cook 1 to 2 minutes more. Spread on toasted
bread and serve.

Italian Beef Appetizer (Carpaccio)

8 servings

    2 pounds *uncooked* prime beef top round,
       trimmed and thinly sliced into 12 to 18 pieces
       Fresh lemon juice
       Olive oil
    2 to 3 tablespoons capers, rinsed, drained and
       minced
    2 to 3 tablespoons minced fresh parsley
       (preferably Italian)

    3 to 4 mushrooms, thinly sliced
       Freshly ground pepper

Gently pound meat on work surface until paper thin.
Arrange 2 to 3 slices in center of each serving plate.
Sprinkle generously with lemon juice. Brush oil
lightly over meat. Combine capers and parsley in
small bowl. Top each slice of meat with 1 teaspoon
of mixture. Surround meat with 3 to 4 mushroom
slices. Season with pepper and serve.

Mushrooms with Pearl Onions (Funghi e Cipolline)

6 to 8 servings

    4 to 5 dried Italian mushrooms

    1⅓ cups (10 ounces) frozen pearl onions

    2 tablespoons (¼ stick) butter
    2 tablespoons olive oil
    1 tablespoon minced fresh parsley (preferably
       Italian)
       Pinch of freshly ground pepper
    1⅓ cups (10 ounces) fresh mushrooms (large ones
       cut into 2 or 3 pieces)

    ¾ cup dry Marsala
    1 teaspoon tomato paste
    ½ beef bouillon cube or ½ teaspoon meat extract
       Salt

Combine mushrooms and ½ cup lukewarm water in
medium bowl and let soak at least 30 minutes. Drain
mushrooms in cheesecloth-lined colander set over

bowl, reserving liquid. Squeeze mushrooms dry and chop coarsely.

Bring 1 quart salted water to boil in medium saucepan over medium-high heat. Add onions, return water to boil and cook about 4 minutes. Drain well.

Combine butter and olive oil in large skillet over medium-high heat. Stir in parsley and pepper. Increase heat to high, add onions, fresh and dried mushrooms and cook 1 minute.

Stir in reserved mushroom liquid. Combine Marsala, tomato paste and bouillon in small bowl and blend into mushroom mixture. Cook over medium-high heat 1 to 2 minutes. Season with salt. Cover, reduce heat to low and cook 10 minutes, stirring occasionally. Adjust seasoning. Serve immediately.

Red, White and Green Lasagne (Vincisgrassi)

This lasagne freezes better uncooked.

6 to 8 servings

Pasta
    6 13 × 3-inch fresh egg pasta rectangles (about 1 pound), homemade or commercial
    3 13 × 3-inch fresh spinach pasta rectangles (about ½ pound), homemade or commercial

Sauce
    ¼ cup (½ stick) unsalted butter
    ¼ cup olive oil
    1 large carrot, quartered
    1 large onion, quartered
    1 pound ground veal
    ½ cup *each* coarsely chopped chicken hearts and giblets
    ½ cup dry white wine
    1 cup chicken broth
    2 tablespoons tomato sauce
    1 cup (about) milk
    ½ cup coarsely chopped chicken livers
    6 large mushrooms, coarsely chopped (optional)
       Salt and freshly ground pepper

Bésciamella
    ¼ cup (½ stick) butter
    ⅓ cup all purpose flour
    2 cups milk
       Freshly grated nutmeg
       Salt and freshly ground pepper

    6 to 9 tablespoons freshly grated Parmesan cheese

    3 tablespoons butter, broken into small pieces
    1 tablespoon melted butter

For pasta: Bring salted water to boil in large saucepan over medium-high heat. Add pasta rectangles one at a time and cook until *al dente*. Drain; spread out on dampened kitchen towels.

For sauce: Heat ¼ cup butter and ¼ cup oil in large saucepan over medium-high heat. Add carrot and onion and sauté until softened, about 10 minutes. Remove vegetables from oil and discard. Stir in veal, chicken hearts and giblets. Gradually blend in wine. Cook until wine has evaporated. Reduce heat, add broth and tomato sauce and simmer 1 hour, stirring in milk as necessary to keep sauce from becoming too thick. Add chicken livers and mushrooms to sauce and simmer another 30 minutes. Season with salt and pepper to taste.

For bésciamella: Melt butter in medium saucepan over medium heat. Blend in flour. Gradually add milk and cook, stirring constantly until mixture has thickened, about 4 minutes. Season with nutmeg, salt and pepper to taste.

To assemble: Preheat oven to 375°F. Generously butter 9 × 13-inch straight-sided dish. Arrange 3 egg pasta rectangles in bottom of pan. Dot with 10 to 12 tablespoons sauce, then dot sauce with about ⅔ cup bésciamella. Sprinkle 2 to 3 tablespoons Parmesan cheese over. Dot with 3 teaspoons butter. Repeat above layering with one layer of spinach pasta and another layer of egg pasta. Bake until casserole is hot and bubbly, about 30 minutes. Top with 1 tablespoon melted butter and serve.

Lamb with Sweet-Sour Sauce (Agnello al Cinghiale)

A variation of a traditional Italian method of preparing wild boar.

8 servings

    2 garlic cloves, minced
    1 tablespoon dried rosemary, crumbled
    1 teaspoon crushed juniper berries
    1 clove, crushed
       Salt and freshly ground pepper
    1 6-pound crown roast of lamb or 3 2-pound racks of lamb
    3 cups red wine
    1 cup red wine vinegar

       Olive oil

Sauce
    2 tablespoons unsweetened cocoa
1½ tablespoons sugar
    2 tablespoons minced pine nuts
    2 tablespoons minced pitted prunes
    2 tablespoons minced golden raisins
    2 to 3 strips orange peel

Combine garlic, rosemary, juniper berries, clove, salt and pepper in small bowl. Cut small slits between ribs of lamb and fill with garlic mixture. Transfer lamb to large plastic bag. Mix wine and vinegar in medium bowl and pour over lamb. Seal bag tightly. Marinate lamb in refrigerator for 24 hours, turning occasionally to redistribute liquid.

Preheat oven to 325°F. Pour enough olive oil into roasting pan to cover bottom. Drain lamb, reserving marinade. Pat meat dry and transfer to roasting pan. Roast lamb until tender and thermometer inserted in thickest part of meat without touching bone registers 140°F, about 25 minutes.

For sauce: Strain marinade into medium saucepan. Add cocoa and sugar and stir until dissolved. Add pine nuts, prunes, raisins and orange peel. Place over medium heat and bring to simmer. Cook, reducing liquid by half. Strain sauce again and set aside.

Transfer lamb to warm serving platter and tent with foil. Skim fat from pan juices. Add juices to sauce. Return mixture to medium heat and simmer, stirring, until heated through. Taste and adjust seasonings. Slice lamb and top each serving with 3 tablespoons of sauce.

Rice with Artichokes and Olives (Risotto alla Viviana)

6 to 8 servings

Artichokes
    2 artichokes
    1 lemon, halved
    4 cups water
        Juice of 1 lemon

Rice
¼ cup (½ stick) butter
    1 medium onion, thinly sliced

1½ cups arborio rice or long-grain rice
    2 cups chicken broth, heated
    2 cups beef broth, heated

    3 tablespoons olive oil
  12 green Sicilian olives, pitted and thinly sliced
        Salt and freshly ground pepper

For artichokes: Wash and drain artichokes. Remove any tough outer leaves. Cut off stems and trim. Slice stems into thin rounds. Rub lemon over each slice to prevent discoloring. Combine water and lemon juice in large bowl. Add stem rounds. Cut artichokes lengthwise and with melon scoop or sturdy teaspoon, remove and discard fuzzy choke, scraping to clean thoroughly. Cut artichokes into thin wedges and rub with lemon. As each artichoke is cleaned, drop into acidulated water. Set aside.

For rice: Melt butter in large saucepan over medium-high heat. Add onion and sauté until translucent. Stir in rice and cook until grains crackle. Add hot broths, stirring once. Reduce heat to medium-low, cover and cook, stirring twice, about 10 minutes.

Heat olive oil and olives in medium saucepan over medium-high heat. Drain artichoke wedges and stems thoroughly and pat dry. Add to skillet and sauté until crisp-tender, about 6 minutes. Stir artichoke mixture into rice. Cook, uncovered, until rice is tender and liquid is evaporated. Season with salt and pepper and serve immediately.

Genoa-Style Spinach (Spinaci all'Olio Genovese)

4 to 6 servings

    2 pounds fresh spinach, stemmed, cooked and drained
⅓ cup seedless golden raisins plumped in white wine and drained
¼ cup toasted pine nuts
        Pinch of freshly grated nutmeg

¼ cup olive oil
    2 tablespoons chopped fresh parsley
    4 anchovy fillets, cut into small pieces
        Salt and freshly ground pepper

Combine spinach, raisins, pine nuts and nutmeg in medium bowl.

Heat olive oil in large saucepan over medium heat. Add parsley and anchovies, reduce heat to low and stir until anchovies are dissolved. Stir in spinach mixture, cover and cook over very low heat about 5 minutes. Season with salt and pepper. Transfer to serving dish and serve immediately.

Fantasy Salad
(Insalata di Fantasia)

A refreshing party salad any time of year. Use whatever greens are in season.

20 servings

Salad
> Tender inner leaves of 1 head of lettuce, torn into bite-size pieces
> 1 *each* red, yellow and green bell pepper, seeded and cut into bite-size pieces
> 2 carrots, shredded
> 2 small cucumbers, unpeeled, cut into bite-size pieces
> 1 large red onion, slivered
> 3 to 4 ounces *each* rughetta,* chicory and red-leaf lettuce, torn into bite-size pieces

Mustard Anchovy Dressing
> 4 2-ounce cans anchovy fillets (about 30), drained
> 1 7½-ounce jar cocktail onions (about 30), drained
> 3 tablespoons Dijon mustard
> 2 cups olive oil
> 1¼ cups wine vinegar
> Freshly ground white pepper
> 1 cup halved pitted black olives

For salad: Combine all ingredients in large glass salad bowl and set aside.

For dressing: Combine anchovies, onions and mustard in processor and mix until smooth. Add oil and vinegar and blend 5 seconds. Season with pepper to taste. Pour over greens and toss well. Top with black olives and serve.

*Available in specialty produce markets.

Piedmont-Style Almond Cake
(Torta di Mandorle
alla Piemontese)

12 servings

> ½ cup golden raisins, plumped in hot water and drained
> Flour

> ⅓ cup sugar
> ⅓ cup whole almonds, shelled, skinned and toasted

> 6 eggs
> ¾ cup sugar

> ½ cup finely ground corn flour
> ¼ cup cake flour
> 3 tablespoons potato flour
> ½ teaspoon baking powder
> 2 tablespoons Cognac or brandy
> 1 teaspoon almond extract
> ¼ cup (½ stick) unsalted butter, melted and cooled

Butter and flour 10-inch tube pan and set aside. Preheat oven to 350°F. Coat raisins with flour, shaking off excess flour.

Combine ⅓ cup sugar and almonds in processor and mix using on/off turns until finely ground.

Combine eggs and ¾ cup sugar in top of double boiler set over simmering water. Beat until mixture is warm, about 3 to 5 minutes. Remove from heat and continue beating until mixture is cool and very fluffy, about 5 or 6 minutes.

Combine flours and baking powder in sifter. Sift into egg mixture a little at a time, folding in very gently with whisk. Fold in almond-sugar mixture, Cognac and almond extract. Stir in melted butter and raisins. Turn mixture into prepared pan. Bake until cake is golden brown and tester inserted in center comes out clean, about 45 minutes. Invert cake onto rack and cool.

Can be served plain or frosted with favorite light-colored icing. Sprinkle with toasted slivered almonds.

Provençal Buffet

THE MENU

Zucchini Salad with Saffron

Pepper Salad

Onion and Raisin Salad

Chick-Pea and Anchovy Salad

Salade Niçoise

Vegetables à la Grecque

Marinated Scampi

Eggplant Mold

Beef en Daube

Baked Fish Niçoise

Lemon and Almond Pie

Serves 6 to 24

A burst of color for the buffet table. In the background, roasted Pepper Salad provides a bright contrast to Marinated Scampi topped with Parmesan and bread crumbs. In the foreground, a spectacular Eggplant Mold.

THE STRATEGY

This menu, inspired by the sunny flavors of the South of France, offers a rich choice of dishes suitable for a party of six or a gala dinner for twenty-four. The beef or the fish accompanied by one or two salads and the Lemon Almond Pie constitute a delicious menu for six. To amply serve twelve, simply double the recipes for one entrée and three or four salads; double the recipes of the entire menu for a brilliant dinner for twenty-four. Please note that the Shopping List and Countdown have been keyed to the number of servings that a single recipe yields.

Shopping List

   3 pounds shrimp or prawns (preferably sized 15 to 20 to the pound)
3½ to 4 pounds beef chuck or round roast
   1 pig's foot (optional)
 ¾ pound lean bacon
   5 to 6 pounds white fish (preferably including heads)
 ½ cup chicken stock plus additional 1½ to 2 cups chicken stock (optional; see recipe for Vegetables à la Grecque)
1½ cups (or more) veal or beef stock
1½ pounds small zucchini
   3 shallots (1 onion can be substituted)
   3 large red peppers
   3 large green peppers
   3 to 4 lemons
2½ pounds small boiling onions plus 20 to 25 additional
   2 large onions plus 1 medium onion
      Bermuda or other mild onion for garnish
   7 large garlic cloves plus 6 (sized to taste)
 ¾ pound fresh green beans
   1 small cucumber (½ large can be substituted)
   7 medium tomatoes
   3 to 4 small eggplants (about 2 pounds)
  10 tomatoes (sized to taste) (4 cups canned Italian-style plum tomatoes can be substituted)
   8 tomatoes (sized to taste) (3 cups regular canned tomatoes can be substituted)
   1 pound carrots plus 1 additional carrot
   1 to 2 oranges
   1 pound mushrooms
      Fresh dill

      Fresh parsley
      Fresh basil (chervil can be substituted)
      Fresh thyme
      Raisins
      If preparing Vegetables à la Grecque, an additional 2 pounds of any *one* of the following: mushrooms, cucumber, zucchini, cauliflower, cabbage, green beans or artichoke bottoms
   1 cup plain yogurt
   2 sticks unsalted butter
   6 eggs
      Parmesan cheese
      Milk for soaking anchovies
      Breadcrumbs
   2 cups cooked chick-peas (garbanzo beans) (use dried or canned)
   1 cup ground blanched almonds
1⅓ cups plus 1 tablespoon all purpose flour
1¼ cups sugar (about)
3⅔ cups olive oil
      White wine vinegar
      Safflower oil
      Vegetable oil
      Pinch of saffron
      Dill seed
      Salt
      Black pepper
      Whole black or white peppercorns
      Coriander seed (¼ cup plus 1 teaspoon)
      Bay leaves
      Whole cloves
      Dried thyme
      Paprika
      Vanilla
      Dark brown sugar
   1 7-ounce can tuna packed in oil
   1 can anchovy fillets plus 10 to 12 additional fillets
1½ cups tomato juice (optional; see recipe for Baked Fish Niçoise)
      Tomato paste
      Pitted black olives (¾ cup)
      Italian black olives or Greek olives (¼ cup)
1½ cups white wine (optional; see recipe for Baked Fish Niçoise)
 ¼ cup dry white wine plus additional dry white wine (for soaking raisins)
   2 cups red wine

Special Equipment

10-inch flan ring (10-inch pie plate can be substituted)

Tips

All the recipes can be doubled.

Countdown

4 days ahead
Prepare Vegetables à la Grecque. Let cool, cover and refrigerate.

2 days ahead
Prepare marinade for Beef en Daube. Add meat and refrigerate overnight.

1 day ahead
Make Zucchini Salad with Saffron and refrigerate.
Prepare Pepper Salad and refrigerate.
Make Marinated Scampi and refrigerate.
Prepare Eggplant Mold. Let cool, cover and refrigerate (do not unmold).
Finish Beef en Daube. Let cool slightly, cover and refrigerate.

Morning of buffet
Prepare Onion and Raisin Salad and store at room temperature.
Make Chick-Pea and Anchovy Salad and store at room temperature.
Assemble Salade Niçoise and refrigerate.
Prepare Baked Fish Niçoise if serving cold or at room temperature.

About 6 hours before serving
Make Lemon and Almond Pie.

About 3 hours before serving
Prepare Baked Fish Niçoise to point of baking if serving hot; refrigerate sauce.

About 1 hour before serving
Remove all salads from refrigerator and bring to room temperature.
Finish Baked Fish Niçoise if serving hot.
Rewarm Beef en Daube over very low heat.

Wine Suggestions

In Provence the choice to accompany such a varied feast would be several bottles of chilled Tavel rosé or perhaps a Bandol—red, white or rosé. A youthful and slightly chilled red wine would also do the trick. Try a Beaujolais from France or a Gamay Beaujolais from California.

THE RECIPES

Zucchini Salad with Saffron

6 servings

 5 tablespoons olive oil
1½ pounds small zucchini, thinly sliced
 3 shallots or 1 onion, finely chopped
  Pinch of saffron infused in 2 tablespoons boiling water
 1 teaspoon dill seed or 2 teaspoons chopped fresh dill
 1 teaspoon sugar
  Salt and freshly ground pepper

 4 to 5 tablespoons white wine vinegar
  Fresh dill or parsley (garnish)

Heat oil in large skillet over low heat. Add zucchini and shallot or onion and cook 5 minutes, stirring occasionally *(do not allow mixture to brown)*. Add dissolved saffron, dill, sugar, and salt, pepper and vinegar to taste. Continue cooking until zucchini is just tender, about 5 minutes. Transfer to salad bowl and let cool slightly. Cover and chill. To serve, bring to room temperature and sprinkle with dill or parsley.

Salad is best if served within 24 hours.

Pepper Salad

4 to 6 servings

> 3 large red peppers
> 3 large green peppers
> 5 tablespoons olive oil
> 2 tablespoons fresh lemon juice
> ¼ teaspoon salt
>   Freshly ground pepper
> 1 tablespoon chopped fresh parsley
> 2 teaspoons chopped fresh basil or chervil
>   (optional)

Preheat oven to 450°F. Place peppers on baking sheet and roast until soft and skin is black, about 30 minutes. Let cool slightly. Peel off skin and cut peppers into strips. Combine oil, lemon juice, salt and pepper in deep bowl. Add peppers and toss gently to coat. Cover and marinate at room temperature 1 to 2 hours. Mix in parsley and basil or chervil just before serving.

Salad can be prepared ahead and marinated in refrigerator up to 24 hours. Bring to room temperature before serving.

Onion and Raisin Salad

4 servings

> ¼ cup raisins
>   Dry white wine
>
> 2 tablespoons (or more) olive oil
> 2 tablespoons (or more) dark brown sugar
>   Salt and freshly ground pepper
> 1½ pounds small boiling onions, blanched and peeled

Place raisins in small bowl, cover with wine and let soak for 1 hour.

Heat oil in 10-inch skillet over medium-high heat. Stir in sugar, salt and pepper. Reduce heat and add onions in single layer. Cook, shaking pan frequently, until onions are browned and nicely caramelized. (If necessary, add a little more oil and sugar.)

Drain raisins; add to onions and shake pan over low heat until raisins are heated through. Cover and let cool to room temperature. Transfer to dish just before ready to serve.

Chick-Pea and Anchovy Salad

4 servings

> 2 cups cooked chick-peas (garbanzo beans), drained and rinsed
> 1 can anchovy fillets, soaked in small amount of milk, drained and chopped
>   Vinaigrette (see following recipe)
> 3 to 4 slices Bermuda or other mild onion, divided into rings (garnish)
> 1 tablespoon chopped fresh parsley (garnish)

Combine chick-peas, anchovies and Vinaigrette in medium bowl and stir well. Transfer to serving dish. Cover and let stand at least 1 hour (or up to 12 hours) at room temperature. Just before serving, garnish with onion and parsley.

Vinaigrette

> 2 tablespoons fresh lemon juice
> 1 large garlic clove, crushed
>   Freshly ground pepper
> ¼ cup safflower oil
> 2 tablespoons olive oil

Combine lemon juice, garlic and pepper in small bowl. Whisk in oils.

Salade Niçoise

6 servings

> ¾ pound fresh green beans, cut into thirds
> 1 teaspoon salt
>
> 1 7-ounce can tuna packed in oil, drained and flaked
>   Vinaigrette (see following recipe)
> 1 small or ½ large cucumber, peeled and thinly sliced
> 10 to 12 anchovy fillets, soaked in milk, drained and split lengthwise
> ¼ cup Italian black olives or Greek olives, halved and pitted
> 3 medium tomatoes, peeled, seeded and cut into quarters

Add green beans and salt to 1 quart rapidly boiling water. Return to boil and cook beans until just tender, about 15 minutes. Transfer to icy water using slotted spoon. Let cool completely. Drain thoroughly.

Place tuna in shallow serving dish or salad bowl. Cover with green beans and moisten with some of Vinaigrette. Overlap cucumber slices to cover beans.

Spoon Vinaigrette over, reserving only a small amount. Arrange anchovies in lattice pattern over cucumbers. Put olive halves, rounded side up, in center of each lattice. Arrange tomato around edge of salad and brush with remaining Vinaigrette. Cover and chill up to 8 hours before serving.

Vinaigrette

2 tablespoons fresh lemon juice
1 garlic clove, crushed
  Salt and freshly ground pepper
6 tablespoons olive oil

Combine lemon juice, garlic, salt and pepper in small bowl. Whisk in olive oil.

Vegetables à la Grecque

This method is a basic preparation for many different vegetables. Vegetables à la Grecque must be cooked over very high heat, with liquid constantly at a rolling boil, in order for oil and liquid to emulsify and thicken the sauce. If serving several types of vegetables à la Grecque, each should be cooked individually (always with small boiling onions) and served in separate bowls.

6 to 8 servings

¼ cup coriander seed
1 tablespoon whole peppercorns
4 branches thyme
3 bay leaves
3 to 4 parsley sprigs

1½ to 2 cups water (substitute chicken stock when preparing mushrooms, cucumbers or artichokes)
¼ cup dry white wine
2 tablespoons tomato paste
2 tablespoons fresh lemon juice

¼ cup vegetable oil
¼ cup olive oil
20 to 25 small boiling onions

Vegetables
2 pounds of any *one* of the following:
  Mushrooms, quartered if large
  Cucumbers, cut into short lengths and pared into olive shapes
  Zucchini, cut into thick slices
  Cauliflower, separated into florets
  Cabbage, ribs only (save leaves for another use)

Green beans, ends removed
Artichoke bottoms, rubbed with cut lemon and sliced into 6 pieces

4 medium tomatoes, peeled, seeded and coarsely chopped
2 teaspoons salt

Combine coriander, peppercorns, thyme, bay leaves and parsley sprigs and tie in cheesecloth bag; set aside.

Combine water or stock, wine, tomato paste and lemon juice; set aside.

Heat oils in large stockpot until haze forms. Add onions and sauté until lightly browned, about 3 minutes. Add vegetable (see preceding list), chopped tomatoes, salt, spice bag and tomato paste mixture. *(There should be enough liquid barely to cover vegetables; add more water or stock if necessary.)*

Bring to rapid boil and boil hard until vegetables are tender. Allow about 9 minutes for mushrooms, cucumber and zucchini; about 15 minutes for cauliflower, cabbage and beans; about 20 to 25 minutes for artichoke bottoms.

Discard spice bag. Taste for seasoning; vegetables should be highly seasoned. Allow to cool to room temperature and serve.

Vegetables can be prepared ahead. Let cool, then cover and refrigerate up to 48 hours.

Marinated Scampi

8 servings

3 pounds raw shrimp or prawns (preferably 15 to 20 to the pound)
½ cup olive oil
½ cup breadcrumbs, toasted
½ cup freshly grated Parmesan cheese
2 garlic cloves, crushed

½ cup olive oil
3 tablespoons fresh lemon juice
  Salt and freshly ground pepper
2 tablespoons chopped fresh parsley (garnish)

Split shrimp lengthwise but leave in shells. Mix ½ cup olive oil, breadcrumbs, cheese and garlic and spread over cut surface of shrimp. Place on rack in broiler pan. Broil until browned, about 2 to 4 minutes.

Arrange shrimp in serving dish. Combine remaining olive oil with lemon juice, salt and pepper. Spoon over shrimp and let stand until cool. Cover and marinate in refrigerator for at least 1 hour (or up to 24 hours). To serve, bring to room temperature and sprinkle with chopped fresh parsley.

Eggplant Mold

6 to 8 servings

    3 to 4 small eggplants (about 2 pounds), stems
      discarded, cut into ⅜-inch slices
      Salt

  ⅔ cup olive oil
    1 medium onion, finely chopped
  10 tomatoes, peeled, seeded and chopped or 4
      cups Italian-style plum tomatoes, drained and
      chopped
    1 large garlic clove, crushed
      Salt and freshly ground pepper

    1 cup plain yogurt

  ½ cup chicken stock

Sprinkle eggplant slices with salt and set aside for 30 minutes to draw out bitter juices. Rise thoroughly with cold water and let dry on paper towels.

Heat 2 tablespoons oil in large skillet until haze forms. Add onion and sauté until lightly browned. Add tomatoes, garlic and salt and pepper and cook, stirring occasionally, until mixture is thick and pulpy, about 20 to 25 minutes. Remove ⅓ of mixture for sauce and set aside.

Preheat oven to 350°F. Heat remaining oil in large skillet and brown eggplant. Place 1 slice in bottom of 2-quart charlotte mold or other mold. Halve remaining slices. Begin arranging slices in overlapping concentric circles; spread with a little tomato mixture and yogurt. Continue layering until all of eggplant, yogurt and tomato mixture have been used, ending with layer of eggplant. Cover with foil and bake until eggplant is very tender, about 40 to 50 minutes. Let cool completely in mold.

Meanwhile, prepare sauce. Simmer reserved tomato mixture with stock in small saucepan until heated through, about 2 to 3 minutes. Let cool to room temperature. To serve, unmold eggplant onto platter; spoon sauce around base.

Eggplant and sauce can be prepared up to 24 hours ahead. Keep covered in refrigerator and bring to room temperature.

Beef en Daube

Daube is best made a day before serving so flavors can mellow. This method of cooking is intended for a less tender cut of meat, which is cooked so thoroughly it can then be cut with a spoon.

6 servings

3½ to 4 pounds beef chuck or round roast, cut
      into 1-inch cubes

Marinade
    2 cups red wine
    2 large onions, sliced
    1 carrot, sliced
    2 tablespoons wine vinegar
  ¼ cup parsley sprigs
    6 peppercorns
    3 large garlic cloves, crushed
    3 whole cloves
    1 teaspoon coriander seed
    4 strips orange peel

  ¾ pound lean bacon
    1 pig's foot, well washed (optional)
    8 tomatoes, peeled, seeded and chopped or 3
      cups drained and chopped canned tomatoes
    1 pound carrots, sliced into rounds
    1 pound mushrooms, sliced
    1 pound small boiling onions
    2 large garlic cloves, minced
      Bouquet garni (4 strips orange peel, 1
      teaspoon dried thyme, 1 large parsley sprig
      and 1 bay leaf)
1½ cups (or more) veal or beef stock

      Salt and freshly ground pepper

Put meat in deep bowl and add marinade ingredients. Cover and refrigerate 24 hours, turning meat occasionally to marinate evenly.

Cook bacon until crisp; drain well. Remove meat from bowl. Strain marinade, pressing vegetables to remove as much moisture as possible; discard vegetables. In 10- to 12-quart oval roaster or Dutch oven with tight-fitting lid, layer ingredients in following order: bacon, beef cubes, pig's foot, tomatoes, carrots, mushrooms, onions, garlic, strained marinade and bouquet garni. Add 1½ cups stock and bring slowly to boil. Cover and simmer until beef is tender, 2 to 3 hours, checking occasionally to see if additional stock is needed.

Uncover and continue cooking until sauce is slightly reduced and broth is rich and flavorful. Season with salt and pepper. Remove pig's foot; using fork, pull meat in shreds from bone and return meat to pot. Discard bouquet garni. Let daube cool slightly, then cover and refrigerate overnight.

To serve, remove fat from surface. Let daube simmer over direct heat or in oven until heated through. Taste and adjust seasoning as necessary.

Baked Fish Niçoise

8 servings

  ½ cup olive oil
  3 garlic cloves, crushed
  1 tablespoon paprika
 1½ teaspoons dried thyme
  6 tablespoons tomato paste
 1½ cups white wine or tomato juice
    Salt and freshly ground pepper

  5 to 6 pounds white fish* (preferably including heads), cleaned and scaled

  ¾ cup pitted black olives
  1 lemon, halved lengthwise and thinly sliced (garnish)

Preheat oven to 350°F. Heat oil in small pan. Add garlic and cook 2 minutes. Remove from heat and stir in paprika, thyme, tomato paste, wine or juice, and salt and pepper. Return to heat and simmer 2 to 3 minutes; set aside.

Wash fish; discard fins and trim tails to "V." Set in oiled baking dish or roasting pan and score deep diagonal slashes 2 inches apart (fish will cook more evenly). Spoon sauce over top.

Bake about 10 minutes per pound, basting frequently, until fish flakes easily when tested with fork; add olives last 10 minutes of cooking time. Transfer to platter and spoon sauce over top. Decorate with overlapping slices of lemon.

Baked Fish Niçoise can be prepared ahead and served either hot or cold. If serving hot, prepare fish to point of baking 2 to 3 hours before serving, then cover and refrigerate. Just before ready to bake, pour cold sauce over top and bake according to directions. To serve fish cold or at room temperature, bake up to 8 hours before serving.

*Red snapper, mullet and bass are particularly suitable for this recipe. Quantities needed depend on whether fish is plump and if it includes head. With bony fish allow 1 pound per person; for plump fish without head allow 10 to 12 ounces per person. Fish can be any size, but all must be the same size for even cooking. Allow the following cooking times: For fish weighing 2 to 3 pounds—12 minutes per pound; for fish 3 to 6 pounds—10 minutes per pound; for fish 6 to 12 pounds—9 minutes per pound.

Lemon and Almond Pie

Makes 1 10-inch pie

Pastry
 1⅓ cups plus 1 tablespoon sifted flour
  ⅓ cup sugar
  ¼ teaspoon salt
  ⅓ cup unsalted butter, well chilled and cut into small pieces
  3 egg yolks
  ½ teaspoon vanilla

Filling
  3 eggs
  ¾ cup sugar
  7 tablespoons lemon juice
  1 heaping tablespoon finely grated lemon peel
  ⅔ cup unsalted butter, melted
  1 cup ground blanched almonds

For pastry: Combine flour, sugar and salt and blend well. Cut in butter until mixture resembles coarse meal. Beat yolks with vanilla. Add to flour mixture and blend until dough forms ball. Flatten dough into disc. Wrap in plastic and refrigerate 1 hour or longer.

Position rack in lower third of oven and preheat to 375°F. Roll dough out onto lightly floured board to thickness of about ⅛ inch. Fit into 10-inch pie plate or flan ring; trim excess dough 1 inch beyond rim of pan. Flute edges. Line crust with waxed or parchment paper. Set slightly smaller pan or pie plate inside crust and fill with dried beans. Bake 10 to 12 minutes. Let cool slightly before removing inside pan, then let pastry stand until completely cooled.

For filling: Beat eggs and sugar together thoroughly until light and lemon colored. Stir in lemon juice and peel. Add butter and almonds. Pour into pastry and bake until filling is golden brown and set, 25 to 30 minutes. Serve at room temperature.

Pie can be baked 6 to 8 hours ahead, but is best baked and served on same day.

Seasonal
Celebrations

ᵆ

EVERY SEASON OF THE YEAR has its own temperament. Each has different weather, a different look and pace, a different set of holidays and, of course, different food. And there are occasions when any host or hostess, no matter how untraditional and iconoclastic, wants to celebrate by giving a party that is completely appropriate to the particular time of year. This is especially true on the big national and religious holidays, but there are many other days in the calendar that you may also want to mark with a special menu—the day the first spring flowers open, for example, bringing with them those perfect early vegetables; or that day in summer when it's finally warm enough to go to the beach or have a big picnic; or the fall harvest, perhaps, when the moon is huge and the markets are bulging with the best seasonal produce. You might even want to observe those two favorite unofficial holidays, April Fool's and Halloween, with a whimsical dinner that fits the spirit of the day.

No matter what the season, there is always something to celebrate. The festive menus in this chapter are designed to take you through the year in style. We begin, naturally enough, on New Year's Eve (page 209), presenting a trio of menus that will ring in the new with a flourish extravagant enough to last all winter. Our suggestion for a spring party is a bounteous Easter feast with the flavors of the Greek islands (page 219), on to summertime, when the living is easy and the greatest variety of fresh produce is at its peak. Our warm-weather menus are designed to be easy on the cook—no one wants to spend too much time in the kitchen at this time of year—and include a down-home, all-American Fourth of July picnic (page 229) that will work just as well anytime the outdoors beckons.

November and December are times for stuffing the turkey, trimming the tree, decking the halls and gathering family and friends together for special meals. Our fall-winter holiday menus combine traditional ingredients with new twists for a trio of great dinners from which no one, even Tiny Tim, will go away hungry.

Everyone has his or her favorite season and special days. These party menus will help make yours all the more memorable.

ᵆ

A Gala
New Year's Eve

THE MENU

9:00 P.M. · *Preambles in the Kitchen*

Sausages   Two-Toned Braided Loaves

Saucisson en Croûte

Baked Kentucky Ham   Cream Biscuits

Midnight · **Toast to the New Year**

Oysters on the Half Shell

Rabbit Terrine   Toasted Pain de Mie

1:00 A.M. · *Supper*

Oxtail Ragoût in Madeira

Green Noodles with Parmesan

Salad of Endive, Watercress, Beets

Chintz and Velvet Holiday Cake   Tuiles

Serves 20

*Champagne, Two-Toned Braided Loaves and an assortment of mustards
are part of the ingredients for the "first movement" of a
wonderfully orchestrated New Year's Eve feast.*

THE STRATEGY

Ring in the new year with the perfect open house party idea—a three-part buffet that begins at 9 p.m. with an informal charcuterie in the kitchen, then moves on to an elegant toast to the new year at midnight, followed by a sophisticated supper at 1 a.m. All of the dishes are prepared ahead so the host or hostess can join in the celebration and start the new year with the easiest party ever.

Shopping List

2½ pounds pork shoulder
 1 pound pork fat, cut into sheets ⅛ inch thick, plus ½ pound additional pork fat (will be ground)
 1 13-pound fresh Kentucky or country ham
 1 veal knuckle
 1 5- to 6-pound rabbit
 ½ pound veal leg
 ¼ pound regular ham
 ¼ pound lean belly of pork
 ¼ pound pork back fat
10 pounds oxtails (have butcher cut into joints for serving)
 6 to 7 cups chicken broth
   Oysters to serve on half shell at midnight as desired
   Assorted purchased charcuterie-type sausages as necessary to supplement 9 p.m. menu as desired
 6 garlic cloves
 7 large onions
 6 carrots
 1 leek
 2 large white turnips
 5 bunches endive
 1 bunch watercress
 2 large or 4 small beets
1¼ pounds candied pineapple
 1 pound seedless raisins
 ¾ pound candied cherries
 1 pound golden raisins
1¼ pounds citron
 ½ pound currants
   Parsley
   Fresh or dried chervil (for bouquet garni)
   Oranges (for ¼ pound peel cut into thin shreds)

 1 cup plain yogurt
20 eggs
 ¾ to 1 cup whipping cream plus about 4 tablespoons
2¾ sticks butter, plus additional butter for melted butter (see recipe for Cream Biscuits)
 6 sticks unsalted butter, plus additional 6 tablespoons (¾ stick) unsalted butter or beef drippings (see recipe for Oxtail Ragoût in Madeira)
   Milk
   Cornmeal
 ½ pound shelled hazelnuts
 1 pound plus 1 cup sliced almonds
 ½ pound blanched almonds or pecans
7½ envelopes active dry yeast
 3 ounces unsweetened chocolate
 1 cup (8 ounces) almond paste
4½ cups powdered sugar
26 cups (about) all purpose flour, plus additional all purpose flour for oxtails
2½ cups whole wheat flour
 3 cups sugar (about)
 ½ cup firmly packed brown sugar
   Additional 2 cups sugar *or* 1 cup firmly packed brown sugar and 1 cup sugar
   Mustard of choice for vinaigrette
   Olive oil or other vegetable oil
   Vinegar of choice for vinaigrette
   Oil of choice for vinaigrette
   Assorted mustards (for sausages and Saucisson en Croûte)
   Dried rosemary
   Dried thyme
   Salt
   Coarse salt
   Black pepper
   Bay leaf
   Cinnamon
   Mace
   Nutmeg
   Ground cloves
   Baking powder
   Baking soda
   Cream of tartar
   Vanilla
 1 cup bourbon
1½ fifths Madeira
 1 cup dry white wine

½ cup brandy
1¾ cups Cognac, plus additional Cognac for storing cake layers for Chintz and Velvet Holiday Cake
Sherry

Special Equipment

2-quart terrine or pâté mold (loaf pan can be substituted)
Pain de mie pan (13 × 4 × 3¼ inches) (four 9 × 5-inch loaf pans can be substituted)
8-quart braising pan (2 deep skillets can be substituted and oxtail mixture divided between)
12-inch springform pan

Countdown

1 month ahead
Prepare Two-Toned Braided Loaves and freeze.
Make Toasted Pain de Mie and freeze.
Bake Tuiles; let cool, transfer to plastic bags and freeze.

5 days ahead
Begin preparation of black fruitcake portion of Chintz and Velvet Holiday Cake.

3 days ahead
Prepare cake layers for Chintz and Velvet Holiday Cake and store at room temperature.

1 day ahead
Prepare sausages for Saucisson en Croûte and refrigerate.
Make Rabbit Terrine and refrigerate.
Prepare Oxtail Ragoût in Madeira; let cool and refrigerate.
Remove Tuiles from freezer and thaw in refrigerator overnight.
Remove Two-Toned Braided Loaves from freezer and thaw in refrigerator overnight.
Remove Toasted Pain de Mie from freezer and thaw in refrigerator overnight.
Purchase sausages (and special mustards), oysters and green noodles to supplement buffet as desired according to each menu.
Soak ham for Baked Kentucky Ham as directed.

Mix vinaigrette for Salad of Endive, Watercress, Beets and refrigerate.

Morning of buffet
Finish Baked Kentucky Ham.

Late afternoon of buffet
Finish Saucisson en Croûte.
Prepare icing and glaze for Chintz and Velvet Holiday Cake and assemble layers.

About 8:15 p.m.
Prepare Cream Biscuits.

About 8:45 p.m.
Rewarm Two-Toned Braided Loaves in low oven if desired.
Assemble purchased sausages and mustards.
Slice ham and arrange on platter.

About 11:30 p.m.
Rewarm Toasted Pain de Mie in low oven if desired.
Unmold Rabbit Terrine onto serving platter.
Ready Oysters on the Half Shell.

About 12:15 a.m.
Begin rewarming Oxtail Ragoût over medium-low heat, stirring occasionally.
Assemble vegetables for salad.

About 12:30 a.m.
Begin boiling water for Green Noodles with Parmesan (if using).
Remix vinaigrette.

Just before serving
Add vinaigrette to salad and toss lightly.
Cook noodles; drain well. Add butter and Parmesan cheese to taste.
Set out desserts with main buffet or wait a bit until guests have almost finished supper.

Wine Suggestions

With the preambles (at 9:00 p.m.) serve a chilled Beaujolais Nouveau—a crisp, fruity wine from the harvest of the waning year. At midnight toast the New Year with French Champagne or the best California sparkler you can find (try Piper-Sonoma). With supper drink a mature red Bordeaux or California Cabernet Sauvignon.

THE RECIPES

Two-Toned Braided Loaves

Makes 7 to 8 loaves

Sponge #1 (White Bread)
  2 envelopes active dry yeast
  ½ cup warm water (100°F to 115°F)
  2 cups all purpose flour
  ¾ to 1 cup water

Sponge #2 (Whole Wheat Bread)
  2 envelopes active dry yeast
  ½ cup warm water (100°F to 115°F)
  2 cups whole wheat flour
  ¾ to 1 cup water

White Bread
  3 tablespoons olive or other vegetable oil
  2 to 2¼ cups all purpose flour
  1 tablespoon coarse salt
  ½ cup plain yogurt

Whole Wheat Bread
  3 tablespoons olive or other vegetable oil
  ½ cup plain yogurt
  ½ cup whole wheat flour
  1½ to 1¾ cups all purpose flour
  1 tablespoon coarse salt

    Cornmeal

  1 egg yolk
  1 tablespoon milk

For sponges: Make each sponge separately. In each instance, dissolve yeast in warm water in large mixing bowl and let proof. Add flour and water a little at a time, working in well after each addition to make quite a soft dough. When sponges are thoroughly mixed, cover with plastic wrap and refrigerate at least 12 hours or up to 36 hours.

    For white bread: Punch down sponge #1. Add oil and blend well. Combine 2 cups flour and salt and gradually add to mixture along with yogurt to make soft dough. Turn out onto lightly floured board. Using remaining flour (or more if necessary), knead dough until smooth, elastic and resilient to the pressure of your fingers, at least 10 minutes. Shape into ball and place in oiled bowl, turning to coat entire surface. Cover with plastic wrap and let stand at room temperature until doubled in bulk, about 1 to 1½ hours.

    For whole wheat bread: Punch down sponge #2. Add oil and blend well. Gradually add yogurt and

whole wheat flour. Combine 1½ cups all purpose flour with salt and add gradually to mixture to make soft dough. Turn out onto lightly floured board. Using remaining all purpose flour (or more if necessary), knead dough until smooth, elastic and resilient to the pressure of your fingers, at least 10 minutes. Shape into ball and place in oiled bowl, turning to coat entire surface. Cover with plastic wrap and let stand at room temperature until doubled in bulk, approximately 1 to 1½ hours.

    When both doughs have doubled, punch down and transfer to lightly floured board. Divide each into ¼-pound pieces and shape into balls about the size of a medium orange. Cover lightly with towel.

    Preheat oven to 400°F. Grease baking sheets and dust lightly with cornmeal. To assemble loaves, roll each ball of dough in palms of your hands into long, slender 12-inch strand. Join one wheat with one white to make one 24-inch strand, pinching securely at center. Cut into 8-inch lengths. Join strands, pinching together one end to form a knob, and braid loosely.

    Place loaf on prepared sheet. Cover with towel while braiding remaining dough. Beat yolk with milk and use to glaze loaves. Bake until loaves sound hollow when tapped on top and bottom, about 25 minutes. Cool on racks.

Saucisson en Croûte

20 servings

Sausage
2½ pounds pork shoulder, coarsely ground
  ½ pound pork fat, coarsely ground
  1 cup bourbon
  4 garlic cloves, finely chopped
  2 tablespoons rosemary
  1 tablespoon dried thyme
  1 tablespoon salt
  1 tablespoon freshly ground pepper

Brioche
1½ envelopes active dry yeast
  2 tablespoons sugar
  ½ cup warm water (100°F to 115°F)
  1 cup (2 sticks) butter, melted
1½ teaspoons salt
  4 to 4¼ cups all purpose flour
  4 eggs

2 egg yolks
3 tablespoons whipping cream
Assorted mustards

For sausage: Combine all ingredients in large bowl. Fry a small amount in skillet, taste and adjust seasoning if necessary.

Form into 2 sausage-shaped rolls about 7 inches long and 2 inches in diameter. Wrap sausages in a double thickness of cheesecloth, twisting ends of cloth securely. Tie ends with string.

Poach sausages in boiling salted water just to cover for about 35 to 40 minutes, or until internal temperature registers 170°F. Remove from pan and chill in cheesecloth overnight.

For brioche: Combine yeast, sugar and warm water and let proof. Blend melted butter and salt in separate bowl. Combine 4 cups flour, 4 eggs, butter and yeast in mixing bowl and beat by hand until smooth, adding flour as necessary to make dough easy to handle. Transfer to buttered bowl, turning to coat entire surface. Cover and let stand in warm draft-free area until doubled in bulk, 1 to 1½ hours.

Preheat oven to 375°F. Butter baking sheet. Remove cheesecloth from sausages. Punch dough down. Divide in half and roll each half on lightly floured surface to thickness of ⅓ inch. Place sausage in center of each and wrap neatly, tucking in ends and then bringing sides together to overlap. Place seam side down on prepared sheet and let stand 3 minutes. Beat yolks with cream and use to glaze dough. Bake until brioche is lightly browned, about 35 minutes. Cool slightly before slicing. Serve with assorted mustards.

Baked Kentucky Ham

20 servings

1 13-pound fresh Kentucky or country ham

1 fifth Madeira
½ cup firmly packed brown sugar

Soak ham in enough water to cover for 24 hours, turning several times.

Preheat oven to 350°F. Remove ham from water and place skin side down on a rack in roasting pan. Pour Madeira over ham. Cover tightly with foil and roast 3½ hours. Remove from oven and discard foil. Let stand until cool. Remove skin. Rub brown sugar evenly over ham. Carve in thin slices.

Sliced Saucisson en Croûte and Baked Kentucky Ham.

Cream Biscuits

Makes about 12 biscuits

  2 **cups all purpose flour**
  1 **tablespoon baking powder**
  2 **teaspoons sugar**
  1 **teaspoon salt**
  ¾ **to 1 cup whipping cream**
     Melted butter

Preheat oven to 425°F. Butter baking sheet or square baking pan. Sift first 4 ingredients into large bowl. Fold in enough cream to make soft dough that can be handled easily. Turn out onto floured board and knead about 1 minute. Pat to thickness of ½ to ¾ inch. Cut into rounds or squares, dip in melted butter and place on prepared baking sheet (do not crowd; biscuits should not touch). Bake until golden, about 15 to 18 minutes. Serve hot.

This recipe can be doubled to serve 20 to 24.

Rabbit Terrine

An unusual pâté that makes an interesting first course or picnic dish.

20 servings

Stock
     Bones from 5- to 6-pound rabbit
  1 **veal knuckle, cracked**
  3 **large onions**
  2 **carrots**
  1 **leek**
  1 **cup dry white wine**
  1 **cup water**
  ½ **teaspoon freshly ground pepper**
  2 **or 3 pinches *each* of rosemary and thyme**
     Bouquet garni (parsley, bay leaf and chervil)
     Salt

Forcemeat
  1 **5- to 6-pound rabbit, boned (about 2 pounds meat)**
  ½ **pound veal leg**
  ¼ **pound ham, chopped**
  ½ **pound lean belly of pork, chopped**
  ¼ **pound pork back fat, chopped**
  ½ **cup brandy**
  2 **teaspoons salt**
     Pinch *each* of rosemary and thyme

  1 **pound pork fat, cut into sheets ⅛ inch thick (for lining the terrine)**

For stock: Combine all ingredients except salt in large pot. Bring to boil, skimming off foam as it rises to surface. Reduce heat and simmer 1 hour. Strain. Return liquid to saucepan and reduce by half over high heat. Add salt to taste.

For forcemeat: While stock is cooking, chop most of the rabbit meat and the veal, reserving some large pieces of both. Combine chopped rabbit and veal with remaining ingredients for forcemeat and marinate until stock is done.

Preheat oven to 325°F. Line a 2-quart terrine, pâté mold or loaf pan with pork fat sheets, reserving some for top. Alternate layers of forcemeat with the pieces of rabbit and veal, beginning and ending with forcemeat. Cover with remaining sheets of pork fat. Pour ¼ cup reduced stock over top. Cover with foil, set in roasting pan and pour hot water into pan. Bake until set, about 2 hours. Remove from oven and cool. Weight top and refrigerate overnight, until stock is jellied and fat is firm.

Toasted Pain de Mie

Makes 1 large loaf

  2 **envelopes active dry yeast**
  1½ **cups warm water (100°F to 115°F)**
  2 **teaspoons sugar**
  6 **to 6½ cups all purpose flour**
  1 **tablespoon coarse salt**
  ¾ **cup (1½ sticks) unsalted butter**

Combine yeast, ½ cup warm water and sugar in large bowl and let proof. Combine 6 cups of flour with salt in another mixing bowl and blend well. Cut butter into flour using two knives, being careful not to overwork. Add another ¼ cup warm water to proofed yeast. Add flour mixture, incorporating it with one hand while adding remaining ¾ cup warm water with the other (dough should be sticky and stiff).

Turn dough out onto floured board and work it well for at least 10 minutes, slapping, beating, punching and kneading thoroughly. When smooth, let rest a few minutes. Shape into ball and place in buttered bowl, turning to coat entire surface. Cover dough with plastic wrap and let rise in warm, draft-free area 1½ hours.

Punch dough down and let rest 3 to 4 minutes, then again knead vigorously 3 to 4 minutes. Shape into ball and return to buttered bowl. Cover and let stand in warm, draft-free area 45 minutes to 1 hour to rise again.

Generously butter pain de mie (13½ × 4 × 3¾ inch) pan.* Punch dough down and let rest another 3 to 4 minutes. Knead a third time, then shape carefully into loaf and fit into pan. Let rise until almost doubled, about 1 hour.

About 15 minutes before baking, preheat oven to 400°F. Butter inside of lid of bread pan. Cover pan and place in oven. *Immediately* reduce temperature to 375°F. After 30 minutes, turn pan on one side. Bake 5 minutes. Turn pan to other side and bake an additional 5 minutes. Set pan upright; remove lid.

Continue baking until bread is golden brown, about 12 to 15 minutes. Turn loaf out of pan and set directly on oven rack. Bake until bread is a beautiful color and sounds hollow when tapped with knuckles, about 3 to 5 minutes. Remove from oven and cool thoroughly on wire rack before slicing.

*If pain de mie pan is not available, use four 9 × 5-inch loaf pans. Top with baking sheet and weight with bricks or other heavy objects and bake without turning.

Oxtail Ragoût in Madeira

20 servings

- 10 **pounds oxtails, cut into joints for serving**
  Flour
  Salt and freshly ground pepper

- 6 **tablespoons oil**
- 6 **tablespoons (¾ stick) unsalted butter *or* beef drippings from broiler pan**
- 4 **large onions, thinly sliced**
- 4 **carrots, cut julienne**
- 2 **large white turnips, peeled and cut julienne**
- 3 **tablespoons rosemary**
- 2 **teaspoons thyme**
- 1 **bay leaf**
- 6 **to 7 cups chicken broth**
- ½ **fifth Madeira**

  Chopped fresh parsley

Preheat broiler. Dust oxtails with flour and place on broiler rack. Broil until nicely browned and crispy around the edges, turning once, about 15 minutes,

sprinkling with salt and a few grindings of pepper as they brown.

Heat oil and butter or beef drippings in 8-quart braising pan over medium heat. Add onion and sauté until limp and golden. Add oxtails, carrots, turnips, rosemary, thyme and bay leaf. Stir in chicken broth (there should be just enough barely to cover oxtails) and bring to boil over high heat, skimming off foam that rises to the surface. Continue to boil and skim 5 minutes. Reduce heat, cover and simmer 3 to 3½ hours, adding more liquid if it reduces too much (it should just cover oxtails). Test meat for tenderness by piercing with point of small, sharp knife; it should penetrate meat easily. Add Madeira and cook covered for 10 minutes. Taste broth for seasoning, adding salt, pepper and additional herbs as necessary. Cool ragoût. Skim off fat.

To serve, warm ragoût until heated through. Remove oxtails and vegetables to large serving bowl using slotted spoon. Reduce broth over high heat for 2 or 3 minutes. Ladle over meat and vegetables. Sprinkle with parsley.

Salad of Endive, Watercress, Beets

The mustardy vinaigrette is a nice counterpoint to the hearty ragout.

4 to 6 servings

- 5 **bunches endive, separated into leaves**
- 1 **bunch watercress**
- 2 **large or 4 small beets, washed, peeled and shredded**

Mustard Vinaigrette
- 2 **garlic cloves**
- ¼ **cup oil**
- 2 **tablespoons mustard**
- 2 **tablespoons vinegar**
  Salt and freshly ground pepper

Arrange endive leaves around outer edge of salad bowl. Mound the watercress in center. Top with shredded beet.

Combine all ingredients for vinaigrette in processor and mix until smooth. Taste and adjust seasoning as necessary. Pour over salad and toss gently.

Recipe can be doubled or tripled, as necessary; adjust shopping list accordingly.

Chintz and Velvet Holiday Cake

25 to 30 servings

Black Fruitcake
1 pound candied pineapple, cut into thin shreds
1 pound seedless raisins
½ pound candied cherries, halved
½ pound golden raisins
½ pound citron, cut into thin shreds
½ pound currants
¼ pound orange peel, cut into thin shreds
1¼ cups Cognac

½ pound shelled hazelnuts

2 cups sifted all purpose flour

1 teaspoon cinnamon
½ teaspoon mace
½ teaspoon baking soda
Pinch of nutmeg
Pinch of ground cloves

½ cup (1 stick) unsalted butter
2 cups sugar *or* 1 cup firmly packed brown
  sugar mixed with 1 cup sugar
6 eggs
3 ounces unsweetened chocolate, grated

Cognac

White Fruitcake
1 pound sliced almonds
¾ pound citron, cut into thin shreds
½ pound blanched almonds or pecans
½ pound bleached golden raisins
¼ pound candied cherries
¼ pound candied pineapple, cut into thin shreds
4 cups sifted all purpose flour

1½ cups (3 sticks) unsalted butter
2 cups sugar
6 eggs, separated
½ cup Cognac
¼ cup Sherry
1 teaspoon cream of tartar

Cognac

Marzipan Icing
1 cup (8 ounces) almond paste
½ cup powdered sugar
¼ cup (½ stick) unsalted butter, room temperature,
  cut into pieces
3 to 4 teaspoons whipping cream

Vanilla Glaze
4 cups powdered sugar
¼ cup cold water
1 teaspoon vanilla

For black fruitcake: Two days before baking, combine first 7 ingredients with 1 cup Cognac in large mixing bowl and toss lightly. Cover and refrigerate.

On day of baking, toast hazelnuts in 350°F oven about 30 minutes. Chop coarsely or leave whole if you wish.

Preheat oven to 275°F. Generously butter 12-inch springform pan. Line bottom with parchment paper; butter paper. Sprinkle fruit mixture with ½ cup flour and mix well. Stir in hazelnuts.

In separate bowl, combine remaining 1½ cups flour with cinnamon, mace, baking soda, nutmeg and cloves.

Cream butter with sugar until light and fluffy using electric mixer. Beat eggs lightly and add with chocolate and remaining ¼ cup Cognac, blending well. Add flour mixture a little at a time, beating well after each addition. Pour batter over fruit-nut mixture and mix well using your hands.

Spoon into prepared pan and bake until cake tests done, about 2½ to 3 hours. Let stand at room temperature at least 1 hour. Sprinkle with additional Cognac. Remove from pan and wrap in foil or store in airtight container.

For white fruitcake: Preheat oven to 275°F. Generously butter 9-inch springform pan. Line bottom with parchment paper; butter paper. Combine first 6 ingredients in large mixing bowl and toss lightly. Sift ½ cup flour over mixture and blend well.

Cream butter, gradually adding sugar. Beat egg yolks and add, mixing thoroughly. Add Cognac and Sherry alternately with remaining 3½ cups sifted flour, blending well. Fold in fruit-nut mixture. Beat egg whites until stiff and glossy, folding in cream of tartar just before incorporating into batter. Thoroughly fold whites into batter.

Spoon batter into prepared pan and bake until cake tests done, about 1½ to 2 hours. (Any remaining batter can be baked in buttered loaf pan 1½ hours.) Let stand at room temperature at least 1 hour. Sprinkle with additional Cognac. Remove from pan and wrap in foil or store in airtight container.

For icing: Combine all ingredients in processor or blender and mix thoroughly until smooth and of spreading consistency.

For glaze: Combine 1 cup powdered sugar with the water in saucepan and cook over medium-low

The glorious two-toned fruitcake is wreathed in greens and Christmas balls.

heat, skimming several times, until syrup spins thread when small quantity is dropped from spoon (220°F). Stir in enough powdered sugar to make creamy consistency (it should not be thick). Stir in vanilla. Remove from heat and set pan over hot water. Continue stirring until glaze is lukewarm and pourable.

To assemble: Place black fruitcake on serving plate; top with white layer. Spread top with icing. Pour glaze over icing, allowing it to drizzle down sides of cake. Slice very thinly to serve.

Tuiles

A classic French almond cookie that takes its name from its shape, similar to curved terra-cotta roof tiles. Delicate and crisp, tuiles are a lovely partner for sherbet. Be sure to shape the cookies while they are hot and pliable.

Makes about 1 dozen large cookies

6 tablespoons (¾ stick) **butter, room temperature**
½ cup **sugar**
1 cup **sliced almonds**
2 **egg whites**
⅓ cup **sifted all purpose flour**
  Pinch of salt

Preheat oven to 400°F. Butter heavy-duty baking sheet. Thoroughly cream butter and sugar. Stir in almonds, egg whites, flour and salt. Drop batter onto baking sheet by tablespoonfuls, leaving enough space to allow for spreading. Bake about 10 minutes, or until cookies are golden brown around the edges and slightly yellow in center. Remove from sheet using spatula and immediately press onto rolling pin. Let stand several minutes. Remove and cool on rack.

This recipe can be doubled to serve 24; adjust shopping list accordingly.

A Greek Islands Easter

THE MENU

Stuffed Grape Leaves

Creamy Seafood in Shells

*Stuffed Leg of Lamb
Wrapped in Pastry*

Lemon Artichokes

Stuffed Tomatoes

Spring Green Salad

Orzo and Rice Pilaf

Cheese-Filled Bread

Honey and Cheese Pie

Serves 6

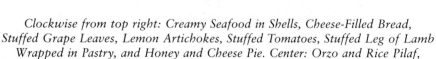

*Clockwise from top right: Creamy Seafood in Shells, Cheese-Filled Bread,
Stuffed Grape Leaves, Lemon Artichokes, Stuffed Tomatoes, Stuffed Leg of Lamb
Wrapped in Pastry, and Honey and Cheese Pie. Center: Orzo and Rice Pilaf,
Spring Green Salad and a traditional ornamental bread.*

THE STRATEGY

Here is a special menu filled with the fresh flavors of spring—all with a Greek accent: pastry-wrapped lamb, lemony artichokes, stuffed tomatoes, bread filled with three cheeses and a traditional dessert, rich Honey and Cheese Pie. Add strong Greek coffee, good brandy and unsalted pistachios to complete this inspired feast from the Mediterranean.

Shopping List

3¼ cups chicken broth
  3 cups rich chicken broth plus additional broth if reheating thawed Dolmáthes
  1 pound lean ground lamb
  ¼ pound whitefish
  ¼ pound sea scallops
  ¼ pound small shrimp
  ¾ pound lean ground pork
  1 5- to 6-pound leg of lamb, trimmed and boned
  1 medium onion plus 1 medium-large onion
  3 lemons
 16 green onions
  1 orange (for peel)
  2 to 3 large garlic cloves
  6 firm ripe tomatoes

  6 large artichokes
 10 ounces fresh spinach or one 10-ounce package frozen chopped spinach
  1 head romaine
  1 head bronze lettuce
  1 bunch large red radishes
  1 1-quart jar grape leaves in brine or about 4 dozen fresh grape leaves.
    Fresh dill (1¼ cups chopped) (dried dillweed can be substituted)
    Parsley
    Fresh mint for garnish plus additional ½ cup chopped fresh mint (dried can be substituted)
    Glacéed apricots (optional; see recipe for Melópitta Nissiótiki)
  1 pound ricotta cheese
  ¾ pound Muenster cheese
  ½ pound Swiss cheese
  ¼ pound mozzarella cheese
  4 cups plus 1 tablespoon milk
 12 eggs
 5½ sticks butter
    Parmesan cheese (2 tablespoons grated)
    Feta cheese (½ cup crumbled)
  ¾ cup orzo (rice-shaped pasta)
 1¼ cups short-grain rice

Ingredients for the Easter feast.

Breadcrumbs
Pine nuts (⅓ cup)
 1 envelope plus 1½ tablespoons active dry yeast
 ¾ cup honey
 1¼ cups unbleached all purpose flour
 11 cups (about) all purpose flour
Sugar (¼ cup)
Olive oil (about 1 cup)
White vinegar
Salt
Black pepper
White pepper
Ground cumin
Rosemary
Arrowroot or cornstarch
Tomato paste

Special Equipment

Six 4-inch scallop shells (see recipe for Creamy Seafood in Shells)

Tips

The following recipes can be doubled: Stuffed Grape Leaves, Creamy Seafood in Shells and White Sauce, Lemon Artichokes and Lemon Sauce, Stuffed Tomatoes, Spring Green Salad and Vinaigrette, Orzo and Rice Pilaf.

Countdown

1 week ahead
Prepare Stuffed Grape Leaves and freeze (can also be prepared up to 3 days ahead and just refrigerated).

1 day ahead
Make Honey and Cheese Pie and store at room temperature.
Mix Vinaigrette for Spring Green Salad and refrigerate.

Prepare Cheese-Filled Bread and store at room temperature.
Remove Stuffed Grape Leaves from freezer and thaw in refrigerator overnight.

Morning of dinner
Prepare White Sauce for Creamy Seafood in Shells and set aside at room temperature.
Blend stuffing mixture for lamb and refrigerate.
Prepare artichokes for Lemon Artichokes. Cover with damp paper towel and set aside at room temperature.
Make tomato cups for Stuffed Tomatoes and let drain at room temperature.
Assemble salad ingredients for Spring Green Salad in serving bowl and refrigerate.

About 2 hours before serving
Prepare lamb with flavored butter and stuffing as directed and do initial roasting; meanwhile, prepare pastry and set aside to rise for 1 hour.

About 1 hour before serving
Proceed with lamb recipe and finish as directed.
Finish Stuffed Tomatoes.
Finish Lemon Artichokes.

About 45 minutes before serving
Prepare Orzo and Rice Pilaf.

About 30 minutes before serving
Make Creamy Seafood in Shells.

Just before serving
Reheat Cheese-Filled Bread in low oven if desired.
Drizzle Vinaigrette over salad.
Make Lemon Sauce for artichokes.
Rewarm Stuffed Grape Leaves in small amount of broth or water over very low heat.

Wine Suggestions

With the seafood serve a crisp Sauvignon Blanc, such as the ones by Concannon, Sterling, Sonoma Vineyards or Preston. The lamb will work well with a Cabernet Sauvignon from California or Bordeaux, or a snappy Zinfandel such as the ones by Edmeades, Lytton Springs or Devlin.

To Prepare Fresh Grape Leaves

Use the tender leaves of wild or cultivated grape-vines although the bottled, brined variety works equally well. Wild Concord vines in the New England area yield good leaves in May and June. Pick the choice ones by counting down from the tip of a vine and selecting the third and fourth leaves. Farther down the leaves will be too tough. Snip stems from leaves, pile in stacks of a dozen and drop each stack into boiling water, pressing leaves down for a few seconds until they are pliable. Lift out, drain and cool. Can be dampened slightly and stored several days in a plastic bag, then used to make Dolmáthes.

Tips and Tricks

Separate egg yolks easily by nipping a small hole in the one end of the eggshell and draining out the whites first.

Make a main meal of stuffed vine leaves by using the largest ones and filling them with 3 table-spoons meat mixture. Can be made ahead and served cold as a main luncheon course.

Substitutes for Greek cheeses that may be used in authentic Greek recipes are ricotta for *miz-ithra*, Parmesan for *kephalotiri* and Muenster for *haloumi*.

When using feta cheese, which is very salty, omit salt in recipes.

Refrigerate leftover unstuffed grape leaves for up to a month in their original covered jar and brine.

Rub trimmed and cut artichoke surfaces all over with the cut surface of a lemon to prevent discoloration.

Instead of pilaf, little new potatoes may be served with the lamb. Simply boil in jackets until tender. Then toss them in melted butter with pepper, salt and a generous amount of chopped fresh mint for a different flavor.

Pit fresh apricots by inserting the point of a clean, small screwdriver at stem end and pushing the pit through and out.

If you want to be authentically Greek for your party, serve anise-flavored Oúzo as an aperitif, straight or mixed with water (it will become cloudy).

Get more juice from a lemon by rolling it first on a hard surface, pressing down firmly to soften it.

Use dried orange peel to flavor teas and stuffings. Peel the orange skin in a continuous piece, then hang it up to dry for about 2 days. Cut up and store in a jar or box, unrefrigerated.

THE RECIPES

Stuffed Grape Leaves (Dolmáthes)

Makes 4 to 5 dozen

- ¼ cup olive oil
- 1 medium onion, finely chopped
- 1 pound lean ground lamb
- ½ cup short-grain rice
- ½ cup chopped fresh dill or 1 tablespoon dried dillweed
- ⅓ cup pine nuts
- ¼ cup water

- 2 tablespoons tomato paste
  Freshly ground pepper
  Salt (if fresh leaves are used)

- 1 1-quart jar grape leaves in brine, well rinsed, or about 4 dozen fresh grape leaves, blanched in boiling water 2 to 3 minutes until pliable

- ¾ cup rich chicken broth
- 3 tablespoons fresh lemon juice
- 1 lemon, thinly sliced (garnish)

Heat oil in large skillet. Add onion and sauté until translucent. Add meat, stirring to break into pieces.

1. *The filling is spooned onto grape leaf, which is rolled up and stacked in a Dutch oven* (**2**) *to simmer.*

Add rice, dill, pine nuts, water and tomato paste. Season to taste with pepper, and salt, if necessary. Cook over medium heat until water is absorbed, about 10 minutes.

Cover bottom of Dutch oven with layer of grape leaves. Stuff remaining leaves by placing leaf shiny side down, on palm of hand, with base of leaf toward wrist and tip toward middle finger. Put a spoonful of meat mixture in center. Fold base over stuffing, then fold sides of leaf over (like an envelope), tucking edges in snugly. Roll up and tuck tip of leaf beneath to prevent unrolling. Arrange tip side down in pan.

Add broth to within 1 inch of top layer. Use any leftover leaves to cover top layer. Place plate upside down over top layer and press. Cover and cook over medium heat until rice is tender, about 30 minutes. Sprinkle with lemon juice and cook 5 minutes longer. Let cool to room temperature, or chill thoroughly. Serve garnished with lemon slices.

Stuffed Grape Leaves can be prepared 2 to 3 days before serving and refrigerated, or they may be frozen. If frozen, thaw overnight in refrigerator, then add a little broth or water before gently reheating.

Creamy Seafood in Shells (Thalasiná se Ostrakón)

This first course can also be served as a supper main dish.

6 servings

  2 tablespoons (¼ stick) butter
  2 green onions, minced
  ¼ pound whitefish, boned and cut into ½-inch pieces
  ¼ pound sea scallops, halved or quartered
  ¼ pound small shrimp, shelled and deveined
  2 tablespoons chopped fresh parsley
     Salt and freshly ground white pepper
  ¾ cup White Sauce (see following recipe)
  2 hard-cooked eggs, coarsely chopped
  6 4-inch scallop shells
  2 tablespoons fine dry breadcrumbs
  2 tablespoons freshly grated Parmesan cheese

Preheat oven to 375°F. Melt butter in large skillet over medium heat. Add green onion and cook until just soft. Add fish, scallops and shrimp and simmer gently until scallops and shrimp are opaque and fish flakes when tested with fork. Stir in parsley, and salt and pepper to taste. Remove from heat. Fold in White Sauce and chopped egg. Divide mixture among shells. Sprinkle with breadcrumbs and cheese and place on baking sheet. Bake until lightly browned and bubbly, 15 to 20 minutes.

White Sauce

Makes 1 1/2 cups

3 tablespoons butter
2 1/2 tablespoons all purpose flour
1 1/2 cups hot milk
   Salt and freshly ground white pepper

Melt butter in saucepan over low heat. Gradually stir in flour, blending well. Slowly add milk, stirring constantly until sauce thickens. Season to taste with salt and pepper. Remove from heat and keep covered until ready to use.

Stuffed Leg of Lamb Wrapped in Pastry (Bouty Arniou Ghemisto Zimaropeplomeno)

6 to 8 servings

Stuffing
3/4 pound lean ground pork
3 green onions, chopped
1 egg, lightly beaten
1/2 cup chopped fresh parsley
1 tablespoon finely minced orange peel
3/4 teaspoon ground cumin
1/2 teaspoon freshly ground pepper
   Salt

Pastry
2 tablespoons sugar
1 1/2 tablespoons active dry yeast
1/2 cup warm water (105°F to 115°F)
6 cups all purpose flour
1 teaspoon salt
1/2 cup (1 stick) butter, diced
1 1/2 cups milk, room temperature

Lamb
1 5- to 6-pound leg of lamb, trimmed and boned
3 tablespoons butter, softened
2 to 3 large garlic cloves, crushed or pressed

1 teaspoon salt
3/4 teaspoon freshly ground pepper
1 tablespoon crushed rosemary

1 egg yolk
1 tablespoon milk

   Fresh mint leaves (garnish)

For stuffing: Combine all ingredients and blend well. Cover and refrigerate.

For Pastry: Dissolve sugar and yeast in water and let stand until foamy and proofed. Combine flour and salt in large bowl. Using your hands, rub butter into flour until it is absorbed. Make well in center of flour and pour in yeast and milk. Still using hands, push flour from sides of bowl into center and mix to form dough. Knead several minutes until smooth. Place in lightly oiled bowl and turn to coat. Cover with plastic wrap and let stand in warm area until doubled, about 1 hour.

For lamb: Preheat oven to 450°F. Set butterflied lamb skin side down on working surface. Pound to flatten slightly. Mix butter, garlic, salt and pepper to a paste. Rub half thoroughly into lamb. Spread with stuffing and reshape leg. Sew closed with kitchen string; tie crosswise at 1-inch intervals and twice around length to hold stuffing. Rub outside with remaining butter mixture, then rub with rosemary. Set on rack in roasting pan and roast 20 minutes. Reduce oven temperature to 350°F and roast an additional 40 minutes. Let cool, then remove string and brush off excess rosemary.

Lightly oil shallow roasting pan. Knead dough once again. Roll out enough dough on lightly floured surface to make rectangle 1/4 inch thick, large enough to enclose lamb completely with 1-inch overlap. Set lamb on one end of rectangle. Beat yolk with milk and brush some on edges of dough. Fold dough over lamb. Press seams together; trim and reserve excess dough. Set seam side down in roasting pan and brush with some of yolk mixture.

Preheat oven to 450°F. Roll excess dough into long thin ropes. Braid in threes to make braid long enough to go around top perimeter of lamb. (Remaining dough can also be made into smaller and thinner ropes and/or worked into more intricate designs such as leaves, initials, tiny birds, flowers and coiled snakes inside the encircling braid, all symbols of Easter in Greece.) Brush decorations with yolk mixture. Bake until pastry sets, about 15 minutes. Reduce oven temperature to 300°F and bake an additional 20 to 30 minutes (use meat thermometer to check doneness). Transfer to heated serving platter and garnish with mint. Allow to stand several minutes before slicing.

1. *Leftover dough is worked into a long braid that (2) wreathes the Easter roast.*

Lemon Artichokes (Anghináres Avgholémono)

---

6 servings

  6 **large artichokes**
½ **cup white vinegar**

  1 **medium-large onion, finely diced**
½ **cup chopped fresh dill**
⅓ **cup olive oil**
1½ **cups chicken broth**
¼ **cup fresh lemon juice**
    Salt and freshly ground pepper

Lemon Sauce (see following recipe)

Trim base from artichokes; remove hard outer leaves and cut off top third. Bring enough water to cover artichokes to boil with vinegar in large pan. Add artichokes and boil 15 to 20 minutes. Drain. When cool, remove chokes.

Line bottom of casserole with onion and dill. Arrange artichokes over and sprinkle with oil. Cook uncovered over medium heat about 10 minutes. Combine broth, lemon juice and salt and pepper and pour over artichokes. Cover and cook until tender and juice is reduced, about 45 minutes. Transfer to serving platter and fill centers with warm Lemon Sauce.

Lemon Sauce

2 egg yolks
3 tablespoons fresh lemon juice
1 teaspoon arrowroot or cornstarch
  Salt and freshly ground pepper
1 cup chicken broth

Whisk egg yolks in nonaluminum saucepan until frothy. Add lemon juice, arrowroot and salt and pepper. Slowly whisk in broth. Cook over medium heat, stirring constantly, until sauce thickens; *do not boil.* Keep warm.

Stuffed Tomatoes (Domátes Ghemistés)

6 servings

6 firm ripe tomatoes
  Salt

¼ cup olive oil
5 green onions, coarsely chopped
10 ounces fresh spinach, coarsely chopped, or 1 10-ounce package frozen chopped spinach, thawed and well drained
¼ cup chopped fresh parsley
¼ cup chopped fresh dill or 1 tablespoon dried dillweed
  Freshly ground pepper
½ cup crumbled feta cheese

Slice ½ inch from top of each tomato. Scoop out pulp and seeds; chop pulp and reserve. Lightly salt tomato cavities and let drain on paper towels.

Heat oil in large skillet. Add onion and sauté until tender. Add tomato pulp, spinach, parsley, dill and pepper. Cook uncovered over high heat until most of liquid is absorbed, about 5 minutes. Remove from heat and stir in all but 2 tablespoons cheese. Set aside to cool.

Preheat oven to 375°F. Lightly oil large baking dish. Divide stuffing among tomato shells, filling lightly. Sprinkle with remaining feta. Place in dish and bake until tomatoes are cooked through but not splitting, about 20 minutes.

Spring Green Salad (Maroulosaláta)

6 servings

1 head romaine, crisped
1 head bronze lettuce, crisped
1 bunch large red radishes, sliced
⅓ to ½ cup Vinaigrette (see following recipe)

Separate inner romaine leaves from outer ones. Use outer leaves and bronze lettuce to line sides of salad bowl. Arrange smaller leaves in center. Sprinkle radishes over top. Just before serving, drizzle Vinaigrette over entire salad.

Vinaigrette

Makes about ½ cup

⅓ cup olive oil
  Juice of 1 lemon
  Salt and freshly ground pepper

Combine ingredients in small bowl and mix well with fork or whisk.

Orzo and Rice Pilaf (Thítono Piláfi)

6 servings

1 cup (2 sticks) butter
6 green onions, white part only, finely chopped
¾ cup orzo*
¾ cup short-grain rice
3 cups rich chicken broth, heated
  Salt and freshly ground pepper

Heat butter in large skillet over medium heat. Add onion and sauté until just translucent. Add orzo and stir until grains are golden. Add rice and stir about 2 minutes. Blend in broth and salt and pepper to taste. Bring to boil, then reduce heat, cover tightly and simmer until rice is tender and liquid is absorbed, about 30 minutes.

*Orzo, a pasta that looks similar to barley, is available in Greek markets.

Cheese-Filled Bread

Serve this hot or cold.

6 to 8 servings

Filling
- ¾ pound Muenster cheese, grated
- ½ pound Swiss cheese, grated
- ¼ pound mozzarella cheese, grated
- 2 eggs, lightly beaten
- ½ cup chopped fresh mint leaves or 1 tablespoon dried mint
  Freshly ground white pepper

Dough
- ½ cup warm water (105°F to 115°F)
- 1 envelope active dry yeast
- 1 tablespoon sugar

- 6 tablespoons (¾ stick) butter
- 1 cup warm milk (110°F to 115°F)
- 1 tablespoon sugar
- 1 teaspoon salt

- 3¾ to 4 cups all purpose flour

- 1 egg yolk

For filling: Combine all ingredients in mixing bowl and set aside.

For dough: Combine water, yeast and 1 tablespoon sugar and let stand until foamy and proofed, about 10 minutes.

Meanwhile, melt butter in small saucepan over very low heat. Remove from heat and blend in milk, sugar and salt.

Place 3½ cups flour in large mixing bowl and make well in center. Pour yeast and milk mixtures into center and stir until dough forms. Dust dough with flour as necessary and knead in bowl or on lightly floured board until dough is smooth and pliable but not stiff, about 5 minutes. Roll dough into circle 22 to 24 inches in diameter.

Preheat oven to 375°F. Butter 9 × 1½-inch round cake pan. Line pan with dough, letting excess hang evenly all around edge. Spoon filling into dough. Fold dough evenly into pleats around pan and then over filling, with edges of pleats meeting at center top. Twist to form knob. Bake until light golden brown, about 45 minutes. Brush top with lightly beaten yolk and return to oven until bread is golden brown, about 15 minutes. Remove from pan immediately; let cool several minutes on rack before slicing into wedges.

Honey and Cheese Pie (Melópitta Nissiótiki)

6 to 8 servings

Crust
- 1¼ cups unbleached all purpose flour, sifted
- 1 tablespoon sugar
- 5 to 6 tablespoons butter, well chilled and cut into pieces
- 3 tablespoons (or more) ice water

Filling
- 1 pound ricotta cheese
- ¾ cup honey
- 3 medium eggs, lightly beaten
- 1 teaspoon grated lemon peel

  Glacéed apricots (optional garnish)

For crust: Combine flour and sugar in large bowl. Mix in butter until evenly distributed and mixture resembles small peas. Add 1 tablespoon water and blend well. Add remaining water and mix gently until dough pulls away from sides of bowl. Transfer dough to plastic bag and form into ball. Flatten into 8-inch disc and chill about 30 minutes.

Preheat oven to 350°F. Roll dough out on lightly floured board to thickness of about ⅛ inch. Fit into 9-inch pie plate and trim excess dough 1 inch beyond rim of pan. Flute edges. Line crust with waxed or parchment paper. Set slightly smaller pan or pie plate inside crust and fill with dried beans. Bake 10 to 15 minutes. Let cool slightly before removing inside pan, then cool completely.

For filling: Combine cheese and honey in mixing bowl. Add eggs and lemon peel and mix thoroughly. Pour filling into cooled crust and bake at 350°F until top is golden brown, about 1 hour. Serve at room temperature decorated with apricots, if desired.

Classic Summer Picnic

THE MENU

Old South Fried Chicken

Barbecued Ribs with
Back Bay Sauce

Early Dutch Coleslaw

Heritage Baked Beans

Dilled Potato Salad

Buttermilk Custard Pie

Serves 12

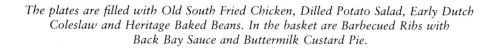

The plates are filled with Old South Fried Chicken, Dilled Potato Salad, Early Dutch Coleslaw and Heritage Baked Beans. In the basket are Barbecued Ribs with Back Bay Sauce and Buttermilk Custard Pie.

THE STRATEGY

The great all-American foods of summer—fried chicken, zesty barbecued ribs, crispy coleslaw, potato salad, baked beans and delectable desserts—inspired this delicious menu. All the dishes can be prepared well ahead, with only some last-minute barbecuing for the outdoor chef. And for added convenience, all the dishes are easily transported, so you can opt for a flower-filled meadow or the beach rather than your own backyard.

Shopping List

3 2½-to 3-pound frying chickens
7 to 8 pounds country pork ribs *or* 3 to 4 racks beef back ribs
1 pound bacon (preferably deep-smoked country type)
4 garlic cloves plus 2 teaspoons minced garlic
4 large onions plus 1¼ cups minced
6 pounds new potatoes
   Sweet red onion (⅔ cup finely chopped)
   Green cabbage (7 cups shredded)
   Pimiento (½ cup chopped)
   Celery (¼ cup minced)
   Green pepper (¼ cup minced)
   Parsley (3 tablespoons minced plus garnish)
   Fresh dill (⅔ cup minced) plus additional dill for garnish
3 cups evaporated milk
1 cup milk
4 cups (1 quart) buttermilk
¾ stick unsalted butter
¼ stick butter plus additional 3 tablespoons butter or bacon fat (see recipe for Early Dutch Coleslaw)
12 eggs
   Sour cream (½ cup)
2 pounds dried Great Northern beans
1½ cups finely ground cornmeal
4½ cups vegetable oil
1½ cups (about) cider vinegar
1 cup light olive oil
3¼ cups (about) all purpose flour
1½ pounds dark brown sugar plus additional 2 tablespoons dark or light brown sugar
2⅓ cups (about) sugar

2 cups bottled chili sauce
   Wine vinegar (1 tablespoon) (cider vinegar can be substituted; see recipe for Dilled Potato Salad)
   Salt
   Black pepper
   Worcestershire sauce
   Hot pepper sauce
   Dry mustard
   Dijon mustard
   Celery seed
   Bay leaf
   Ground cloves
   Paprika
   Lemon extract
   Cake flour (⅓ cup)
   Unbleached all purpose flour (¾ cup)

Special Equipment

Barbecue
Insulated container if transporting warm foods to another location

Tips

All the recipes can be doubled.

Countdown

1 week ahead
Make chili sauce for Barbecued Ribs with Back Bay Sauce. Let cool, transfer to jar and refrigerate.

5 days ahead
Prepare dressing for Early Dutch Coleslaw. Let cool, transfer to container and refrigerate.

3 days ahead
Make pie crust for Buttermilk Custard Pie and refrigerate.
Finish coleslaw as directed and refrigerate.
Make Heritage Baked Beans to point noted in recipe and refrigerate.

2 days ahead
Finish Buttermilk Custard Pie and refrigerate.
Finish Heritage Baked Beans.
Prepare milk marinade for Old South Fried
    Chicken; add chicken and refrigerate
    overnight.

1 day ahead
Prepare Dilled Potato Salad and refrigerate.
Finish Old South Fried Chicken and refrigerate.

Morning of picnic
Roast ribs as directed; let cool.

About 1½ hours before serving
Prepare charcoal grill for ribs; rewarm sauce over
    medium-low heat.

About 1 hour before serving
Begin barbecuing ribs, basting frequently with
    warm sauce.

Just before serving
Reheat Heritage Baked Beans.

Wine Suggestions

Al fresco dining calls for casual quaffing wines. A crisp Johannisberg Riesling, such as the ones by Chateau St. Jean, Jekel, Ventana or Obester, would be delightful with this picnic. Equally nice would be a jug of Soave, Gallo Sauvignon Blanc or Almaden Monterey Chablis.

THE RECIPES

Old South Fried Chicken

Revered, authentic southern fried chicken. Should be prepared a day or more in advance for best flavor.

12 servings

- 3 2½- to 3-pound frying chickens, cut into pieces.
- 3 cups evaporated milk
- 2 tablespoons Worcestershire sauce

- 1½ cups all purpose flour
- 1½ cups finely ground cornmeal
- 1½ teaspoons salt
- ⅛ teaspoon freshly ground pepper

- 4 cups vegetable oil
    Parsley sprigs (garnish)

Arrange chicken in shallow bowl(s). Combine milk and Worcestershire in another bowl. Pour over chicken. Cover and refrigerate about 8 hours.

Drain chicken and pat dry with paper towels. Mix flour, cornmeal, salt and pepper in large plastic bag. Add chicken pieces in batches and shake to coat. Remove from bag, shaking off excess.

Heat oil in wok, deep fryer or skillet to 365°F. Add chicken legs (do not crowd pan) and fry, turning to brown evenly, about 15 to 20 minutes. (Increase heat if temperature drops below 350°F; decrease heat if temperature exceeds 375°F.) Remove legs with slot-ted spoon and drain on paper towels. Repeat with thighs, frying 15 minutes, and breasts, frying 10 minutes or until evenly browned. Cool at room temperature. Transfer to large container with tight-fitting lid and refrigerate. Garnish dish with parsley sprigs before serving.

Barbecued Ribs with Back Bay Sauce

The traditional Boston sauce can be prepared a week ahead and refrigerated.

12 servings

- 7 to 8 pounds country pork ribs or 3 to 4 racks beef back ribs, trimmed of all excess fat
- 1 cup all purpose flour seasoned with 1 tablespoon paprika, 1 to 2 teaspoons minced garlic and ¼ teaspoon freshly ground pepper

- 2 cups bottled chili sauce
- ½ cup minced onion
- 2 tablespoons brown sugar
- 2 tablespoons cider vinegar
- 2 teaspoons dry mustard
- 6 dashes of hot pepper sauce
- 4 dashes of Worcestershire sauce

For ribs: Preheat oven to 325°F. Combine ribs and seasoned flour in plastic bag in batches and shake well to coat. Arrange ribs rounded side up in shallow baking pan. Bake until thermometer inserted in thickest part of meat (without touching bone) registers 150°F and ribs are browned and tender, about 1½ hours for country pork ribs or 45 minutes for beef back ribs. Let cool.

Combine chili sauce, onion, sugar, vinegar, mustard, hot pepper sauce and Worcestershire sauce in medium saucepan and bring to boil over medium-high heat. Reduce heat to low and simmer mixture about 15 minutes.

Meanwhile, prepare charcoal grill. Remove sauce from heat and pour over ribs, turning to coat thoroughly. Grill ribs over moderately hot coals, basting frequently with sauce, until ribs are crisp, about 15 minutes per side. Cut ribs into serving pieces, transfer to platter and serve immediately.

Early Dutch Coleslaw

The dressing for this delicious coleslaw dates back to the first Dutch settlers in America. Dish can be prepared three days ahead. Surround with cabbage leaves for attractive serving.

12 servings

Dressing
    3 eggs
 ¾ cup cider vinegar
 1½ tablespoons dry mustard
    2 teaspoons sugar (optional)
    1 teaspoon salt
 ½ teaspoon celery seed
 ⅛ teaspoon freshly ground pepper

    3 tablespoons butter or bacon fat
    2 tablespoons all purpose flour
    1 cup milk

Coleslaw
    7 cups shredded green cabbage
 ¾ cup minced onion
 ½ cup chopped pimiento
 ½ cup sour cream
 ¼ cup minced celery
 ¼ cup minced green pepper
    3 tablespoons minced fresh parsley
      Salt and freshly ground pepper

For dressing: Combine eggs, vinegar, mustard, sugar, salt, celery seed and pepper in medium mixing bowl and beat until smooth. Set aside.

Melt butter in heavy nonaluminum 1½-quart saucepan over medium heat. Stir in flour and cook, whisking constantly, about 3 minutes, reducing heat if necessary so flour does not brown. Pour in milk and continue whisking until sauce begins to simmer. Cook, whisking constantly, about 5 minutes. Reduce heat to just below simmer, stir in egg mixture and cook until sauce thickens; do not boil or eggs will curdle. Remove from heat and let cool. Season to taste. Transfer dressing to container, cover and refrigerate up to 5 days.

For coleslaw: Combine cabbage, onion, pimiento, sour cream, celery, pepper and parsley in large mixing bowl and toss lightly. Add dressing and toss again. Season with salt and pepper to taste. Cover and refrigerate 1 to 3 days.

Heritage Baked Beans

Bake this savory dish in the cool of evening and reheat before leaving for picnic. Beans will stay hot for several hours in insulated container.

12 servings

    2 pounds dried Great Northern beans

    2 garlic cloves, chopped
    1 large onion, chopped
    1 bay leaf
 ⅛ teaspoon ground cloves

    1 pound bacon (preferably deep-smoked country type), finely chopped
    3 large onions, minced
 1½ pounds dark brown sugar
    2 garlic cloves, minced
 ¼ to ½ cup cider vinegar
 ¼ cup Dijon mustard
    1 teaspoon salt
 ¼ teaspoon freshly ground pepper
 ⅛ teaspoon ground cloves

Add dried beans to heavy 6-quart saucepan. Cover with 2 inches boiling water. Let stand 2 to 3 hours. Discard any beans that float to surface.

Add garlic, chopped onion, bay leaf and cloves to beans and mix well. Place over medium heat and bring to gentle simmer. Reduce heat, cover partially and simmer until beans are tender, approximately 1½ to 2 hours.

Meanwhile, cook bacon in heavy nonaluminum 5-quart saucepan or Dutch oven over medium heat until browned (but not crisp), about 10 minutes. Spoon off all but 6 tablespoons fat. Add minced onion. Reduce heat to medium-low, cover and cook until onion is soft and translucent, about 20 minutes. Stir in sugar, garlic, ¼ cup vinegar, mustard, salt, pepper and cloves. Remove saucepan from heat.

Remove beans from liquid using slotted spoon and add to bacon mixture, blending well. Taste and add more vinegar if desired. If mixture appears dry, add several spoonfuls of bean liquid. (*Can be prepared to this point, and refrigerated overnight.*)

Preheat oven to 325°F. Bake beans, uncovered, about 4 to 5 hours, stirring every hour to prevent scorching and adding some reserved bean liquid if mixture appears dry; beans should be thick and caramelized. Let cool, cover and chill (*can be refrigerated up to 2 days*).

If transporting, reheat beans in oven or over direct heat. Cover and wrap in several layers of newspaper. Transport in insulated container.

Dilled Potato Salad

12 servings

- 3 egg yolks, room temperature
- 1 tablespoon Dijon mustard
- 1 tablespoon wine vinegar or cider vinegar
- 1 cup light olive oil
- ½ cup vegetable oil
  Salt and freshly ground pepper

- ⅔ cup minced fresh dill
- 6 pounds new potatoes, boiled, peeled and diced
- ⅔ cup finely chopped sweet red onion
  Fresh dill sprigs (optional garnish)

Combine yolks, mustard and vinegar in processor or blender and mix until thick and smooth, about 2 minutes. With machine running, gradually add oils through feed tube in slow steady stream, stopping machine occasionally to be sure oil is being absorbed (add 2 tablespoons very hot water if mixture begins to separate), until mayonnaise is very thick. Season with salt and pepper.

Transfer to large container and blend in dill. Gently fold in potatoes and onion, coating well. Refrigerate overnight. Garnish with fresh dill sprigs.

Buttermilk Custard Pie

A cheesecake-like custard pie recipe from early southern kitchens.

12 servings

- ½ cup all purpose flour
- 2 tablespoons (¼ stick) butter, room temperature
- 6 egg yolks
- 1½ to 2 cups sugar
- 4 cups (1 quart) buttermilk
- 2 teaspoons lemon extract
- 1 12-inch Pie Crust, baked and cooled (see following recipe)

Position rack in center of oven and preheat to 425°F. Combine flour and butter in medium bowl and mix well. Whisk in yolks, 1½ cups sugar, buttermilk and extract and beat until smooth. Taste and add additional sugar if desired. Pour into prepared Pie Crust. Bake 10 minutes; reduce heat to 350°F and continue baking until knife inserted between edge and center of filling comes out clean, about 45 to 50 minutes. Cool to room temperature. Refrigerate until serving time. (*Can be prepared up to 2 days ahead.*)

Pie Crust

- ¾ cup unbleached all purpose flour
- ⅓ cup cake flour
- 2 tablespoons sugar
- ⅛ teaspoon salt
- 6 tablespoons (¾ stick) unsalted butter, chilled and cut into small pieces
- 3 to 4 tablespoons ice water

Combine flours, sugar and salt in processor and mix well. Add butter and blend using on/off turns until mixture resembles coarse meal. Add water and mix using on/off turns just until dough begins to mass together. Gather dough into ball, wrap in plastic and refrigerate 1 to 24 hours. (To mix by hand, combine flours, sugar and salt in bowl. Cut in butter, using pastry blender, until mixture resembles coarse meal. Add water and toss mixture with fork until moistened. Gather dough into ball, wrap and chill from 1 to 24 hours.)

Grease 12-inch pie plate and set aside. Roll dough out on lightly floured surface into large circle. Fit into prepared pie plate; flute edges. Refrigerate 1 to 8 hours.

Preheat oven to 400°F. Line pastry with foil and weight with dried beans or rice. Bake 10 minutes. Discard foil and beans and continue baking until crust is golden brown, about 4 minutes. Cool.

Garden-Fresh Summer Menu

THE MENU

Pasta del Sol

*Roasted Small Birds
on Pâté-Topped Croutons*

Three-Green Salad with Warm Brie

*Liqueur-Marinated
Blueberries and Strawberries*

Blanche's Macaroon Cake

Serves 8

*In the foreground, an impressive platter of Roasted Small Birds accompanied by
Mushroom-Pancetta Sauce; upper right, Three-Green Salad with
Warm Brie and colorful Pasta del Sol.*

THE STRATEGY

Here is perfect entertaining for summer—a versatile menu that spotlights the fresh bounty of the season without any last-minute fuss. The first course, Pasta del Sol, can be altered to suit whatever looks best from garden or greengrocer. An elegant main course—which can be made ahead in easy stages—a bright salad garnished with melting wedges of brie and two simple-to-prepare do-ahead desserts round out this inspired summer dinner party.

Shopping List

½ to ⅔ pound chicken livers
20 slices pancetta or bacon
8 Cornish game hens (with livers)
   Chicken stock (½ cup plus additional to thin pasta sauce if necessary)

Additional chicken stock (¼ cup or more, preferably double strength)
1½ cups green beans
2 medium zucchini or 4 small zucchini
1½ cups very small broccoli florets
16 small mushrooms plus 4 cups coarsely chopped
2 cups fresh blueberries
1 cup fresh strawberries
   Asparagus (1½ cups chopped)
   Green bell pepper (1½ cups cut julienne)
   Red bell pepper (1 cup cut julienne)
   Fresh peas (¾ cup shelled) (frozen petits pois can be substituted)
   Fresh Chinese pea pods (¾ cup; frozen can be substituted)
   Green onion (¼ cup chopped)
   Garlic (1 teaspoon finely chopped)

A still life of summer's bounty.

Italian or regular curly-leaf parsley (½ cup
coarsely chopped plus additional sprigs for
garnish)
Fresh green chilies (1 teaspoon finely chopped;
red pepper flakes can be substituted)
Fresh basil leaves (about ½ cup coarsely
chopped; dried can be substituted)
Shallot (¾ to 1 cup minced plus 8 teaspoons
finely minced)
Deer tongue lettuce*
Buttercrunch lettuce*
Oak leaf lettuce*
Coconut (2 cups grated fresh; packaged flaked
coconut can be substituted)
8 wedges Brie (each about 4 inches long
with 1-inch-wide base)
1 3-ounce package cream cheese
6 eggs
1 cup milk
1 stick butter or margarine
1¼ sticks butter
5 tablespoons clarified butter plus additional
clarified butter for croutons and game hens
Additional 8 teaspoons butter (clarified if
desired)
Parmesan cheese (⅔ cup grated plus additional
for table)
1 pound fettuccine or spaghetti (if not using
homemade)
1 loaf white bread (preferably homemade)
Pine nuts (½ cup)
3 cups cake flour
3 cups sugar
Olive oil
Vegetable oil
Worcestershire sauce
Salt
Coarse salt
Black pepper
Dried tarragon (preferably French)
Vegetable shortening
Vanilla extract
Almond extract
Powdered sugar for garnish
1 cup dry Sherry
Orange liqueur (¼ cup)
Cognac (¼ cup)
Dry white wine (½ cup)

*Any combination of three different fresh greens can be
used for salad.

Special Equipment

Covered barbecue (optional; game hens can also be
oven roasted)
10-inch tube pan with removable bottom
Small loaf pan

Countdown

1 day ahead
Prepare Blanche's Macaroon Cake; let cool. Wrap
tightly in plastic and overwrap in foil. Refrig-
erate overnight.
Defrost game hens in refrigerator overnight if using
frozen.
Make fettuccine or spaghetti if using homemade
and let dry overnight.
Blanch all vegetables for Pasta del Sol and
refrigerate.
Make chicken liver pâté for Roasted Small Birds on
Pâté-Topped Croutons.

Morning of dinner
Prepare olive oil–basil mixture for pasta; add vege-
tables and heat through. Set aside at room
temperature.
Cook butter-stock-wine sauce for pasta and set
aside at room temperature.
Make basting sauce for Roasted Small Birds on
Pâté-Topped Croutons and set aside.
Assemble "surprises" for game hens and set aside.
Make croutons for game hens and set aside.
Prepare mushroom-pancetta sauce for game hens
and set aside.
Reduce Sherry for game hens and set aside.
Mix Liqueur-Marinated Blueberries and Strawber-
ries and refrigerate.

About 1½ hours before serving
Ready barbecue for game hens if not roasting in
oven.
Assemble game hens as directed and begin roasting.
Ready greens for salad.

About 1 hour before serving
Mix lemon–olive oil dressing for Three-Green
Salad with Warm Brie.

About 30 minutes before serving first course
Begin boiling water for pasta.
Toss greens with dressing and arrange on individ-
ual plates; set aside.

Just before serving first course
Cook pasta and reheat sauce; add vegetables as
    directed.

Just before serving main course
Reheat mushroom-pancetta sauce and finish with
    Sherry reduction as directed. Assemble game
    hens on plates.
Bake Brie for salad; set atop individual servings.

Just before serving dessert
Spoon berries into individual dishes.
Sprinkle cake with powdered sugar.

Wine Suggestions

With the pasta dish serve a crisp, dry Sauvignon
Blanc, a white Bordeaux, a light California Chardonnay or an Italian dry Orvieto. The main course
will match up nicely with a good red Bordeaux, a
Cabernet Sauvignon or Merlot from California. For
dessert pour a fine late harvest Johannisberg Riesling,
such as those by Chateau St. Jean, Joseph Phelps or
Felton-Empire.

THE RECIPES

Pasta del Sol

*Use whatever green vegetables are the freshest and
the best, and supplement with frozen vegetables if
you like. Use equal amounts (approximately 1½
cups) of all vegetables except peas, Chinese pea
pods and red pepper.*

6 to 8 appetizer servings

1½ cups green beans, trimmed and cut into 1¼-inch
    lengths
 2 unpeeled medium zucchini, cut lengthwise into
    sixths and cut into 1¼-inch lengths, or 4
    unpeeled small zucchini, quartered lengthwise
    and cut into 1¼-inch lengths (about 1½ cups)
1½ cups very small broccoli florets
1½ cups chopped asparagus (cut about 1 to 1¼
    inches long)
1½ cups green pepper julienne (cut 1¼ inches long)
 1 cup red pepper julienne (cut 1¼ inches long)
 ¾ cup fresh peas or frozen petits pois
 ¾ cup fresh or frozen Chinese pea pods (as small
    as possible)
    Boiling salted water

 3 tablespoons olive oil
 ¼ cup chopped green onion
 1 teaspoon finely chopped fresh garlic
 ½ cup coarsely chopped Italian parsley or ½ cup
    finely minced curly-leaf parsley
 1 teaspoon finely chopped fresh green chilies or
    scant ½ teaspoon crushed red pepper flakes

   Salt and freshly ground pepper
 ½ cup (about) coarsely chopped fresh basil leaves
    or 2 teaspoons dried, crumbled

 ¼ cup (½ stick) butter
 ½ cup chicken stock
 ½ cup dry white wine

 1 tablespoon olive oil or vegetable oil
 1 teaspoon salt
 1 pound fettuccine or spaghetti (preferably
    freshly made)

 ⅔ cup freshly grated Parmesan cheese
 ½ cup toasted pine nuts
    Additional chicken stock (optional)
    Freshly grated Parmesan cheese

Blanch each of the vegetables separately in rapidly
boiling water until just tender, about 2 to 3 minutes
per vegetable (peas will take only 1 minute if fresh
or 30 seconds or less if frozen). Drain each vegetable
well after cooking. Refresh in cold water and drain
again; pat dry if necessary. Combine all vegetables in
large bowl and set aside.

   Heat olive oil in large skillet over medium heat.
Add green onion and garlic and sauté about 3 minutes; *do not brown*. Add parsley, chiles and salt and
pepper to taste and sauté an additional 2 minutes.
Blend in basil.

   Add more oil to skillet if necessary. Add vegetables and stir gently to heat through, 1 to 2 minutes.
Set aside.

For sauce, melt butter in Dutch oven or large deep skillet (large enough to accommodate pasta and vegetables) over low heat. Stir in stock and wine and bring to simmer. Cover and set aside.

Bring large quantity of water to boil with 1 tablespoon oil and 1 teaspoon salt. Add pasta and stir with wooden spoon to separate. Cook until pasta is *al dente.*

Reheat sauce if necessary. Add pasta and half of vegetable mixture and toss gently to mix. Add remaining vegetables with Parmesan and pine nuts and toss again. Add more stock if mixture seems too dry (sauce should not be soupy). Divide among heated plates and serve immediately, passing additional Parmesan at table.

Roasted Small Birds on Pâté-Topped Croutons

For a surprise touch, a small strip of bread topped with parsley, mushrooms and Italian bacon is placed in each bird before roasting. The birds are perched on a pâté-topped crouton and then napped with a mushroom-pancetta sauce redolent of Sherry and tarragon. The chicken liver pâté can be made one day ahead, and the basting sauce early on the day of serving.

8 servings

Basting Sauce
5 tablespoons clarified butter
¼ cup dry Sherry
Dash of coarse salt (optional)
Freshly ground pepper
1½ tablespoons dried tarragon (preferably French), crumbled

Chicken Liver Pâté
¼ cup (½ stick) butter
½ to ⅔ pound chicken livers, cut into small pieces
¼ cup minced shallot
¼ cup Cognac, slightly reduced
Worcestershire sauce
Salt and freshly ground pepper

1 3-ounce package cream cheese, cut into small pieces

Surprise
8 parsley sprigs (preferably Italian)
16 small mushrooms (about ½ inch in diameter), sautéed lightly in butter

4 slices pancetta or blanched bacon, sautéed until crisp and cut into 24 pieces about 1 inch square
8 crustless 1 × 3-inch strips thinly sliced white bread

Mushroom-Pancetta Sauce
8 slices pancetta or blanched bacon, cut into ¼-inch dice

2 tablespoons (¼ stick) butter
½ teaspoon oil
4 cups coarsely chopped mushrooms
½ to ¾ cup minced shallot
8 livers from game hens, finely chopped
2½ tablespoons dried tarragon (preferably French), crumbled
Freshly ground pepper (optional)

Croutons
8 very thin slices homemade bread
Clarified butter

8 Cornish game hens, about 1 pound each (livers reserved)
8 teaspoons butter (clarified, if desired)
8 teaspoons finely minced shallot
3 teaspoons dried tarragon (preferably French), crumbled
Coarse salt and freshly ground pepper

Clarified butter
8 strips pancetta or blanched bacon

1 cup dry Sherry

½ cup (or more) chicken stock, preferably double strength

For basting sauce: Heat butter in small saucepan over medium heat. Add Sherry, salt and pepper and bring to boil. Remove from heat and add tarragon. Cover and set aside.

For pâté: Chill a small loaf pan. Melt butter in skillet over medium heat. Add livers, shallot and Cognac and sauté until livers are cooked but still pink inside. Stir in Worcestershire. Taste and adjust seasoning with salt and pepper. Remove from heat and let cool.

Transfer mixture to processor or blender. Add cream cheese and mix until smooth. Pack into chilled pan. Cover tightly and refrigerate for at least 6 hours or overnight.

For surprise: Place 1 sprig parsley, 2 mushrooms and 3 pieces pancetta or bacon on each bread strip. Set aside.

For sauce: Cook pancetta in small skillet over medium heat until crisp. Remove with slotted spoon and set aside. *Do not clean the skillet;* set aside.

Melt 2 tablespoons butter in Dutch oven or very large skillet over medium-low heat. Add oil and mix well. Add mushrooms and sauté until lightly browned about 5 minutes. Add shallot and sauté several minutes longer. Blend in pancetta, livers, tarragon and pepper. Remove from heat and set aside.

For croutons: Toast bread lightly. Set on rack and brush with clarified butter while still warm. Set croutons aside.

Rinse birds and pat dry. Rub cavity of each with 1 teaspoon butter. Sprinkle 1 teaspoon shallot and ¼ teaspoon tarragon in each. Season cavities with salt and pepper. Sprinkle additional pinch of tarragon over each bird and place 1 surprise in each cavity. Truss birds.

Prepare barbecue equipped with cover or preheat oven to 350°F. Brush roasting pan(s) with some of basting sauce. Rub underside of birds with clarified butter and set in pan(s). Brush skins with some of basting sauce. Lay 1 slice pancetta over breast of each bird.

Roast in covered barbecue or oven 5 minutes. Spoon some of basting sauce over tops of birds. Continue roasting, basting every 10 or 15 minutes, until birds test done and juices run clear, about 50 to 55 minutes for barbecue or about 1 hour for oven (cover loosely with small pieces of foil if birds brown too quickly). Transfer birds to heated platter. Discard pancetta and remove strings or pins. Keep birds warm in low oven with door ajar to prevent drying.

Boil Sherry in small saucepan until reduced to ½ cup. Remove from heat.

Reheat mushroom-pancetta sauce. Add 3 tablespoons of the Sherry. Taste and add remaining Sherry if necessary (to mellow liver flavor). Deglaze pan used to sauté pancetta with ¼ cup chicken stock. Add to sauce. Pour off fat from roasting pan(s). Add any browned bits clinging to bottom of pan to sauce. Continue cooking until heated through, adding more stock if mixture seems too dry (sauce should be thickened but not soupy).

To serve, arrange croutons on individual heated plates. Top with slice of pâté. Set bird on pâté and spoon enough mushroom-pancetta sauce over to moisten croutons also. Pass rest of sauce separately.

Three-Green Salad with Warm Brie

Substitute any crisp, fresh lettuce from your garden or market.

8 servings

Lemon–Olive Oil Dressing
⅔ cup light olive oil
⅓ cup fresh lemon juice
  Salt and freshly ground white pepper

  Deer tongue lettuce
  Buttercrunch lettuce
  Oak leaf lettuce
8 wedges of Brie, each about 4 inches long and 1 inch wide at base

Combine oil, lemon juice, salt and pepper and whisk to blend well. Allow to stand at least 1 hour at room temperature.

Preheat oven to 350°F. Tear lettuce into large bowl. Whisk dressing over greens and toss well. Divide among serving plates. Arrange Brie on baking sheet and bake until warmed but not runny, about 1 minute. Top each salad with wedge of cheese and serve immediately.

Liqueur-Marinated Blueberries and Strawberries

This dessert is the perfect complement to Blanche's Macaroon Cake.

8 servings

2 cups fresh blueberries
1 cup fresh strawberries
¼ cup orange liqueur

Combine berries in bowl and pour liqueur over. Cover and refrigerate several hours. Spoon berries and some liqueur into clear glass or crystal compotes, wine glasses or goblets.

Blanche's Macaroon Cake

This cake benefits from being made a day ahead. Wrap tightly in plastic and foil and refrigerate overnight. Serve with marinated berries.

12 to 16 servings

   6 **eggs, separated (room temperature)**
 ¾ **cup vegetable shortening**
 ½ **cup (1 stick) margarine or butter, room temperature**
   3 **cups sugar**
 ½ **teaspoon almond extract**
 ½ **teaspoon vanilla extract**

   3 **cups sifted cake flour**
   1 **cup milk**
   2 **cups grated fresh or packaged flaked coconut**

   Powdered sugar (garnish)

Preheat oven to 300°F. Generously grease and flour 10-inch tube pan with removable bottom, shaking out excess. Beat yolks with shortening and margarine using electric mixer at high speed. Gradually add sugar and continue beating until light and fluffy. Add extracts and beat until well blended.

Reduce mixer speed to low. Add flour in fourths alternately with milk, beginning and ending with flour. Beat in coconut, blending well.

Beat egg whites in separate bowl until stiff but not dry. Gently fold into batter using scraper or balloon whisk, blending thoroughly. Turn into prepared pan. Bake until tester inserted near center of cake comes out clean, about 2 hours. Cool in pan on wire rack 20 to 30 minutes. Remove cake from pan and let cool completely. Dust top lightly with powdered sugar before serving.

The Great All-American Thanksgiving

THE MENU

Golden Caviar in Iced Ring Mold

Country Tomato Soup

Pumpkin Biscuits

Herb Biscuits

*Double-Stuffed Turkey with Herbed
Sausage and Onion Dressing*

Root Vegetable Puree

Ginger Pear Pickles

Green Beans in Red Pepper Butter

Glazed Carrots and Chestnuts

Currant Bars

Cranberry-Cassis Mousse

Serves 12

*Tender, golden Double-Stuffed Turkey is the centerpiece of an
unforgettable Thanksgiving dinner.*

THE STRATEGY

This is a traditional feast with all the trimmings—some classic, and some classics updated. Native American ingredients such as cranberries and pumpkin are delicious and colorful accompaniments to the star of the show—a golden roast turkey stuffed with a homemade Herbed Sausage and Onion Dressing. Cooling Cranberry-Cassis Mousse and flavorful Currant Bars provide the sweet finish.

Shopping List

American golden caviar
3 cups rich brown stock (preferably homemade)
2½ quarts (10 cups) rich beef stock
5¾ cups chicken broth plus additional 4 cups chicken broth *or* chicken stock
1 12- to 14-pound turkey (with liver, heart, neck and gizzard)
1½ pounds boneless lean pork
1 pound boned and skinned chicken (or additional turkey meat)
1 pound fresh pork fat or rindless salt pork
3 pounds ripe tomatoes plus 3 additional tomatoes
Fresh tiny peas (½ cup shelled) (optional)
1 medium onion plus 1 cup minced and 1 cup chopped
4 large Bermuda onions
Celery leaves (⅓ cup minced)
3 pounds carrots or baby carrots
1 medium carrot plus 1 cup chopped plus 1½ cups finely diced
1 medium celery stalk plus 1 cup chopped plus 1 cup minced
15 medium-size ripe pears
2 limes
5 red bell peppers
3 pounds green beans
1 cup dried currants
5 cups cranberries
½ pound whole fresh chestnuts
Lemons (wedges for garnish plus juice)
Green onion for garnish plus additional green onion for optional garnish
Leeks (2 cups minced; white part only)
Turnips (1 cup chopped plus 1½ cups finely diced)
Parsley (2 sprigs plus ½ cup chopped plus

additional parsley minced for garnish)
Rutabaga (1½ cups finely diced)
Parsnip (1½ cups finely diced)
Celery root (2 cups finely diced)
Fresh ginger (1 cup thinly sliced)
Additional carrot, celery and turnip to make ½ cup (total) finely diced
2 cups milk
4 cups whipping cream
9 eggs
8 sticks butter
3¼ sticks unsalted butter plus additional unsalted butter for garnish
French or Italian bread (12 cups dry bread cubes)
15 cups all purpose flour
7 cups (about) sugar
1 cup light brown sugar
Dark or light brown sugar (2 to 3 tablespoons)
Powdered sugar (for garnish on Currant Bars)
1 cup plus 2 teaspoons oil
3 cups plus 2 tablespoons white vinegar
6 cinnamon sticks
3 envelopes dry yeast
Red wine vinegar (5 tablespoons)
Salt
Black pepper
White pepper
Ground ginger
Whole nutmeg
Cinnamon
Allspice
Ground cloves
Whole cloves (¼ cup)
Ground sage
Thyme, ground and dried
Bay leaves
Dried summer savory
Dried sage
Celery salt
Ground rosemary
Cornstarch
Baking powder
Vanilla
Arrowroot
1 cup canned pumpkin
2 cups cranberry juice cocktail
1 cup apple juice
Currant jelly (½ cup)

2⅓ cups dry white wine
  Brandy (⅓ cup)
  Crème de cassis (about ¾ cup)
1 small package paraffin
2 bunches yellow button chrysanthemums
1 bunch brown and yellow variegated chrysanthemums
  Fern leaves

Special Equipment

5-inch diameter glass bowl
11 × 6 (or 7)-inch charlotte mold
2½-quart decorative deep mold (soufflé dish can be substituted)

Tips

All the recipes can be doubled except the turkey and Cranberry-Cassis Mousse. Biscuit dough is easier to work with if prepared in two batches.

Countdown

1 month ahead
Make pastry for Currant Bars and freeze.

3 weeks ahead
Make Ginger Pear Pickles and refrigerate.

1 week ahead
Prepare decorative iced ring mold for golden caviar and freeze.

4 days ahead
Make red pepper butter for Green Beans in Red Pepper Butter.

2 days ahead
Remove pastry for Currant Bars from freezer and thaw in refrigerator overnight.
Prepare Cranberry-Cassis Mousse and freeze.
Prepare cassis sauce and refrigerate.
Make Herbed Sausage.

1 day ahead
Prepare Herbed Sausage stuffing; cover tightly and refrigerate.
Finish Currant Bars and store in airtight container.
Make Root Vegetable Puree to point noted in recipe and refrigerate.
Bake Herb Biscuits; wrap tightly and store at room temperature.

Bake Pumpkin Biscuits; wrap tightly and store at room temperature.
Prepare Country Tomato Soup to point noted in recipe; let cool and refrigerate.
Make Glazed Carrots and Chestnuts to point noted in recipe, draining chestnuts well. Refrigerate carrots and chestnuts separately.

Morning of dinner
Unmold Cranberry-Cassis Mousse onto serving platter and return to freezer.
Cook beans for Green Beans in Red Pepper Butter and set aside at room temperature.
Let Herbed Sausage and Onion Dressing stand at room temperature.

1 hour later (about 4 hours before serving for a 12- to 14-pound turkey)
Begin stuffing and roasting turkey.

When turkey is done (about 45 minutes before serving)
Tent turkey with foil to keep warm; prepare sauce.

About 30 minutes before serving
Bake Root Vegetable Puree to heat through.
Begin rewarming Country Tomato Soup over medium-low heat, stirring occasionally.

About 10 minutes before serving
Finish Green Beans in Red Pepper Butter.
Rewarm Herb Biscuits and Pumpkin Biscuits in low oven if desired.

Just before serving appetizer
Invert decorative ice ring onto serving platter; fill bowl with American Golden Caviar.
Let cassis sauce stand at room temperature until dessert time.

Just before serving soup
Add chopped tomato to soup and heat through.

About 20 minutes before dessert
Let Cranberry-Cassis Mousse stand at room temperature to soften slightly before serving (time will vary with warmth of kitchen, but mousse should not be served directly from freezer).

Wine Suggestions

The wines for this home-grown feast should be American. Serve a crisp, dry Sauvignon Blanc with the iced ring mold. With the turkey pour a slightly chilled Gamay Beaujolais or a Zinfandel by DeLoach, Cassayre-Forni or Christian Brothers.

THE RECIPES

Golden Caviar in Iced Ring Mold

This striking frozen flower mold can be prepared 1 week ahead.

12 servings

　1　small package paraffin

　1　gallon water, boiled and chilled

　2　bunches yellow button chrysanthemums (reserve some for garnish)
　1　bunch brown and yellow variegated chrysanthemums (reserve some for garnish)
　　　Fern leaves

　　　American golden caviar
　　　Thinly sliced dark bread
　　　Unsalted butter, lemon wedges and chopped green onion (garnishes)

Invert glass bowl 5 inches in diameter in center of 11 × 6 (or 7)-inch charlotte mold. Melt paraffin in top of double boiler set over simmering water. Spoon paraffin around glass bowl to provide seal so water cannot flow through. Carefully remove excess paraffin with razor blade. Let cool until set. Freeze mold for 15 minutes.

　Fill area between charlotte mold and glass bowl with chilled boiled water and freeze until ¼ inch of ice has formed around bowl and in mold, about 2 to 3 hours. Pour remaining ice water off into container and set aside. Freeze mold for 30 minutes.

　Arrange 12 sprigs of yellow button chrysanthemums around bottom of mold. Pour reserved ice water over flowers to depth of ¼ inch. Freeze about 30 minutes. Arrange variegated chrysanthemums around mold, interspersing with fern leaves. Repeat layering, ending with 1½ to 2 inches ice water at top of mold. Freeze until firm, preferably overnight.

　Shortly before serving, run sharp thin knife around inside of mold, dip bottom very briefly into hot water and invert onto serving platter with 1-inch lip. Fill bowl in center of mold with caviar. Decorate with reserved flowers. Serve with bread and garnishes.

Country Tomato Soup

12 servings

　¼　cup (½ stick) butter
　2　cups minced leek (white part only)
2½　quarts rich beef stock
　3　pounds ripe tomatoes (about 10 medium), peeled, cored, seeded and chopped (juice reserved and strained)
　5　tablespoons red wine vinegar
　¼　cup sugar
　⅓　cup dry white wine
　3　heaping tablespoons cornstarch
　　　Salt and freshly ground pepper

　½　cup uncooked tiny peas (optional garnish)
　½　cup minced green onion (optional garnish)

Melt butter in heavy large saucepan over medium-high heat. Reduce heat to low and add leek. Cover and let sweat until transparent (do not brown), about 10 to 14 minutes. Add stock and reserved strained tomato juice and simmer another 10 minutes. Stir in vinegar and sugar. Combine wine and cornstarch in small mixing bowl, stirring until well blended. Whisk cornstarch mixture into soup. *(Soup can be prepared ahead up to this point, covered and refrigerated.)* Add chopped tomatoes and simmer 3 to 5 minutes. Season with salt and pepper.

　To serve, ladle soup into tureen or individual serving bowls; garnish with peas and onion, if desired.

Pumpkin Biscuits

Makes 40 biscuits

　½　cup warm water (105°F to 115°F)
1½　envelopes dry yeast
　　　Pinch of sugar
6¾　cups all purpose flour
　1　cup milk (scalded and cooled)
　1　cup canned pumpkin
　1　cup firmly packed light brown sugar
　½　cup (1 stick) melted butter

2 teaspoons ground ginger
1 teaspoon salt
½ teaspoon freshly grated nutmeg
¼ teaspoon *each* ground cinnamon, allspice and cloves

Generously grease large mixing bowl. Lightly grease baking sheet.

Combine water, yeast and sugar in another large bowl and let stand until foamy and proofed, about 15 minutes. Stir in flour, cooled milk, pumpkin, brown sugar, butter, ginger, salt, nutmeg, cinnamon, allspice and cloves. Mix until soft dough forms. Transfer to floured work surface and knead until dough is smooth and elastic, about 10 minutes (or use dough hook of electric mixer and mix 8 to 10 minutes). Place dough in greased bowl, turning to coat entire surface. Cover and let rise in warm, draft-free area until doubled, about 2½ hours.

Turn dough out onto floured work surface and roll to thickness of about 1 inch. Dip 2-inch biscuit cutter into flour and cut out biscuits. Arrange close together on prepared baking sheet. Cover and let rise until doubled in volume, about 45 to 60 minutes.

Preheat oven to 350°F. Bake until biscuits sound hollow when tapped on bottoms, about 25 minutes.

Herb Biscuits

Makes 40 biscuits

½ cup warm water (105°F to 115°F)
1½ envelopes dry yeast
    Pinch of sugar
6 cups all purpose flour
1 cup milk (scalded and cooled)
1 cup minced onion
½ cup sugar
½ cup (1 stick) butter, melted
⅓ cup minced celery leaves
1½ teaspoons ground sage
1 teaspoon celery salt
1 teaspoon ground thyme
½ teaspoon freshly ground pepper

Generously grease large mixing bowl. Lightly grease baking sheet.

Combine water, yeast and sugar in another large bowl and let stand until foamy and proofed, about 15 minutes. Stir in flour, cooled milk, onion, sugar,

butter, celery leaves, sage, salt, thyme and pepper. Mix until soft dough forms. Transfer to floured work surface and knead until dough is smooth and elastic, about 10 minutes (or use dough hook of electric mixer and mix 8 to 10 minutes). Dough will be quite stiff. Place dough in greased bowl, turning to coat entire surface. Cover and let rise in warm, draft-free area until doubled in volume, about 2½ hours.

Turn dough out onto floured work surface and roll to thickness of about 1 inch. Dip 2-inch biscuit cutter into flour and cut out biscuits. Arrange close together on prepared baking sheet. Cover and let rise until doubled in volume, about 45 to 60 minutes.

Preheat oven to 350°F. Bake until biscuits sound hollow when tapped on bottoms, about 25 minutes.

Double-Stuffed Turkey

12 servings

1 12- to 14-pound turkey, rinsed and thoroughly patted dry
2½ cups Herbed Sausage (see following recipes)
8 to 10 cups Herbed Sausage and Onion Dressing (see following recipes)
    Salt and freshly ground pepper
1 turkey liver, minced

½ cup (1 stick) butter
½ cup oil
1 medium onion, chopped
1 medium carrot, chopped
1 celery stalk, chopped

    Brown Turkey Stock (see following recipe)
½ cup dry white wine

2 tablespoons (¼ stick) butter
2 tablespoons all purpose flour
½ cup (total) finely diced carrot, celery and turnip, blanched 45 seconds and drained

Loosen skin over turkey breast, thighs and drumsticks with fingers, being careful not to puncture skin. Pat ¼- to ½-inch layer of Herbed Sausage between skin and flesh of breast, thighs and drumsticks, adding any remainder to Herbed Sausage and Onion Dressing. Season neck cavity with salt and pepper. Fill with some of Herbed Sausage and Onion Dressing. Fold skin over and truss. Add minced liver to remaining dressing. Salt and pepper breast cavity and fill with dressing (do not pack tightly; dressing expands during roasting). Truss breast cavity.

Preheat oven to 325°F. Melt butter with oil in small saucepan over medium heat. Brush turkey with mixture. Place bird on its side on rack in large shallow pan and roast 1 hour, basting with butter mixture every 30 minutes. Turn turkey on other side and continue roasting 2 hours, basting with butter mixture every 30 minutes and turning pan for even browning as necessary. Turn bird breast side up. Reduce heat to 300°F. Add chopped onion, carrot and celery to pan juices. Continue roasting and basting until thermometer inserted in thickest part of thigh or breast registers 175°F to 180°F, about 45 minutes (tent turkey with foil if it begins browning too quickly). Transfer to heated large serving platter. Discard trussing; cover turkey loosely with aluminum foil. (Bird will stay warm 45 minutes.)

Bring Brown Turkey Stock to simmer over low heat. Spoon off excess fat from pan juices and discard. Add pan juices to stock. Deglaze pan with white wine, scraping up any browned bits. Blend wine mixture into stock.

Combine butter and flour in small saucepan over low heat and mix well. Gradually stir into stock until desired consistency. Add diced carrot, celery and turnip. Transfer to sauceboat and serve hot. Carve turkey at table.

Brown Turkey Stock

Makes 4½ cups

 ½ cup oil
 1 turkey neck, heart and gizzard
 1 cup *each* chopped onion, carrot, celery and turnip
 3 tomatoes, peeled, cored, seeded and coarsely chopped
 4 cups (1 quart) chicken broth or stock
 1½ cups dry white wine
 2 parsley sprigs
 ½ teaspoon salt
   Bouquet garni (2 bay leaves, 1 teaspoon *each* dried thyme, sage and summer savory)

Heat oil in large saucepan over medium-high heat. Add turkey neck, heart and gizzard, Stir in onion, carrot, celery and turnip and sauté until well browned. Blend in tomatoes, chicken broth or stock,

white wine, parsley, salt and bouquet garni. Simmer, uncovered, about 1½ hours. Cover partially and cook another 1½ hours. Strain stock into large saucepan, pressing vegetables with back of spoon to extract as much liquid as possible.

Herbed Sausage and Onion Dressing

Makes about 10 cups

 4 large Bermuda onions, unpeeled
 12 cups dry bread cubes (preferably good-quality French or Italian bread)
 3 cups whipping cream
 2½ cups Herbed Sausage (see following recipe)
 2 tablespoons (¼ stick) butter
 1 cup minced celery
 ½ cup chopped fresh parsley
 1 tablespoon celery salt
 1 generous tablespoon dried summer savory, crumbled
 2 teaspoons ground rosemary
 2 teaspoons ground sage
 1 teaspoon dried thyme, crumbled
 1 teaspoon freshly ground pepper
 1 teaspoon oil

Preheat oven to 400°F. Lightly grease baking sheet. Arrange onions on sheet. Roast 1 hour. Cool; peel and mince (you should have about 2½ cups).

Combine bread cubes and whipping cream in bowl and set aside.

Cook Herbed Sausage, covered, in large skillet over medium heat, about 10 to 12 minutes. Transfer to large mixing bowl using slotted spoon. Drain bread cubes and squeeze dry; pat lightly with paper towel. Add to sausage. Blend in 2¼ cups onions (reserve remainder for Green Beans in Red Pepper Butter, page 250), tossing to blend well.

Heat 2 tablespoons butter in same skillet. Add minced celery and sauté until transparent. Add to sausage mixture with all remaining ingredients except oil and blend thoroughly.

Heat 1 teaspoon oil in small skillet over medium-high heat. Add 1 tablespoon dressing and cook through. Taste and adjust seasoning for remaining uncooked dressing mixture. Refrigerate.

Let stand at room temperature 1 hour before stuffing turkey.

Herbed Sausage

Makes about 5 cups

1½ pounds boneless lean pork, cut into 1-inch cubes
  1 pound boneless, skinless chicken or turkey, cut into 1-inch cubes
  1 pound fresh pork fat or rindless salt pork, cut into ½-inch cubes, simmered in water 10 minutes and drained
 ⅓ cup brandy
  1 tablespoon celery salt
  2 teaspoons ground sage
  2 teaspoons ground rosemary
  1 teaspoon freshly ground pepper
 ½ teaspoon dried thyme, crumbled
 ½ teaspoon dried summer savory, crumbled
 ½ teaspoon freshly grated nutmeg

  1 teaspoon oil

Grind pork, chicken and pork fat in batches in processor. Transfer to large mixing bowl. Add all remaining ingredients except oil and blend.

Heat 1 teaspoon oil in small skillet over medium-high heat. Add 1 tablespoon of Herbed Sausage mixture and cook through. Taste and adjust seasoning for remaining uncooked sausage mixture. Cover and refrigerate.

Herbed Sausage is best if refrigerated overnight to mellow. Let stand at room temperature for about 1 hour before using.

Root Vegetable Puree

12 servings

5¾ cups chicken broth
1½ cups *each* finely diced carrot, turnip, rutabaga and parsnip
  2 cups finely diced celery root
 ¾ cup (1½ sticks) unsalted butter, softened
  2 to 3 tablespoons brown sugar
    Freshly ground white pepper

    Minced fresh parsley (garnish)

Lightly grease 3-quart round baking dish and set aside. Bring chicken broth to boil in large saucepan over medium-high heat. Add carrot, turnip, rutabaga, parsnip and celery root and cook until tender, about 35 minutes. Strain. Transfer vegetables to processor or blender and puree. Turn into large bowl of electric mixer. Add butter, sugar and pepper and blend well.

Transfer to prepared baking dish and cover with foil. *(Can be prepared ahead to this point and refrigerated.)*

Preheat oven to 350°F. Bake puree until just warmed through. Remove foil and continue baking for 5 minutes. Top with parsley and serve.

Ginger Pear Pickles

12 servings

15 medium pears, peeled, cored, seeded and quartered
  4 cups (1 quart) water
  2 tablespoons white vinegar

  5 cups sugar
  3 cups white vinegar
  1 cup water
  1 cup apple juice
  1 cup thinly sliced, peeled fresh ginger (reserve peel)
  6 cinnamon sticks
 ¼ cup whole cloves
  2 limes, thinly sliced

Combine pears, water and 2 tablespoons vinegar in large bowl and let stand for 10 minutes.

Combine sugar, 3 cups vinegar, water, apple juice and ginger in large saucepan and bring to boil over high heat. Tie ginger peel, cinnamon sticks, cloves and lime in cheesecloth and add to saucepan. Cover and boil 8 to 10 minutes. Drain pears well. Add to sugar mixture and continue boiling until pears are translucent, about 10 minutes. Transfer pears and syrup to large bowl. Let cool slightly, then cover and refrigerate until well chilled. Remove pears from syrup using slotted spoon and arrange in serving bowl. Remove spices from syrup (add to pears if desired). Pour syrup over pears.

Ginger Pear Pickles can be prepared ahead and refrigerated up to 3 weeks.

Green Beans in Red Pepper Butter

12 servings

Red Pepper Butter
  2 tablespoons (¼ stick) butter
  2 red bell peppers, shredded

  ¾ cup (1½ sticks) unsalted butter, room
    temperature
  ¼ cup onion reserved from Herbed Sausage and
    Onion Dressing recipe (page 248)
    Juice of 1 lemon
    Salt and freshly ground pepper

  3 pounds green beans, washed and trimmed

  2 tablespoons (¼ stick) unsalted butter
  3 red bell peppers, cored, seeded and cut julienne

For butter: Melt butter in medium saucepan over medium-high heat. Add shredded peppers and sauté until crisp-tender. Transfer to platter using slotted spoon and set aside.

Combine ¾ cup butter with onion in processor and mix well. Add sautéed peppers, lemon juice, salt and pepper and mix until smooth, 30 seconds.

Bring 2 quarts water to boil in large saucepan over high heat. Add beans and cook 8 to 10 minutes (cook longer if softer beans are desired). Drain beans well; place in ice water and let soak 2 to 3 minutes then drain again.

Ten minutes before serving, melt 2 tablespoons butter in large saucepan over medium-high heat. Add julienne peppers and sauté 2 minutes. Reduce heat to low, add green beans and half of red pepper butter, stirring to blend well. Save remaining red pepper butter for future use with vegetables. Cover and simmer until beans are heated through, about 3 to 4 minutes. Transfer to large serving bowl and serve immediately.

Glazed Carrots and Chestnuts

12 servings

  ½ pound whole chestnuts
  3 cups rich brown stock (preferably homemade)

  ¾ cup (1½ sticks) butter
  3 pounds carrots, cut into 2½- to 3-inch pieces
    and quartered lengthwise, or 3 pounds whole
    baby carrots
  2 teaspoons sugar

Combine chestnuts in medium bowl with enough boiling water to cover. Let soak 1 hour. Drain chestnuts well; remove as much skin as possible. Transfer chestnuts to medium saucepan. Add 1 cup stock and simmer over low heat 20 minutes. Set aside.

Melt butter in large saucepan over medium-high heat. Add carrots and sugar and cook, stirring constantly, about 5 minutes. Add remaining 2 cups stock and cook until carrots are tender and liquid is reduced to syrupy glaze, about 15 to 20 minutes. *(Can be prepared ahead to this point, covered with aluminum foil and refrigerated.)*

Just before serving, drain chestnuts well. Add to carrots and heat through. Transfer to platter and serve immediately.

Currant Bars

Makes 24 to 28 bars

Pastry
  ½ cup (1 stick) butter, room temperature
  ¼ cup sugar
  1 egg yolk
  2 cups all purpose flour
  1 teaspoon baking powder
  1 teaspoon cornstarch
  1 teaspoon vanilla
  3 tablespoons water (about)

Filling
  1 cup dried currants
  ½ cup currant jelly
  2 tablespoons crème de cassis

  2 tablespoons all purpose flour
  1 egg white
  1 tablespoon water
    Powdered sugar

For pastry: Combine butter and sugar in large mixing bowl and beat until light and fluffy. Add egg yolk and continue beating until well blended. Slowly stir in 2 cups flour with baking powder and cornstarch, mixing well. Add vanilla and enough water to make dough pliable. Chill 30 minutes. *(Can be prepared ahead and frozen.)*

For filling: Combine currants, jelly and crème de cassis in small saucepan and soften over low heat. Remove from heat.

Position rack in center of oven and preheat to 375°F. Lightly oil baking sheet and set aside. Divide dough into 4 equal parts and roll into cylinders. Flour 16-inch sheet of waxed paper. Place 1 pastry cylinder on paper and roll into 10 × 4-inch rectangle ¼ inch thick. Trim edges. Repeat with 3 more sheets of waxed paper and 3 cylinders.

Blend 2 tablespoons flour into filling. Spoon ¼ of filling down center of each rectangle. Fold each long side of rectangles over to meet in center. Combine egg white and 1 tablespoon water in small mixing bowl. Brush each rectangle with egg wash. Cut each into 6 to 7 pieces, depending on size desired. Arrange bars on prepared baking sheet. Bake 18 to 20 minutes. Let cool completely. Dust with powdered sugar.

Currant Bars can be prepared ahead, wrapped tightly and frozen.

Cranberry-Cassis Mousse

Makes 2½ quarts

  8 **egg yolks**
  1 **cup cranberry juice cocktail**

  4 **cups freshly cooked sweetened cranberries, cooled and well drained**
 ⅓ **cup crème de cassis**

  1 **cup whipping cream**
  4 **egg whites**
 ½ **cup sugar**

Cassis Sauce
  1 **cup cranberry juice cocktail**
 ¼ **cup water**
  1 **tablespoon arrowroot**

  1 **cup freshly cooked cranberries, cooled and well drained**
 ¼ **cup crème de cassis**

Beat egg yolks in large mixing bowl until thick and lemon colored. Add cranberry juice and continue beating until well blended. Transfer to large saucepan and cook over medium heat, stirring constantly, until mixture thickens and coats spoon heavily (do not boil or yolks will curdle). Remove from heat and allow to cool completely.

Add 4 cups cranberries to cooled custard and blend well. Transfer to large bowl. Chill until mixture begins to thicken, about 30 minutes. Add ⅓ cup crème de cassis and mix thoroughly.

Whip cream in medium bowl until stiff. Beat egg whites in another bowl until foamy. Gradually add sugar to whites, beating until soft peaks form. Gently fold cream into cranberry mixture with spatula; then gently fold in egg whites until completely blended. Pour mixture into decorative 2½-quart mold or soufflé dish. Cover with foil and freeze until firm.

For sauce: Bring cranberry juice to simmer in medium saucepan over low heat. Combine water and arrowroot in cup and add to cranberry juice, blending well. Cook until thickened, stirring constantly, about 10 minutes. Remove from heat. Stir in remaining cranberries and let cool completely. Blend in ¼ cup crème de cassis.

About 5 to 10 minutes before serving, run sharp thin knife around inside edge of mold. Dip bottom of mold very briefly in hot water. Invert mousse onto platter. Serve immediately with cassis sauce. *(Mousse can be unmolded early in day and returned to freezer.)*

Hearty Holiday Feast

THE MENU

Four-Mushroom Consommé

Beef with Port and Butter Pan Juices

Sautéed Escarole

Sweet Potato Puree

*Frozen Champagne Cream in
Chocolate Cups
with Chocolate Sauce*

Serves 8

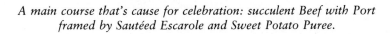

*A main course that's cause for celebration: succulent Beef with Port
framed by Sautéed Escarole and Sweet Potato Puree.*

THE STRATEGY

Here is a spectacular menu highlighting a traditional holiday favorite: sirloin of beef in a superb sauce laced with Port. The menu is simple to prepare, but features lots of innovative touches—a light consommé of four mushrooms, creamy Sweet Potato Puree and Sautéed Escarole. Dessert is a memorable treat designed for chocolate lovers: chocolate cups filled with frozen Champagne cream and garnished with a rich sauce.

Shopping List

      3 cups beef stock (preferably homemade)
      6 cups chicken stock
      1 3½- to 4-pound boneless first-cut sirloin beef roast or fillet (have butcher tie)
    1½ ounces (about) pancetta or unsmoked bacon (¼ cup minced)
      1 ounce dried Polish or Italian (porcini) mushrooms*
      1 ounce dried Japanese shiitaké mushrooms**
      1 pound fresh mushrooms
    1½ pounds escarole
      4 large sweet potatoes or yams (3 pounds total)
        Shallot (5 tablespoons minced)
        Lemons (for juice)
        Enoki mushrooms** or additional fresh mushrooms for garnish
        Garlic (1 teaspoon minced)
    1½ cups whipping cream
      8 eggs
    1½ sticks butter
    1¼ sticks unsalted butter
      9 ounces semisweet chocolate chips
        Salt
        Black Pepper
        White pepper
        Soy sauce
        Red wine vinegar (2 tablespoons)
        Sugar (½ cup)
        Superfine sugar (1 tablespoon)
      1 cup plus 2 tablespoons Tawny Port
        Brut Champagne (¾ cup plus 6 tablespoons)
        Dry Sherry (2 tablespoons)

*Available in specialty food stores.
**Available in oriental markets.

Special Equipment

8 ⅓-cup fluted paper cupcake liners

Tips

All the recipes can be doubled.

Countdown

2 or 3 days ahead
Prepare beef stock for Beef with Port and Butter Pan Juices if using homemade; chill.

1 or 2 days ahead
Prepare chocolate cups. Refrigerate or freeze.

1 day ahead
Prepare Four-Mushroom Consommé. Cover and refrigerate.
Prepare Sweet Potato Puree. Cover and refrigerate.
Prepare Champagne cream. Cover and freeze.

Morning of dinner
Parboil escarole for Sautéed Escarole. Cover and refrigerate.

1½ hours before serving
Prepare Beef with Port and Butter Pan Juices for main course.

20 minutes before serving
Reheat Sweet Potato Puree.

10 minutes before serving
Complete Sautéed Escarole. Reheat consommé.

At serving time
Garnish consommé. Complete dessert.

Wine Suggestions

This meal calls for one wine, but it should be a very good one. Serve a Grand Cru Classé red Bordeaux from 1978, 1975 or 1970, or a fine reserve Cabernet Sauvignon from one of California's best producers (Mondavi, Heitz, Clos du Val, Stag's Leap Wine Cellars, Conn Creek, Beaulieu, Beringer, for example). If you are feeling particularly grand, an extra dry Champagne would go nicely with the dessert.

THE RECIPES

Four-Mushroom Consommé

8 servings

- 1 ounce dried Polish or Italian (porcini) mushrooms
- 1 ounce dried Japanese shiitaké mushrooms
- 6 cups chicken stock
- 1 pound mushrooms, stems minced and caps sliced
- 3 tablespoons minced shallot

- 1 teaspoon salt
- ¼ teaspoon freshly ground pepper
- 2 tablespoons dry Sherry
- 2 teaspoons soy sauce

- 3 egg whites
- 2 eggshells, crumbled

- 3 cups water
  Several drops fresh lemon juice
  Uncooked enoki mushrooms or sliced mushroom caps (garnish)

Four-Mushroom Consommé enhanced with Sherry, soy sauce and a hint of shallot.

Soak dried mushrooms in stock in large saucepan until soft, about 2 hours. Remove with slotted spoon. Discard any hard stems or pieces, then mince mushrooms. Return to saucepan and add minced mushroom stems (reserve sliced caps), shallot, salt and pepper. Bring to simmer over medium-high heat; reduce heat and let simmer 40 minutes, skimming occasionally and keeping level of liquid constant by adding water. Remove saucepan from heat and stir in Sherry and soy sauce.

Beat egg whites with eggshells in 4-quart stainless steel bowl. Whisking constantly, gradually add broth to whites. Return to saucepan, place over medium heat and whisk gently until liquid is simmering. Stop stirring but let *simmer* for 15 minutes (*do not allow to boil*). Egg whites will coagulate and float to top, forming a cap.

Meanwhile, line strainer or sieve with 2 layers of cheesecloth and set over large bowl. Gently ladle consommé into strainer, pressing liquid through cheesecloth with back of ladle. Adjust seasoning.

Combine water and lemon juice in small saucepan and bring to boil. Add sliced mushroom caps and parboil 2 minutes. Drain well. Transfer to clean saucepan and add strained consommé. Bring to simmer. Ladle into bowls and garnish consommé with uncooked mushrooms.

Beef with Port and Butter Pan Juices

8 servings

    3 cups beef stock (preferably homemade)
    1 cup Tawny Port

    1 3½- to 4-pound boneless first-cut sirloin beef
       roast or fillet, tied (room temperature)

    2 tablespoons minced shallot
    2 tablespoons Tawny Port
    2 tablespoons red wine vinegar
    8 tablespoons (1 stick) unsalted butter
    ½ teaspoon salt
    ¼ teaspoon freshly ground pepper

Combine stock and 1 cup Port in 3-quart saucepan and boil until reduced to ¾ cup, about 1 hour. Set mixture aside.

Preheat oven to 450°F. Place roast on rack over shallow roasting pan. Set in oven and immediately reduce temperature to 375°F. Roast until meat ther-mometer inserted in thickest part of meat registers 125°F (for rare), about 1¼ hours. Set meat aside on carving board.

Drain off all but 1 tablespoon fat from roasting pan. Add shallot, remaining Port and vinegar and bring to boil over medium heat, scraping up any browned bits clinging to bottom of pan. Let boil about 1 minute. Transfer sauce to 9- or 10-inch skillet. Add reserved stock and bring to boil over medium-high heat. Reduce heat and simmer 2 minutes. Whisk in butter 1 tablespoon at a time, making sure each piece is fully incorporated before adding next. Add salt and pepper. Taste and adjust seasoning. Pour into sauceboat and keep warm.

Sautéed Escarole

8 servings

    1½ pounds escarole
     4 quarts (1 gallon) water

    ¼ cup (about 1½ ounces) minced pancetta or
       unsmoked bacon
    ¼ cup (½ stick) butter
    1 teaspoon minced garlic
    ¾ teaspoon salt
    ¼ teaspoon freshly ground pepper

Separate escarole leaves and wash well under cold water, discarding any that are bruised or blemished. Tear remaining leaves into 2-inch pieces. Bring water to rolling boil in large pot. Add escarole in 4 or 5 batches and parboil each 1 minute (make sure water returns to boil before adding next batch). Remove with slotted spoon and immediately refresh under cold water to stop cooking process. When cool enough to handle, squeeze out excess moisture.

Brown pancetta in 9- or 10-inch skillet over medium heat until crisp. Add butter and garlic and cook about 30 seconds. Add escarole, salt and pepper and toss until heated through. Taste and adjust seasoning. Serve hot.

Sweet Potato Puree

The secret to this recipe is to bake the potatoes until they are very soft and their natural sugars begin to caramelize.

8 servings

4 large sweet potatoes or yams (3 pounds total)

½ cup (1 stick) butter, room temperature
1¼ teaspoons salt
¼ teaspoon freshly ground white pepper

Preheat oven to 350°F. Pierce potatoes with sharp knife and arrange on baking sheet. Bake until potatoes are completely soft, about 2 hours. Remove from oven and let cool slightly.

Peel potatoes. Transfer pulp to processor or food mill. Add butter, salt and pepper and puree until smooth. Taste and adjust seasoning. Reheat puree in top of double boiler over gently simmering water, stirring occasionally.

Frozen Champagne Cream in Chocolate Cups with Chocolate Sauce

8 servings

Chocolate Cups
  6 ounces (1 cup) semisweet chocolate chips
  8 ⅓-cup fluted paper cupcake liners

Champagne Cream
  ¾ cup brut Champagne
  ½ cup sugar

  5 egg yolks

1½ cups whipping cream

Chocolate Sauce
  6 tablespoons brut Champagne
  3 ounces (½ cup) semisweet chocolate chips
  1 tablespoon superfine sugar
  2 tablespoons (¼ stick) unsalted butter

For cups: Partially melt chocolate in top of double boiler set over hot, not boiling, water. When chocolate is about half melted, remove from heat and let stand to melt completely *(temperature of melted chocolate should not exceed 95°F)*. Dip small brush into chocolate and paint inside of cupcake liners, building up sides thickly or cups will break when paper is removed. Invert onto baking sheet and refrigerate or freeze until hardened. Carefully peel off paper; set cups aside in cool area.

For Champagne cream: Combine ½ cup Champagne with sugar in small saucepan and bring to boil over medium-high heat, washing down any sugar crystals clinging to sides of pan using pastry brush dipped in cold water. Continue boiling *without stirring* until syrup registers 236°F (soft-ball stage) on candy thermometer.

Meanwhile, beat egg yolks in large bowl on high speed of electric mixer until light and lemon colored. When syrup is correct temperature, add to yolks in thin steady stream, beating constantly until mixture is thick and creamy, about 10 minutes. Gradually blend in remaining ¼ cup Champagne. Chill until mixture is thick but not stiff.

Whip cream in chilled bowl until stiff. Fold into Champagne mixture. Cover bowl and set in freezer overnight.

For sauce: Combine ingredients except butter in small saucepan and stir over low heat until chocolate is melted and sugar is dissolved. Whisk in butter. Remove from heat and keep warm.

To serve, spoon some Champagne cream into each chocolate cup. Spoon additional cream onto each chilled dessert plate. Center with chocolate cups. Drizzle some chocolate sauce over cream on plate (not in cup) and serve immediately.

Sauce should not be made ahead.

Frozen Champagne Cream in Chocolate Cups with Chocolate Sauce.

Festive Winter Fare

THE MENU

*Oysters, Ham and Peas
in Brioches*

Shrimp Gratin

Pineapple Sorbet

*Standing Rib Roast of Beef
with Madeira Sauce*

*Rosemary Potatoes with
Caramelized Onion*

Braised Broccoli in Tomato Cups

*Parsnip Puree in
Artichoke Bottoms*

English Trifle

Serves 10

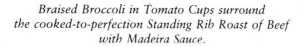

*Braised Broccoli in Tomato Cups surround
the cooked-to-perfection Standing Rib Roast of Beef
with Madeira Sauce.*

THE STRATEGY

This is a sumptuous feast that celebrates the holidays in style. The multicourse menu features elegant traditional touches—oysters in brioche, plump shrimp gratiné, a palate-refreshing Pineapple Sorbet between appetizers and main course and a classic English Trifle—mixed with a lively collection of new dishes, such as braised and pureed vegetables, Rosemary Potatoes with Caramelized Onion and a spectacular Standing Rib Roast of Beef with Madeira Sauce that is the centerpiece of the holiday table. And the step-by-step Countdown lets you get much of the preparation done *before* the Champagne is uncorked to toast the delightful dinner to come.

Shopping List

- 1 cup beef stock
- 1½ pints shucked small oysters with liquor or 4 dozen small fresh
- 3 ounces prosciutto
- 2 pounds medium shrimp
- 1 10-pound standing rib of beef (4 ribs) (have butcher trim, score fat, remove chine and tie onto roast)
- 1 large red bell pepper or 1 large pimiento
- 1 lemon (for juice)
- ½ pound small white mushrooms
- 3 pounds small red boiling potatoes
- 2 pounds small white or yellow onions
- 2 large bunches broccoli
- 5 medium tomatoes
- 1 pound parsnips
  - Garlic (2 tablespoons minced)
  - Shallot (¾ cup minced)
  - Fresh chives (2 tablespoons minced)
  - Fresh parsley (2 tablespoons minced)
  - Carrot (optional; 10 slices for garnish)
  - Buttermilk (5 teaspoons)
- 5½ cups (about) whipping cream
- 2 cups milk
- 16 eggs
- 3 to 3½ sticks plus 1½ tablespoons butter
- 1 stick unsalted butter
- 36 1½-inch almond macaroons
- 1 12-inch pound cake
  - Breadcrumbs (½ cup)
- 1 cup olive oil

- 1 envelope dry yeast
- 2¼ cups (about) all purpose flour
  - Oil (½ cup)
  - Salt
  - Black pepper
  - Whole nutmeg
  - Dill seed
  - Dried thyme
  - Dried rosemary
  - Paprika
  - Brown sugar (2 teaspoons)
  - Cornstarch
  - Vanilla
  - Sugar (about ¾ cup)
- 1 12-ounce jar seedless red raspberry jam
- 10 canned artichoke bottoms
- 2 20-ounce cans pineapple rings
  - Tomato paste
- 4 10-ounce packages frozen raspberries
  - Frozen tiny peas (⅔ cup)
- 1 cup dry white wine
  - Dry vermouth (3 tablespoons)
  - Champagne (amount will vary; see recipe for Pineapple Sorbet)
  - Madeira (½ cup)
  - Amaretto liqueur (⅓ to ½ cup)
  - Cream Sherry (½ to ⅔ cup)

Special Equipment

10 2-ounce brioche molds (4-ounce custard cups can be substituted)

10 individual gratin dishes or scallop shells (any individual broilerproof dishes can be substituted)

12-cup glass bowl or footed trifle bowl (any deep bowl can be used, but clear glass is preferable to display different layers)

Tips

All the recipes can be doubled except the roast and English Trifle.

Countdown

1 to 2 weeks ahead
Make brioches for Oysters, Ham and Peas in Brioches and freeze.
Toast breadcrumbs for Shrimp Gratin and refrigerate.

1 to 2 days ahead
Make Crème Fraîche for brioche filling.
Make trifle to point of adding whipped cream.
Clean broccoli for Braised Broccoli in Tomato Cups. Separate into florets.
Store in refrigerator in plastic bag.
Prepare Pineapple Sorbet. Scoop onto baking sheet and freeze.

Night before
Prepare parsnip puree and refrigerate.
Peel decorative strip around middle of each potato for Rosemary Potatoes with Caramelized Onion. Parboil potatoes, drain and chill.

Morning of dinner
Thaw brioches and peas at room temperature.
Prepare tomato cups for broccoli.
Prepare artichoke bottoms; fill with parsnip puree. Set aside in baking dish.
Mince shallots for Madeira sauce and garlic for broccoli; cover and set aside.
Poach oysters and set aside, covered, in cooking liquid.

4 hours ahead
Rub seasoning into roast; transfer to rack set in roasting pan.
Cook broccoli in boiling water; drain well and pat dry. Refrigerate.
Peel shrimp and drizzle with oil. Sprinkle with seasoning and refrigerate.
Poach mushrooms for Madeira sauce and set aside, uncovered, in liquid.
Whip cream for trifle and finish assembly; refrigerate until serving time.
Chop onions for rosemary potatoes.
Caramelize onions in pan large enough to accommodate potatoes later. Set aside at room temperature.

3 hours ahead
Begin roasting meat in preheated oven.

1 hour ahead
Make sauce for oysters up to point of adding oysters.
Hollow out brioches; toast lightly if desired.

30 minutes before serving
Coat shrimp with breadcrumbs. Arrange in gratin dishes, garnish and set aside at room temperature.
Take cheeses out of refrigerator. Arrange on cheese board and set aside.
Sauté broccoli. Arrange in tomato cups and set aside in baking dish.

15 minutes before serving
Preheat broiler for shrimp.
Bake artichoke bottoms to heat through.
Add oysters and peas to sauce for brioches; warm through gently.
Finish rosemary potatoes and onions.
Transfer roast to serving platter; tent with foil to keep warm.
Finish Madeira sauce.

5 minutes before serving
Warm broccoli in tomato cups in 300°F oven.
Broil Shrimp Gratin.
Spoon oyster filling into brioches.

After appetizers
Divide Pineapple Sorbet among dishes. Let stand at room temperature 5 minutes. Add Champagne and serve.

Wine Suggestions

Start with a crisp but well-rounded dry white wine. Try a Mondavi Fumé Blanc, a Buena Vista Chardonnay, a Ladoucette Pouilly Fumé from France. With the beef, serve a velvety-rich Pinot Noir by Acacia, Smith-Madrone or Carneros Creek, or a Burgundy from the Côte de Nuits. another appropriate wine would be a good Barolo, Barbaresco or Gattinara from Italy. Continue serving the red wine during the cheese course and finish with a light, dry Champagne such as Taittinger or Perrier-Jouet.

THE RECIPES

Oysters, Ham and Peas in Brioches

10 servings

Brioches
  1 envelope dry yeast
2½ teaspoons sugar
 ¼ cup water (105°F to 115°F)
2¼ cups (about) all purpose flour

 ½ cup (1 stick) butter, room temperature
  3 eggs
 ½ teaspoon salt

  2 tablespoons (¼ stick) butter, melted

  1 egg, beaten

Filling
1½ pints shucked small oysters with liquor (or 4 dozen small fresh)

  6 tablespoons (¾ stick) butter
  3 ounces prosciutto, cut julienne
 ¼ cup minced shallot
  3 tablespoons dry vermouth
1½ cups Crème Fraîche (see following recipe)
 ¼ teaspoon freshly grated nutmeg

 ⅔ cup frozen tiny peas, thawed
    Salt and freshly ground pepper

For brioche: Dissolve yeast and ½ teaspoon sugar in ¼ cup warm water in large bowl. Let stand until foamy and proofed, about 10 to 15 minutes. Add ¾ cup flour and stir with fork until blended. Using fingertips, continue blending until mixture forms firm ball, adding more flour as necessary. Nearly fill same bowl with warm water and let stand until dough floats to surface, approximately 15 minutes.

Cream butter thoroughly in food processor. Transfer to another bowl and set aside. Combine remaining flour and sugar with eggs and salt in processor and mix until dough forms ball on top of Steel Knife, about 20 to 30 seconds. Add creamed butter and mix until well blended. Drain yeast dough. Add to processor and mix just until blended. Divide dough in half. Return half to processor and mix until shiny and elastic (consistency of mixture should be between dough and batter). Remove and set aside. Repeat procedure with remaining dough.

Generously flour large bowl. Add dough, cover with towel and let rise in warm, draft-free area until doubled, about 1 hour. Transfer bowl to freezer (do not punch dough down) and chill until firm, about 30 minutes. Transfer to refrigerator for at least 2 hours (or overnight, if desired). Set ten 2-inch brioche molds (or 4-ounce custard cups) on baking sheet and refrigerate at the same time.

Coat chilled molds with melted butter. Turn dough out onto lightly floured surface and divide into 10 equal pieces. Roll each into ball and set in molds. Arrange inverted beverage glasses around molds and drape towel tent-fashion over glasses (do not let towel touch molds or dough will stick). Let dough rise in warm, draft-free area until doubled, about 25 minutes.

Preheat oven to 400°F. Brush top of each brioche with beaten egg. Bake 15 minutes. Reduce oven temperature to 375°F and continue baking until golden brown, about 15 minutes. Unmold brioche onto rack and let cool. *(Can be prepared ahead to this point, wrapped in foil and refrigerated overnight, or frozen for up to 2 weeks.)*

For filling: Drain oysters well (reserve liquor) and set aside. Strain liquor into large measuring cup and add enough water to equal 1½ cups. Transfer to large nonaluminum saucepan and bring to boil over medium-high heat. Add oysters and return to boil. Remove from heat and let stand 1 minute. Cover and set aside. *(Oysters can be prepared several hours ahead. Be sure to serve at room temperature.)*

Melt butter in large skillet or sauté pan over low heat. Add prosciutto and shallot and cook gently until shallot is tender. Increase heat to medium, add vermouth and cook until vermouth has evaporated. Reduce heat to low, add Crème Fraîche and nutmeg and simmer, stirring constantly, until crème is slightly thickened, about 5 to 7 minutes. *(Sauce can be prepared up to 1 hour ahead to this point.)*

Cut thin slice off top of each brioche and set aside for lids. Hollow out centers. Toast brioches lightly if desired. *(Can be prepared 1 hour ahead.)*

Just before serving, bring sauce to simmer over low heat. Drain oysters well. Add to sauce with peas and cook until warmed through. Season with salt and pepper. Divide filling evenly among brioches and cover with lids.

Crème Fraîche

2 cups (1 pint) whipping cream
5 teaspoons buttermilk

Combine cream and buttermilk in jar with tightly fitting lid and shake well. Let mixture stand at room temperature for 1 to 2 days to thicken.

Shrimp Gratin

10 servings

  2 pounds medium shrimp, peeled, deveined, rinsed and patted dry
½ cup oil
  2 tablespoons minced fresh chives
  2 tablespoons minced fresh parsley
1¼ teaspoons salt
¾ teaspoon dill seed
   Freshly ground pepper

½ cup toasted breadcrumbs
  1 large roasted sweet red pepper, seeded and cut into thin strips, or 1 large pimiento, cut into thin strips

Arrange shrimp in single layer in large shallow dish and drizzle with oil. Sprinkle with chives, parsley, salt, dill seed and pepper. Toss shrimp to coat evenly. Rearrange in single layer. Cover dish and refrigerate 4 hours.

About 30 minutes before serving, sprinkle breadcrumbs over shrimp and toss to coat well. Divide shrimp evenly among individual gratin dishes or scallop shells. Top each serving with red pepper or pimiento strips. Set aside at room temperature.

Just before serving, position broiler rack as far below heat source as possible and preheat. Broil shrimp until just pink and breadcrumbs are golden brown, about 5 minutes. Serve hot.

Pineapple Sorbet

10 servings

  2 20-ounce cans pineapple rings, drained (reserve juice)

   Champagne

Arrange pineapple rings on baking sheet and freeze until firm. Cut into small pieces. Transfer to processor. Add ¼ cup reserved pineapple juice and puree

until smooth and creamy. Scoop twenty 1-inch balls of mixture onto baking sheet and freeze.

Arrange two scoops of sorbet in each wine glass or sherbet dish. Let stand at room temperature for 5 minutes. Pour 3 to 4 tablespoons Champagne over each sorbet. Serve immediately.

Standing Rib Roast of Beef with Madeira Sauce

10 servings

  2 teaspoons salt
  1 teaspoon dried thyme, crumbled
  1 teaspoon freshly ground pepper
  1 10-pound standing rib of beef (4 ribs), trimmed, fat scored, chine removed and tied onto roast

Sauce
⅔ cup water
1½ tablespoons butter
   Juice of ½ lemon
¼ teaspoon salt
½ pound small white mushrooms, trimmed (sliced or halved if desired)

¼ cup (½ stick) butter
½ cup minced shallot
  1 cup beef stock
½ cup Madeira
  1 tablespoon tomato paste
   Salt and freshly ground pepper

Combine salt, thyme and pepper in small bowl and blend well. Rub into roast, covering entire surface. Transfer meat to rack in large roasting pan. Let stand at room temperature 1 hour until ready to use.

For sauce: Combine water, butter, lemon juice and salt in nonaluminum medium saucepan and bring to boil over medium-high heat. Reduce heat to low and stir in mushrooms. Cover and cook gently about 5 minutes. Uncover and set aside. *(Can be prepared several hours ahead to this point. Let stand at room temperature until ready to use.)*

Preheat oven to 500°F. Roast meat 10 minutes. Reduce oven temperature to 350°F and continue roasting until meat thermometer inserted in thickest portion of meat (without touching bone) registers 130°F (for rare), about 17 minutes per pound; do not baste. Transfer roast to heated serving platter. Tent with foil and keep warm.

Discard as much fat as possible from roasting pan. Add ¼ cup butter to pan and melt over medium-high heat. Stir in shallot and sauté until tender. Drain mushroom cooking liquid into measuring cup and add water, if necessary, to equal 1 cup. Pour into roasting pan with beef stock, Madeira and tomato paste and blend well. Reduce heat to low and cook, stirring up any browned bits, until liquid is reduced to 2 cups. Stir in mushrooms and cook just until heated through. Season with salt and pepper to taste. Transfer to heated sauceboat. Carve roast at table and serve immediately with sauce.

Rosemary Potatoes with Caramelized Onion

10 servings

  3 **pounds small red boiling potatoes (about 30), unpeeled**

  4 **to 8 tablespoons (½ to 1 stick) butter**
  2 **pounds small white or yellow onions, chopped**
  2 **teaspoons brown sugar**
    Paprika
  1 **to 2 teaspoons dried rosemary, crumbled (or to taste)**
    Salt and freshly ground pepper

Peel decorative strip around middle of each potato. Bring large saucepan of water to boil over medium-high heat. Add potatoes and parboil 10 to 15 minutes. Drain and immediately plunge into ice water to stop cooking process. Drain again. Pat dry and set aside. *(Can be prepared 1 day ahead. Cover and refrigerate.)*

Melt butter in large skillet or sauté pan over medium heat. Add onion, sprinkle with brown sugar and sauté until onion is lightly caramelized. *(Can be prepared several hours ahead to this point. Remove from heat and set aside at room temperature.)* Stir in potatoes. Season with paprika to taste. Continue sautéing until potatoes are glazed and tender. Sprinkle with dried rosemary, tossing mixture to coat evenly. Add salt and pepper. Transfer dish to platter and serve immediately.

Braised Broccoli in Tomato Cups

10 servings

  2 **large bunches broccoli (about 4 pounds), separated into florets with peeled short stems**

  5 **medium tomatoes**

  1 **cup olive oil**
  2 **tablespoons minced garlic**
    Salt and freshly ground pepper

Bring salted water to boil in large saucepan over high heat. Add broccoli and cook, uncovered, until crisp-tender, about 3 to 5 minutes. Drain and immediately plunge into ice water to stop cooking process. Drain; pat dry. *(Can be prepared several hours ahead.)*

Core tomatoes and cut in half crosswise. Carefully remove pulp, leaving ¼- to ½-inch shell. Invert halves on paper towels; set aside and allow to drain. *(Tomato cups can be prepared several hours ahead and refrigerated.)*

Preheat oven to 300°F. Generously butter large baking dish. Heat olive oil in large skillet or sauté pan over medium-high heat until very hot. Remove from heat and stir in garlic. Add broccoli and toss gently to coat. Season with salt and pepper to taste. Arrange broccoli stem side down in tomato cups. Set tomatoes in prepared dish. Bake just until heated through, about 5 to 7 minutes. Arrange tomato cups around roast before serving.

Parsnip Puree in Artichoke Bottoms

10 servings

  1 **pound parsnips, peeled and cut into ½-inch slices**

  ½ **cup (1 stick) unsalted butter**
  1 **teaspoon dried thyme, crumbled**
    Salt and freshly ground pepper
  1 **cup dry white wine**
  ⅔ **cup whipping cream**

  10 **canned artichoke bottoms, well drained**
  10 **carrot slices, cut into flower petal pattern (optional garnish)**

Bring salted water to boil in large saucepan over medium-high heat. Add parsnips and boil about 5 minutes. Drain well and pat dry.

Melt ¼ cup butter in large skillet or sauté pan over medium-high heat. Add parsnip slices, ½ teaspoon thyme, salt and pepper and sauté about 2 minutes. Reduce heat to low and add white wine. Cover and simmer until parsnips are very tender, about 10 minutes. Transfer parsnips and any liquid remaining in pan to processor or blender and puree. Blend in remaining butter and thyme with whipping cream. Season with salt and pepper to taste. *(Can be prepared 1 day ahead and refrigerated.)*

Preheat oven to 350°F. Generously butter large baking dish. Press circular fluted pastry cutter (slightly smaller in circumference than artichoke bottoms) down gently over artichokes to create ridged effect. Arrange artichokes in prepared dish. Spoon parsnip puree into pastry bag fitted with ¼-inch plain or star tip and pipe decoratively into each artichoke bottom, leaving ⅛ inch of fluted rim exposed. *(Can be prepared several hours ahead to this point. Set aside at room temperature.)* Bake until heated through, about 15 to 20 minutes. Garnish each with carrot flower, if desired, and serve immediately.

English Trifle

The ideal do-ahead dessert for Christmas dinner. The recipe requires three batches of custard, and we recommend that you prepare each batch separately to avoid burning or lumping.

10 servings

36 1½-inch almond macaroons
⅓ to ½ cup amaretto liqueur
1 12-ounce jar seedless red raspberry jam

Custard (Makes 1¼ cups)
4 egg yolks
3 tablespoons sugar
10 tablespoons milk
¼ cup whipping cream
2½ teaspoons cornstarch dissolved in 2 tablespoons milk
½ teaspoon vanilla
⅛ teaspoon freshly grated nutmeg

1 12-ounce pound cake, cut into ¼-inch slices (about 16 to 17)
½ to ⅔ cup cream Sherry
4 10-ounce packages frozen raspberries, thawed and thoroughly drained

2 cups (1 pint) whipping cream
2 tablespoons sugar
½ teaspoon vanilla or to taste

Brush flat side of 12 to 15 macaroons with liqueur. Arrange flat sides around sides of 12-cup glass bowl, then line bottom flat side up. Spread generously with red raspberry jam; try not to crush macaroons.

For custard: Whisk yolks in medium saucepan. Gradually add sugar, whisking until mixture is thick and lemon colored, about 1 to 2 minutes. Blend in milk, whipping cream and cornstarch mixture. Place over medium-low heat and cook, stirring constantly, until mixture thickens, about 3 to 5 minutes *(do not boil or mixture will separate)*. Remove from heat and stir until slightly cooled. Blend in vanilla and nutmeg. Transfer to bowl. Repeat twice, for a total of about 3¾ cups custard.

Spoon 1¼ cups custard over raspberry jam layer. Cover with single layer of pound cake slices. Using pastry brush, soak cake generously with ¼ to ⅓ cup Sherry. Spread thin layer of raspberry jam over cake. Top with half of drained raspberries. Carefully spoon another 1¼ cups custard over berries. Repeat layering with remaining pound cake slices, Sherry and jam. Cover with remaining berries. Carefully spread remaining custard over top.

Brush 8 or 9 macaroons with liqueur and arrange over custard flat side down. Place plastic wrap directly on surface of trifle. Refrigerate overnight. *(Can be prepared up to 2 days ahead.)*

About 3 to 4 hours before serving, whip cream in medium bowl until foamy. Add sugar and vanilla and continue beating until stiff but not dry. Spoon over macaroons, swirling top. Crush 10 to 12 macaroons. Sprinkle 1-inch border around outer edge of cream. Refrigerate until serving time.

The perfect finish: delightful English Trifle.

MIX AND MATCH CHART

The 33 menus in this book are just the starting point for countless different dinner parties you can give by mixing and matching recipes. We've begun the process for you here, suggesting two new menus composed of an appetizer, side dish and dessert to go with each of the main dishes.

When using this chart (or creating your own menu) pay careful attention to the quantities each recipe yields: You may have to double or halve some recipes to get the same number of servings for each dish in the menu.

Main Dish	Appetizers	Side Dishes	Desserts
Marinated Boned Lamb with Zinfandel Sauce (6)	Chilled Cream of Watercress Soup (93)	Braised Broccoli in Tomato Cups (264)	Raspberry Sorbet (103)
	Oysters, Ham and Peas in Brioches (262)	Pommes Dauphine (52)	Almond Tulips with Fresh Banana Ice (36)
Game Hens with Spinach-Sage Stuffing (12)	Carrot Soup (74)	Orzo and Rice Pilaf (226)	Cranberry-Cassis Mousse (251)
	Spindled Oysters (125)	Carrot Puree (119)	Coeur à la Crème (6)
Cioppino (19)	Positively West Coast Salad (36)	Stone-Ground Corn Rolls (128)	Buttermilk Strawberry Sherbet (111)
	Three-Green Salad with Warm Brie (240)	Rice with Artichokes and Olives (196)	Lemon Tarts with Caramel (145)
Veal with Pesto and Orzo (23)	Misty Fried Shrimp (177)	Creamy Carrot Timbales (144)	Iced Pear and Apricot Soufflé with Raspberry Sauce (89)
	Four-Mushroom Consommé (255)	Vegetables à la Grecque (203)	Walnut Tart (61)
Grilled Salmon with Tarragon Mayonnaise (36)	Salad of Endive, Watercress, Beets (215)	Matchstick Pommes Frites (12)	Green Grape Tart (25)
	Carpaccio (194)	Stuffed Beet Salad (109)	Sorbet au Cabernet with Sliced Kiwi (53)
Chicken with Braised Garlic and Rosemary (30)	Pasta del Sol (238)	Arugula Salad with Creamy Dijon Dressing (24)	Chocolate Torte (129)
	Country Tomato Soup (246)	Potato Cauliflower Puree (68)	Strawberry-Glazed Sherry Pie (137)
Beef Richelieu with Madeira Sauce (44)	Caviar Mousse (23)	Green Vegetable Medley (75)	Chocolate Sherbet (119)
	Shrimp Shiu Mai (168)	Minted Vegetables (136)	Almond Tulips with Fresh Banana Ice (36)
Boeuf à la Ficelle (51)	Zucchini Salad with Saffron (201)	Potatoes Boulangère (30)	Chocolate Apricot Roll (24)
	Potage Puree Crecy (5)	Cabbage Braised with Vermouth and Pecans (136)	Old St. Mary's Syllabub (128)

Main Dishes	Appetizers	Side Dishes	Desserts
Medallions of Veal in Brown Sauce with Port and Ginger (59)	Mussels à la Nage (85)	Endive-Cress Salad (51)	Honey and Cheese Pie (227)
	Cream of Lentil Soup (41)	Broccoli Timbales (13)	Raspberry Sorbet (103)
Noisettes of Lamb Florentine (68)	Pickled Herb Carrots (128)	Hot Garlic Eggplant (171)	Piedmont-Style Almond Cake (197)
	Vintner's Salad (18)	Corn Pudding (136)	Hazelnut Oeufs à la Neige (13)
Crown Roast of Lamb (74)	Creamy Seafood in Shells (223)	Curried Cauliflower and Potatoes (184)	Minted Pink Grapefruit Ice (67)
	Carrot Soup (74)	Zucchini with Pesto Sauce (144)	Blanche's Macaroon Cake (241)
Lobster Fricassee Primavera with Beurre Blanc (87)	Chicken Liver Toasts (194)	Processor French Bread (18)	Chestnut Roll (44)
	Veal Meatballs with Caper Mayonnaise (65)	Carolina Biscuits (135)	Buttermilk Pie (137)
Lobster with Curried Mayonnaise (93)	Liver Pâté (18)	Sesame Broccoli (117)	Vermouth-Glazed Pears (31)
	Radish and Carrot Salad in Lemon Cups (179)	Saffron Vegetable Rice Medley (186)	Mango Sorbet (105)
Malibu Paella (101)	Anchovy Puffs (73)	Onion and Raisin Salad (202)	Buttermilk-Strawberry Sherbet (111)
	Gingered Tofu (150)	Arugula Salad with Creamy Dijon Dressing (24)	Currant Bars (250)
Salmon with Apples, Pears and Limes (109)	Year-Passing Noodles (176)	Paillasson (60)	Buñuelos (161)
	Mushroom and Pine Nut Salad with Raspberry Vinegar Dressing (60)	Cheese-Filled Bread (227)	Chocolate Torte (76)
Spiced Chicken Strips (117)	Shrimp in Mustard Sauce with Cornbread Rounds (58)	Corn and Cabbage Salad (127)	Frozen Champagne Cream in Chocolate Cups with Chocolate Sauce (257)
	Carpaccio with Watercress Sauce (12)	Genoa-Style Spinach (196)	Peaches Flambéed in Scotch (151)
Southern Maryland Stuffed Ham (126)	Clam Bloody Mary (83)	Likker Pudding (135)	English Trifle (265)
	Eggplant Tempura-Style (50)	Monkey Bread (103)	Walnut Tart (61)
Country Ham and Red Eye Gravy (134)	Lemon Artichokes (225)	Cream Biscuits (214)	Pralines (Serve with fruit) (160)
	Warm Goat Cheese Salad (144)	Dilled Potato Salad (233)	Currant Bars (250)

Main Dishes	Appetizers	Side Dishes	Desserts
Rack of Lamb Moutarde (143)	Shrimp Gratin (263)	Quick Zucchini (6)	Langues de Chats (Serve with fruit) (53)
	Scaloppine of Salmon with Mexican Green Sauce (116)	Rosemary Potatoes with Caramelized Onions (264)	Lemon and Almond Pie (205)
Swiss Enchiladas with Lobster and Shrimp (151)	Guacamole (156)	Refried Beans (160)	Margarita Ice (160)
	Crudités with Fresh Tomato Sauce (115)	Pico de Gallo (156)	Frozen Lemon Cream (119)
Texas-Style Barbecued Chicken (158)	Jalapeños en Escabeche Stuffed with Peanut Butter (149)	Early Dutch Cole Slaw (232)	Peaches Flambéed in Scotch (151)
	Lamb Korma (184)	Green Beans-Open Sesame (111)	Gingersnaps (Serve with fruit) (105)
Steamed Salmon with Black Beans (170)	Springtime Spaghettini (35)	Parsnip Puree in Artichoke Bottoms (264)	Liqueur-Marinated Blueberries and Strawberries (240)
	Crustless Spinach Quiche (115)	Rice and Vegetable Salad (95)	Jalebis (189)
Misty Fried Shrimp (177)	Nat's Grog (149)	Tomatoes Pesto (100)	Ginger Ice Cream (103)
	Saucisson en Croûte (212)	Green Beans in Red Pepper Butter (250)	Lemon Chess Pie (136)
Chicken Tandoori (183)	Spring Green Salad (226)	Chick-Pea and Anchovy Salad (202)	Tuiles (Served with fruit) (217)
	Seafood Quenelles Mousseline (43)	Mushrooms and Pearl Onions (194)	Minted Pink Grapefruit Ice (67)
Lamb with Sweet-Sour Sauce (195)	Pot Stickers (168)	Simmered Vegetables (178)	Langues de Chats (53)
	Shrimp Salad with Mushrooms (66)	Pepper Salad (202)	Kheer (187)
Baked Fish Niçoise (205)	Red, White and Green Lasagna (195)	Stuffed Tomatoes (226)	Lemon Tarts with Caramel (145)
	Rabbit Terrine (214)	Brown Rice Milanese (111)	Margarita Ice (160)
Barbecued Ribs with Back Bay Sauce (231)	Tamales (157)	Fantasy Salad (197)	Iced Pear and Apricot Soufflé (89)
	Mushroom, Fennel and Pepperoni Salad (29)	Ginger Pear Pickles (249)	Buttermilk Pie (137)
Roasted Small Birds on Pâté-Topped Croutons (239)	Peanut Soup (126)	Sautéed Escarole (256)	Chocolate Torte (76)
	Zucchini Salad with Saffron (201)	Yogurt and Fresh Vegetables (186)	Biscuit Tortoni (19)

Main Dishes	Appetizers	Side Dishes	Desserts
Oxtail Ragoût in Madeira (215)	Wine and Champagne Punch (100)	Parathas (186)	Gourmandise with Sautéed Pine Nuts (52)
	Stuffed Grape Leaves (222)	Crusty French Bread (142)	Frozen Lemon Cream (119)
Stuffed Leg of Lamb Wrapped in Pastry (224)	Velouté of Fennel (66)	Cardamom Carrots (68)	Biscuit Tortoni (19)
	Kir Royale with Raspberries (65)	Curried Lentils (185)	Ricotta Almond Torte (69)
Double-Stuffed Turkey (247)	Eggplant Mold (204)	Sweet Potato Puree (256)	Chintz and Velvet Holiday Cake (216)
	Fresh Oysters Dolmades with Lemon and Caviar (83)	Bourbon Squash Rings (128)	Buttermilk Custard Pie (233)
Beef with Port and Butter Pan Juices (256)	Tomato Granité with Pernod (58)	Root Vegetable Puree (249)	Ricotta Almond Torte (69)
	Smoked Trout Salad (11)	Sautéed Leeks (52)	Green Grape Tart (75)
Standing Rib Roast of Beef with Madeira Sauce (263)	Cream of Watercress Soup (43)	Glazed Carrots and Chestnuts (250)	Chocolate Apricot Roll (24)
	Warm Goat Cheese Salad (144)	Broccoli Timbales (13)	Hazelnut Oeufs à la Neige (13)

INDEX

Almonds
  Almond Cake, Piedmont-Style, 197
  Almond Tulips with Fresh Banana
    Ice, 36
  Biscuit Tortoni, 19
  Chintz and Velvet Holiday Cake,
    216
  Chocolate Torte, 76
  Green Grape Tart, 75
  Lemon and Almond Pie, 205
  Likker Pudding, 135
  Rice Pudding, 187
  Ricotta Almond Torte, 69
  Tuiles, 217
  Yogurt Drink, 187
Anchovies
  Anchovy Puffs, 73
  Chick-Pea and Anchovy Salad, 202
  Mustard Anchovy Dressing, 197
  Salade Niçoise, 202
  Spinach, Genoa-Style, 196
Apples
  Glazed May Apples, 75
  Salmon with Apples, Pears and
    Limes, 109
  Wine and Champagne Punch, 100
Apricots
  Chocolate Apricot Roll, 24
  Iced Pear and Apricot Soufflé with
    Raspberry Sauce, 89
Artichokes
  Lemon Artichokes, 225
  Parsnip Puree in Artichoke Bottoms,
    264
  Positively West Coast Salad, 36
  Rice with Artichokes and Olives,
    196
Arugula Salad with Creamy Dijon
  Dressing, 24
Avocados
  Guacamole, 156
  Pico de Gallo (Rooster's Beak), 156

Baked Fish Niçoise, 205
Baked Kentucky Ham, 213
Banana Ice, Almond Tulips with
  Fresh, 36
Barbecued Ribs with Back Bay Sauce,
  231
Basil Bread, 60
Beans
  Heritage Baked Beans, 232
  Joyce's Basque Beans, 6
  Refried Beans, 160
  Steamed Salmon with Black Beans,
    170
  Texas Chili, 159
Beans, Green. See Green Beans
Beef
  Barbecued Ribs with Back Bay
    Sauce, 231

Beef en Daube, 204
Beef Richelieu with Madeira Sauce,
  44
Beef with Port and Butter Pan
  Juices, 256
Boeuf à la Ficelle, 51
Carpaccio, 194
Carpaccio with Watercress Sauce,
  12
Picadillo, 158
Standing Rib Roast of Beef with
  Madeira Sauce, 263
Texas Chili, 159
Beets
  Salad of Endive, Watercress, Beets,
    215
  Stuffed Beet Salad, 109
Benne Biscuits, 100
Beurre Blanc, 87
Beverages
  Champagne Framboise, 73
  Clam Bloody Mary, 83
  Fish House Punch, 126
  Kir Royale with Raspberries, 65
  Margarita Ice, 160
  Nat's Grog, 149
  Old St. Mary's Syllabub, 128
  Wine and Champagne Punch, 100
  Yogurt Drink, 187
Biscuit Tortoni, 19
Blanche's Macaroon Cake, 241
Blueberries and Strawberries,
  Liqueur-Marinated, 240
Boeuf à la Ficelle, 51
Bombay Bread, 85
Bourbon Squash Rings, 128
Bowl of the Wife of Kit Carson, 150
Braised Broccoli in Tomato Cups,
  264
Breads
  Basil Bread, 60
  Benne Biscuits, 100
  Bombay Bread, 85
  Brioches, 262
  Carolina Biscuits, 135
  Chapatis, 186
  Cheese-Filled Bread, 227
  Corn Bread Rounds, 58
  Corn Tortillas, 158
  Cream Biscuits, 214
  Crusty French Bread, 142
  Flour Tortillas, 159
  Herb Biscuits, 247
  Monkey Bread, 103
  Parathas, 186
  Processor French Bread, 18
  Pumpkin Biscuits, 246
  Sage Bread, 75
  Stone-Ground Corn Rolls, 128
  Toasted Pain de Mie, 214
  Two-Toned Braided Loaves, 212

Broccoli
  Braised Broccoli in Tomato Cups,
    264
  Broccoli Timbales, 13
  Sesame Broccoli, 117
Broiled Leg of Lamb, 118
Brown Rice Milanese, 111
Brown Sauce, 58
Brown Stock, 59
Brown Turkey Stock, 248
Buñuelos, 161
Buttermilk Custard Pie, 233
Buttermilk Pie, 137
Buttermilk Strawberry Sherbet, 111

Cabbage
  Cabbage Braised in Vermouth with
    Pecans, 136
  Corn and Cabbage Salad, 127
  Early Dutch Coleslaw, 232
  Pot Stickers, 168
Cakes and Tortes
  Blanche's Macaroon Cake, 241
  Chestnut Roll, 44
  Chintz and Velvet Holiday Cake,
    216
  Chocolate Apricot Roll, 24
  Chocolate Torte, 76, 129
  Piedmont-Style Almond Cake, 197
  Ricotta Almond Torte, 69
Caper Mayonnaise, 66
Cardamom Carrots, 68
Carolina Biscuits, 135
Carpaccio, 194
Carpaccio with Watercress Sauce, 12
Carrots
  Cardamom Carrots, 68
  Carrot Puree, 119
  Carrot Soup, 74
  Creamy Carrot Timbales, 144
  Ginger-Orange Carrots, 13
  Glazed Carrots and Chestnuts, 250
  Paillasson, 60
  Pickled Herb Carrots, 128
  Potage Puree Crecy, 5
  Radish and Carrot Salad in Lemon
    Cups, 179
Cauliflower
  Curried Cauliflower and Potatoes,
    184
  Potato Cauliflower Puree, 68
Caviar
  Caviar Mousse, 23
  Fresh Oyster Dolmades with Lemon
    and Caviar, 83
  Golden Caviar in Iced Ring Mold,
    246
Champagne Framboise, 73
Chapatis, 186
Cheese
  Benne Biscuits, 100

Cheese-Filled Bread, 227
Chicken Enchiladas, 159
Chile con Queso, 156
Coeur à la Crème, 6
Fromage Blanc, 119
Gourmandise with Sautéed Pine
  Nuts, 52
Honey and Cheese Pie, 227
Potatoes Boulangère, 30
Queso, 156
Ricotta Almond Torte, 69
Swiss Enchiladas with Lobster and
  Shrimp, 151
Three-Green Salad with Warm Brie,
  240
Vintner's Salad, 18
Warm Goat Cheese Salad, 144
Chestnut Roll, 44
Chicken
  Bowl of the Wife of Kit Carson,
    150
  Chicken Enchiladas, 159
  Chicken Tandoori, 183
  Chicken with Braised Garlic and
    Rosemary, 30
  Herbed Sausage, 249
  Malibu Paella, 101
  Old South Fried Chicken, 231
  Paper-Wrapped Chicken and Ham,
    169
  Spiced Chicken Strips, 117
  Texas-Style Barbecued Chicken, 158
Chicken Livers
  Chicken Liver Pâté, 239
  Chicken Liver Toasts, 194
Chick-Pea and Anchovy Salad, 202
Chile con Queso, 156
Chiles. *See* Peppers, Hot
Chilled Cream of Watercress Soup,
  93
Chintz and Velvet Holiday Cake, 216
Chocolate and Cocoa
  Chocolate Apricot Roll, 24
  Chocolate Sherbet, 119
  Chocolate Torte, 76, 129
  Frozen Champagne Cream in
    Chocolate Cups with Chocolate
    Sauce, 257
  Ganache, 61
  Ricotta Almond Torte, 69
  Walnut Tart, 61
Chuck's Special Dressing, 11
Cinnamon Sugar Syrup, 161
Cioppino, 19
Clams
  Cioppino, 19
  Clam Bloody Mary, 83
  Clam Pilaf, 87
  Malibu Paella, 101
Coeur à la Crème, 6
Cookies
  Currant Bars, 250
  Gingersnaps, 105
  Langues de Chats, 53
  Tuiles, 217

Corn
  Corn and Cabbage Salad, 127
  Corn Bread Rounds, 58
  Corn Pudding, 136
  Corn Tortillas, 158
  Stone-Ground Corn Rolls, 128
  Tamales, 157
Country Ham and Red Eye Gravy,
  134
Country Tomato Soup, 246
Court Bouillon, 101, 116
Crab
  Cioppino, 19
  King Crab Stir-Fry, 86
Cranberry-Cassis Mousse, 251
Cream Biscuits, 214
Cream of Lentil Soup, 141
Cream of Watercress Soup, 43
Creamy Carrot Timbales, 144
Creamy Dijon Dressing, 24
Creamy Seafood in Shells, 223
Crema Fresca, 159
Crème Fraîche, 263
Croutons, 239
Crown Roast of Lamb, 74
Crustless Spinach Quiche, 115
Crusty French Bread, 142
Cucumber-Stuffed Tomatoes, 95
Currant Bars, 250
Curried Cauliflower and Potatoes,
  184
Curried Lentils, 185
Curried Mayonnaise, 93

Desserts
  Almond Tulips with Fresh Banana
    Ice, 36
  Biscuit Tortoni, 19
  Buñuelos, 161
  Buttermilk Strawberry Sherbet, 111
  Chocolate Sherbet, 119
  Coeur à la Crème, 6
  Cranberry-Cassis Mousse, 251
  English Trifle, 265
  Frozen Champagne Cream in
    Chocolate Cups with Chocolate
    Sauce, 257
  Frozen Lemon Cream, 119
  Ginger Ice Cream, 103
  Hazelnut Oeufs à la Neige, 13
  Iced Pear and Apricot Soufflé with
    Raspberry Sauce, 89
  Mango Sorbet, 105
  Peaches Flambéed in Scotch, 151
  Pineapple Sorbet, 263
  Pralines, 160
  Raspberry Sorbet, 103
  See Cakes and Tortes, Cookies, Pies
    and Tarts
Dilled Potato Salad, 233
Dressings
  Chuck's Special Dressing, 11
  Coleslaw Dressing, 232
  Creamy Dijon Dressing, 24
  Lemon-Olive Oil Dressing, 240

Mustard Anchovy Dressing, 197
Mustard Vinaigrette, 36, 215
Raspberry Vinegar Dressing, 60
Tarragon Mayonnaise, 36
Vinaigrette, 67, 202, 203

Early Dutch Coleslaw, 232
Eggplant
  Eggplant Mold, 204
  Eggplant Tempura-Style, 50
  Hot Garlic Eggplant, 171
Endive-Cress Salad, 51
English Trifle, 265
Escarole, Sautéed, 256

Fantasy Salad, 197
Fennel
  Mushroom, Fennel and Pepperoni
    Salad, 29
  Velouté of Fennel, 66
Fish
  Baked Fish Niçoise, 205
  Cioppino, 19
  Creamy Seafood in Shells, 223
  Grilled Salmon with Tarragon
    Mayonnaise, 36
  Poached Salmon with Raspberry
    Beurre Blanc and Lime Butter
    Sauce, 142
  Salade Niçoise, 202
  Salmon with Apples, Pears and
    Limes, 109
  Scaloppine of Salmon with Mexican
    Green Sauce, 116
  Smoked Trout Salad with Chuck's
    Special Dressing, 11
  Steamed Salmon with Black Beans,
    170
Fish House Punch, 126
Fish Stock, 102
Flour Tortillas, 159
Forcemeat, 214
Four-Mushroom Consommé, 255
Fresh Banana Ice, 36
Fresh Oyster Dolmades with Lemon
  and Caviar, 83
Fresh Raspberry Sauce, 7
Fresh Strawberry Sauce, 7
Fresh Tomato Sauce, 115
Fromage Blanc, 119
Frozen Lemon Cream, 119
Frozen Champagne Cream in
  Chocolate Cups with Chocolate
  Sauce, 257
Frozen Rum Cream, 31
Fruit
  Frozen Lemon Cream, 119
  Iced Pear and Apricot Soufflé with
    Raspberry Sauce, 89
  Lemon Chess Pie, 136
  Lemon Tarts with Caramel, 145
  Lime Butter Sauce, 142
  Minted Pink Grapefruit Ice, 67
  Pineapple-Papaya Chutney, 188
  Raspberry Beurre Blanc, 142
(continued)

Fruit *(continued)*
  Sorbet au Cabernet with Sliced
    Kiwi, 53
  Strawberry-Glazed Sherry Pie, 137
  Vermouth-Glazed Pears, 31

Game Hens
  Game Hens with Spinach-Sage
    Stuffing, 12
  Roasted Small Birds on Pâté-Topped
    Croutons, 239
  Smoked Game Hens, 133
Genoa-Style Spinach, 196
Ginger
  Brown Sauce with Port and Ginger,
    59
  Gingered Tofu, 150
  Ginger Ice Cream, 103
  Ginger-Orange Carrots, 13
  Ginge Pear Pickles, 249
  Gingersnaps, 105
Glazed Carrots and Chestnuts, 250
Glazed May Apples, 75
Golden Caviar in Iced Ring Mold,
  246
Gourmandise with Sautéed Pine
  Nuts, 52
Grapefruit Ice, Minted Pink, 67
Grape Leaves, Stuffed, 222
Green Beans
  Green Beans in Red Pepper Butter,
    250
  Green Beans—Open Sesame, 111
  Salade Niçoise, 202
Green Grape Tart, 75
Green Vegetable Medley, 75
Grilled Salmon with Tarragon
  Mayonnaise, 36
Guacamole, 156

Ham
  Baked Kentucky Ham, 213
  Country Ham and Red Eye Gravy,
    134
  Curing of, 134
  Malibu Paella, 101
  Oysters, Ham and Peas in Brioches,
    262
  Paper-Wrapped Chicken and Ham,
    169
  Rabbit Terrine, 214
  Southern Maryland Stuffed Ham,
    126
Hazelnut Oeufs à la Neige, 13
Herb Biscuits, 247
Heritage Baked Beans, 232
Honey and Cheese Pie, 227
Hot Pepper Chutney, 189
Hot Garlic Eggplant, 171

Iced Pear and Apricot Soufflé with
  Raspberry Sauce, 89
Italian Beef Appetizer, 194

Jalapeños en Escabeche Stuffed with
  Peanut Butter, 149
Jalebis, 189
Joyce's Basque Beans, 6

Kheer, 187
King Crab Stir-Fry, 86
Kir Royale with Raspberries, 65

Lamb
  Broiled Leg of Lamb, 118
  Crown Roast of Lamb, 74
  Lamb Korma, 184
  Lamb Meatballs, 74
  Lamb with Sweet-Sour Sauce, 195
  Marinated Boned Lamb with
    Zinfandel Sauce, 6
  Noisettes of Lamb Florentine, 68
  Rack of Lamb Moutarde, 143
  Stuffed Grape Leaves, 222
  Stuffed Leg of Lamb Wrapped in
    Pastry, 224
Langues de Chats, 53
Leeks, Sauteed, 52
Lemons
  Frozen Lemon Cream, 119
  Lemon and Almond Pie, 205
  Lemon Artichokes, 225
  Lemon Chess Pie, 136
  Lemon-Olive Oil Dressing, 240
  Lemon Tarts with Caramel, 145
  Radish and Carrot Salad in Lemon
    Cups, 179
Lentils
  Cream of Lentil Soup, 141
  Curried Lentils, 185
Likker Pudding, 135
Limes
  Ginger Pear Pickles, 249
  Lime Butter Sauce, 142
  Margarita Ice, 160
  Salmon with Apples, Pears and
    Limes, 109
Liqueur-Marinated Blueberries and
  Strawberries, 240
Liver Pâté, 18
Lobster
  Lobster Fricassee Primavera with
    Beurre Blanc, 87
  Lobster with Curried Mayonnaise,
    93
  Swiss Enchiladas with Lobster and
    Shrimp, 151

Macaroons
  Biscuit Tortoni, 19
  Blanche's Macaroon Cake, 241
  English Trifle, 265
Madeira Sauce, 44, 263
Malibu Paella, 101
Mango Sorbet, 105
Margarita Ice, 160
Marinated Boned Lamb with
  Zinfandel Sauce, 6
Marinated Scampi, 203

Marzipan Icing, 216
Matchstick Pommes Frites, 12
Medallions of Veal in Brown Sauce
  with Port and Ginger, 59
Mexican Green Sauce, 116
Minted Pink Grapefruit Ice, 67
Minted Vegetables, 136
Misty Fried Shrimp, 177
Monkey Bread, 103
Mushrooms
  Four-Mushroom Consommé, 255
  Liver Pâté, 18
  Madeira Sauce, 263
  Mushroom and Pine Nut Salad with
    Raspberry Vinegar Dressing, 60
  Mushroom, Fennel and Pepperoni
    Salad, 29
  Mushroom-Pancetta Sauce, 239
  Mushrooms with Pearl Onions, 194
  Picadillo, 158
  Shrimp Salad with Mushrooms, 66
Mussels
  Malibu Paella, 101
  Mussels à la Nage, 85
Mustard
  Creamy Dijon Dressing, 24
  Mustard Anchovy Dressing, 194
  Mustard Sauce, 58
  Mustard Vinaigrette, 36, 215

Nat's Grog, 149
Noisettes of Lamb Florentine, 68
Noodles, Year-Passing, 176

Old South Fried Chicken, 231
Old St. Mary's Syllabub, 128
Onions
  Herbed Sausage and Onion
    Dressing, 248
  Onion and Raisin Salad, 202
  Pico de Gallo (Rooster's Beak), 156
  Red Onion Relish, 51
  Rosemary Potatoes with
    Caramelized Onions, 264
  Salsa, 158
Open-Face Dumplings, 168
Orzo, 23
Orzo and Rice Pilaf, 226
Oxtail Ragoût in Madeira, 215
Oysters
  Fresh Oyster Dolmades with Lemon
    and Caviar, 83
  Oysters, Ham and Peas in Brioches,
    262
  Spindled Oysters, 125

Paillasson, 60
Parathas, 186
Paper-Wrapped Chicken and Ham,
  169
Parsley Pesto, 23
Parsnip Puree in Artichoke Bottoms,
  264
Pasta
  Misty Fried Shrimp, 177
  Orzo, 23

Orzo and Rice Pilaf, 226
Pasta del Sol, 238
Red, White and Green Lasagne, 195
Springtime Spaghettini, 35
Year-Passing Noodles, 176
Pâté
Chicken Liver Pâté, 239
Rabbit Terrine, 214
Pâte Brisée, 145
Peaches Flambéed in Scotch, 151
Peanut Soup, 126
Pears
Stuffed Pear Pickles, 249
Iced Pear and Apricot Soufflé with
Raspberry Sauce, 89
Salmon with Apples, Pears and
Limes, 109
Vermouth-Glazed Pears, 31
Wine and Champagne Punch, 100
Peas
Oysters, Ham and Peas in Brioches,
262
Pecans
Cabbage Braised in Vermouth with
Pecans, 136
Chintz and Velvet Holiday Cake,
216
Pralines, 160
Peppers, Green and Red
Cioppino, 19
Corn and Cabbage Salad, 127
Green Beans in Red Pepper Butter,
250
Pepper Salad, 202
Red Pepper Jelly, 51
Peppers, Hot
Chile con Queso, 156
Hot Pepper Chutney, 187
Jalapeños en Escabeche Stuffed with
Peanut Butter, 149
Pico de Gallo (Rooster's Beak), 156
Salsa, 158
Texas Chili, 159
Pesto
Parsley Pesto, 23
Pesto Sauce, 144
Tomato Pesto, 100
Picadillo, 158
Pickled Herb Carrots, 128
Pico de Gallo (Rooster's Beak), 156
Pie Crust, 137
Pies and Tarts
Buttermilk Custard Pie, 233
Buttermilk Pie, 136
Green Grape Tart, 75
Honey and Cheese Pie, 227
Lemon and Almond Pie, 205
Lemon Chess Pie, 136
Lemon Tarts with Caramel, 145
Strawberry-Glazed Sherry Pie, 137
Walnut Tart, 61
Piedmont-Style Almond Cake, 197
Pineapple
Chintz and Velvet Holiday Cake,
216

Pineapple-Papaya Chutney, 188
Pineapple Sorbet, 263
Pine Nuts
Gourmandise with Sautéed Pine
Nuts, 52
Mushroom and Pine Nut Salad with
Raspberry Vinegar, 60
Pesto Sauce, 144
Stuffed Grape Leaves, 222
Tomatoes Pesto, 100
Poached Salmon with Raspberry
Beurre Blanc and Lime Butter
Sauce, 142
Pommes Dauphine, 52
Pork
Barbecued Ribs with Back Bay
Sauce, 231
Herbed Sausage, 249
Hot Garlic Eggplant, 171
Pot Stickers, 168
Rabbit Terrine, 214
Stuffed Leg of Lamb Wrapped in
Pastry, 224
Positively West Coast Salad, 36
Potage Puree Crecy, 5
Potatoes
Curried Cauliflower and Potatoes,
184
Dilled Potato Salad, 233
Matchstick Pommes Frites, 12
Paillasson, 60
Pommes Dauphine, 52
Potage Puree Crecy, 5
Potatoes Boulangère, 30
Potato Cauliflower Puree, 68
Rosemary Potatoes with
Caramelized Onions, 264
Pot Stickers, 168
Pralines, 160
Prawns. *See* Shrimp
Pretzels Dipped in Sweet Syrup, 189
Processor French Bread, 18
Pumpkin Biscuits, 246

Quick Zucchini, 6
Queso, 156

Rabbit Terrine, 214
Rack of Lamb Moutarde, 143
Radishes
Radish and Carrot Salad in Lemon
Cups, 179
Rice and Vegetable Salad, 95
Smoked Trout Salad with Chuck's
Special Dressing, 11
Raisin Salad, Onion and, 202
Raspberries
Champagne Framboise, 73
English Trifle, 265
Fresh Raspberry Sauce, 7
Iced Pear and Apricot Soufflé with
Raspberry Sauce, 89
Kir Royale with Raspberries, 65
Raspberry Beurre Blanc, 142
Raspberry Sorbet, 103

Raspberry Vinegar Dressing, 60
Red Eye Gravy, 134
Red Onion Relish, 51
Red Pepper Jelly, 51
Red, White and Green Lasagne, 195
Refried Beans, 160
Relishes
Ginger Pear Pickles, 249
Guacamole, 156
Hot Pepper Chutney, 187
Pineapple-Papaya Chutney, 188
Red Onion Relish, 51
Red Pepper Jelly, 51
Salsa, 158
Rice
Bowl of the Wife of Kit Carson,
150
Brown Rice Milanese, 111
Clam Pilaf, 87
Malibu Paella, 101
Orzo and Rice Pilaf, 226
Rice and Vegetable Salad, 95
Rice Pudding, 187
Rice with Artichokes and Olives,
196
Saffron Vegetable Rice Medley, 186
Stuffed Grape Leaves, 222
White Rice, Decoratively Shaped,
176
Ricotta Almond Torte, 69
Roasted Small Birds on Pâté-Topped
Croutons, 239
Root Vegetable Puree, 249
Rosemary Potatoes with Caramelized
Onions, 264

Saffron Vegetable Rice Medley, 186
Sage Bread, 75
Salade Niçoise, 202
Salads
Arugula Salad with Creamy Dijon
Dressing, 24
Chick-Pea and Anchovy Salad, 202
Corn and Cabbage Salad, 127
Dilled Potato Salad, 233
Early Dutch Coleslaw, 232
Endive-Cress Salad, 51
Fantasy Salad, 197
Mushroom and Pine Nut Salad with
Raspberry Vinegar Dressing, 60
Mushroom, Fennel and Pepperoni
Salad, 29
Onion and Raisin Salad, 202
Pepper Salad, 202
Positively West Coast Salad, 36
Radish and Carrot Salad in Lemon
Cups, 179
Rice and Vegetable Salad, 95
Salade Niçoise, 202
Salad of Endive, Watercress, Beets,
215
Smoked Trout Salad with Chuck's
Special Dressing, 11
Spring Green Salad, 226
(continued)

Salads (continued)
Stuffed Beet Salad, 109
Three-Green Salad with Warm Brie, 240
Vintner's Salad, 18
Warm Goat Cheese Salad, 144
Zucchini Salad with Saffron, 201
Salmon
Grilled Salmon with Tarragon Mayonnaise, 36
Poached Salmon with Raspberry Beurre Blanc and Lime Butter Sauce, 142
Salmon with Apples, Pears and Limes, 109
Scaloppini of Salmon with Mexican Green Sauce, 116
Steamed Salmon with Black Beans, 170
Salsa, 158
Sauces
Back Bay Sauce, 231
Basting Sauce, 239
Beurre Blanc, 87
Brown Sauce, 59
Caper Mayonnaise, 66
Chocolate Sauce, 257
Cinnamon Sugar Syrup, 161
Curried Mayonnaise, 93
Fresh Raspberry Sauce, 7
Fresh Strawberry Sauce, 7
Fresh Tomato Sauce, 115
Lime Butter Sauce, 142
Madeira Sauce, 44, 263
Mexican Green Sauce, 116
Mushroom-Pancetta Sauce, 238
Mustard Sauce, 58
Raspberry Beurre Blanc, 142
Raspberry Sauce, 89
Red Eye Gravy, 134
Red Pepper Butter, 250
Salsa, 158
Sauce Mousseline, 44
Sauce Moutard-Bâtarde, 51
Sweet-Sour Sauce, 196
Tomato, Wine and Cream Sauce, 86
Veal and Tomato Sauce, 143
Watercress Sauce, 12
White Sauce, 224
Zinfandel Sauce, 6
Saucisson en Croûte, 212
Sausages
Herbed Sausage, 249
Herbed Sausage and Onion Dressing, 248
Liver Pâté, 18
Malibu Paella, 101
Mushroom, Fennel and Pepperoni Salad, 29
Saucisson en Croûte, 212
Seafood Sausages with Tomato, Wine and Cream Sauce, 86
Veal Meatballs with Caper Mayonnaise, 65

Sautéed Escarole, 256
Sautéed Leeks, 52
Scallops
Creamy Seafood in Shells, 223
Seafood Quenelles Mousseline, 43
Seafood Sausages with Tomato, Wine and Cream Sauce, 86
Scaloppine of Salmon with Mexican Green Sauce, 116
Seafood
Cioppino, 19
Clam Pilaf, 87
Creamy Seafood in Shells, 223
King Crab Stir-Fry, 86
Lobster Fricassee Primavera with Beurre Blanc, 87
Lobster with Curried Mayonnaise, 93
Malibu Paella, 101
Misty Fried Shrimp, 177
Mussels à la Nage, 85
Oyster Dolmades with Lemon and Caviar, 83
Seafood Quenelles Mousseline, 43
Seafood Sausages with Tomato, Wine and Cream Sauce, 86
Shrimp Gratin, 263
Shrimp in Mustard Sauce, 58
Shrimp Salad with Mushrooms, 66
Shrimp Shiu Mai (Open-Face Dumplings), 168
Spindled Oysters, 125
Swiss Enchiladas with Lobster and Shrimp, 151
Shrimp
Cioppino, 19
Creamy Seafood in Shells, 223
Malibu Paella, 101
Marinated Scampi, 203
Misty Fried Shrimp, 177
Seafood Quenelles Mousseline, 43
Seafood Sausages with Tomato, Wine and Cream Sauce, 86
Shrimp Gratin, 263
Shrimp in Mustard Sauce, 58
Shrimp Salad with Mushrooms, 66
Shrimp Shiu Mai (Open-Face Dumplings), 168
Swiss Enchiladas with Lobster and Shrimp, 151
Simmered Vegetables, 178
Smoked Cornish Hens, 133
Smoked Trout Salad with Chuck's Special Dressing, 11
Smoking process for trout, 11
Sorbets
Mango Sorbet, 105
Pineapple Sorbet, 263
Raspberry Sorbet, 105
Sorbet au Cabernet with Sliced Kiwi, 53
Soups and Stews
Bowl of the Wife of Kit Carson, 150
Carrot Soup, 74

Chilled Cream of Watercress Soup, 93
Cioppino, 19
Country Tomato Soup, 246
Cream of Lentil Soup, 41
Cream of Watercress Soup, 43
Four-Mushroom Consommé, 255
Oxtail Ragoût in Madeira, 215
Potage Puree Crecy, 5
Peanut Soup, 126
Velouté of Fennel, 66
Southern Maryland Stuffed Ham, 126
Spiced Chicken Strips, 117
Spinach
Crustless Spinach Quiche, 115
Genoa-Style Spinach, 196
Noisettes of Lamb Florentine, 68
Oyster Dalmades with Lemon and Caviar, 83
Spinach-Sage Stuffing, 12
Stuffed Tomatoes, 226
Spindled Oysters, 125
Spring Green Salad, 226
Springtime Spaghettini, 35
Squash Rings, Bourbon, 128
Standing Rib Roast of Beef with Madeira Sauce, 263
Steamed Salmon with Black Beans, 170
Stir-frying tips, 171
Stock
Brown Stock, 59
Brown Turkey Stock, 248
Court Bouillon, 101, 116
Dashi (Basic Stock), 176
Fish Stock, 102
Rabbit Stock, 214
Stone-Ground Corn Rolls, 128
Strawberries
Buttermilk Strawberry Sherbet, 111
Coeur à la Crème, 12
Fresh Strawberry Sauce, 7
Liqueur-Marinated Blueberries and Strawberries, 240
Strawberry-Glazed Sherry Pie, 137
Wine and Champagne Punch, 100
Stuffed Beet Salad, 109
Stuffed Grape Leaves, 222
Stuffing, Spinach-Sage, 12
Sweet Potatoes
Likker Pudding, 135
Sweet Potato Puree, 256
Swiss Enchiladas with Lobster and Shrimp, 151

Tamales, 157
Tarragon Mayonnaise, 36
Tempura Batter, 50
Texas Chili, 159
Texas-Style Barbecued Chicken, 158
Three-Green Salad with Warm Brie, 240
Toasted Pain de Mie, 214

Tofu, Gingered, 150
Tomatoes
  Braised Broccoli in Tomato Cups, 264
  Chile con Queso, 156
  Country Tomato Soup, 246
  Cucumber-Stuffed Tomatoes, 95
  Fresh Tomato Sauce, 115
  Hot Pepper Chutney, 187
  Picadillo, 158
  Pico de Gallo (Rooster's Beak), 156
  Salsa, 158
  Stuffed Tomatoes, 226
  Tomatoes Pesto, 100
  Tomato Granité with Pernod, 58
  Tomato, Wine and Cream Sauce, 86
  Veal and Tomato Sauce, 143
Trout Salad with Chuck's Special Dressing, Smoked, 11
Tuiles, 217
Tuna
  Salade Niçoise, 202
Turkey, Double-Stuffed, 247
Two-Toned Braided Loaves, 212

Veal
  Medallions of Veal in Brown Sauce with Port and Ginger, 59
  Rabbit Terrine, 214
  Veal and Tomato Sauce, 143
  Veal Meatballs with Caper Mayonnaise, 65
  Veal with Pesto and Orzo, 23
Vegetables
  Green Vegetable Medley, 75
  Minted Vegetables, 136
  Pasta del Sol, 238
  Rice and Vegetable Salad, 95
  Root Vegetable Puree, 249
  Saffron Vegetable Rice Medley, 186
  Simmered Vegetables, 178
  Springtime Spaghettini, 35
  Vegetables à la Grecque, 203
  Yogurt and Fresh Vegetables, 186
  See also individual vegetables
Velouté of Fennel, 66
Vermouth-Glazed Pears, 31
Vinaigrette, 67, 202, 203, 226
Vintner's Salad, 18

Walnuts
  Endive-Cress Salad, 51
  Vintner's Salad, 18
  Walnut Tart, 61
Warm Goat Cheese Salad, 144
Watercress Sauce, 12
White Sauce, 224
Won Ton Skins, 168

Yams
  Likker Pudding, 135
Year-Passing Noodles, 176
Yogurt
  Chicken Tandoori, 183
  Fromage Blanc, 119
  Lamb Korma, 184
  Yogurt and Fresh Vegetables, 186
  Yogurt Drink, 187

Zinfandel Sauce, 6
Zucchini
  King Crab Stir-Fry, 86
  Quick Zucchini, 6
  Zucchini Salad with Saffron, 201
  Zucchini with Pesto Sauce, 144

CREDITS AND ACKNOWLEDGMENTS

The following people contributed the recipes included in this book:
Elizabeth Andoh 172-179
Sam Arnold 146-151
James Beard 208-217
Paul Bhalla 180-189
Marcia and William Bond 138-145
Anne Byrd 130-137
Hugh Carpenter 164-171
Fifi Crowley 2-7
Diane Darrow and Tom Maresca 258-265
Chuck Flannery-Jones 8-13
Freddi Greenberg 20-25, 26-31, 32-37
Bruce Gregga 90-95
Joan Hoien 54-61
Sally Jordan 46-53
Lynne Kasper 228-233
Gilda Latzky 112-119
Abby Mandel 80-89
Theonie Mark 218-227
Henry Miller 122-129
Iris and Allen Mink 234-241
Vicki Pierson 96-105
Joanna Pruess 62-69
Mary Nell Reck 152-161
Margaret and Franco Romagnoli 190-197
Jack Schneider 14-19, 40-45
Richard Simmons 106-111

Douglas Spingler 242-251
Lisa Stamm and Dale Booher 70-77
Michele Urvater 252-257
Anne Willan 198-205

Writers
The following writers prepared the original *Bon Appétit* articles from which the material in this book has been adapted:
Laurie Glenn Buckle
Diane Darrow and Tom Maresca
June R. Gader
William J. Garry
Freddi Greenberg
Zack Hanle
Diane Harris
Arlene Inge
Lynne Kasper
Bern Keating
Sharon Fay Koch
Jane Lasky
Abby Mandel
Jinx and Jefferson Morgan
Natalie Schram
Michele Urvater
Barbara Varnum
Marilou Vaughan
Jan Weimer
Anne Willan

Photographers
Irwin Horowitz 20, 26, 32, 80, 84, 88, 198, 228, 234, 252, 255, 257, 258, 265
Peter J. Kaplan 67, 69, 122, 126, 127, 129, 130, 133, 135, 137, 172, 177, 178, 242
Brian Leatart 5, 7, 8, 17, 40, 45, 50, 52, 54, 57, 59, 70, 74, 76, 96, 100, 104, 106, 109, 110, 111, 138, 143, 145, 149-152, 155, 157, 161, 169, 170, 180, 185, 188, 190, 192, 208, 213, 217, 218, 223, 225
J. Barry O'Rourke 112, 116-118
Dick Sharpe 38, 78, 120, 162, 206
Skrebneski 90, 94
Dan Wolfe 2, 14, 19, 22, 25, 29, 30, 31, 34, 37, 46, 49, 53, 62, 92, 124, 146, 164, 166, 174, 220, 236

Special thanks to:
Marilou Vaughan, *Editor, Bon Appétit*
Bernard Rotondo, *Art Director, Bon Appétit*
William J. Garry, *Managing Editor, Bon Appétit*
Barbara Varnum, *Articles Editor, Bon Appétit*
Leslie A. Dame, *Assistant Editor, Bon Appétit*

Anthony P. Iacono, *Vice President, Manufacturing, Knapp Communications Corporation*
Philip Kaplan, *Vice-President, Executive Graphics, Knapp Communications Corporation*
Patrick R. Casey, *Vice-President, Production, Knapp Communications Corporation*
Donna Clipperton, *Manager, Rights and Permissions, Knapp Communications Corporation*
G. Dean Larrabee *and* Karen Legier, *Rights and Permissions Coordinators, Knapp Communications Corporation*
Sonsie Conroy
Janet Greenblatt
Edena Sheldon
Sylvia Tidwell

Accessories Information
Page 2: table accessories courtesy of The Brass Tree, 9044 Burton Way, Beverly Hills, CA 90211
Page 14: table accessories courtesy of Williams-Sonoma, P.O. Box 7456, San Francisco, CA 94120; tiles courtesy of International Tile and Supply, 1288 South LaBrea Avenue, Los Angeles, CA 90019
Page 19: table accessories, except porcelain measuring spoons, courtesy of Williams-Sonoma
Page 29: selected table accessories courtesy of Williams-Sonoma
Page 30: table accessories courtesy of Williams-Sonoma
Page 31: table accessories courtesy of Williams-Sonoma
Page 34: table accessories courtesy of Williams-Sonoma

Page 46: table accessories courtesy of The Brass Tree; furniture courtesy of Edward Turrentine/Design Center Antiques, 39 North Raymond Avenue, Pasadena, CA 91103
Page 49: table accessories courtesy of Faire la Cuisine, 8112 Melrose Avenue, Los Angeles, CA 90046 and 3835 Cross Creek Road, Malibu, CA 90265
Page 62: table accessories courtesy of The Brass Tree; furniture courtesy of Edward Turrentine/ Design Center Antiques
Page 92: table accessories courtesy of The Brass Tree; tiles courtesy of International Tile and Supply
Page 124: table accessories courtesy of Faire la Cuisine
Page 146: table accessories courtesy of Tiffany & Company, 9502 Wilshire Boulevard, Beverly Hills, CA 90212
Page 164: table accessories courtesy of The Brass Tree; silk fan courtesy of Geary's North, 351 North Beverly Drive, Beverly Hills, CA 90210
Page 220: table accessories courtesy of The Brass Tree
Page 236: table accessories courtesy of The Brass Tree

The Knapp Press is a wholly owned subsidiary of Knapp Communications Corporation.
Chairman and Chief Executive Officer: Cleon T. Knapp
President: H. Stephen Cranston

Senior Vice-Presidents:
Paige Rense (*Editor-in-Chief*)
Everett T. Alcan (*Corporate Planning*)
Rosalie Bruno (*New Venture Development*)
Harry Myers (*Magazine Group Publisher*)
Betsy Wood Knapp (*MIS Electronic Media*)
L. James Wade, Jr. (*Finance*)

THE KNAPP PRESS
President: Alice Bandy; *Administrative Assistant:* Beth Bell; *Senior Editor:* Norman Kolpas; *Associate Editors:* Jeff Book, Jan Koot, Sarah Lifton, Pamela Mosher; *Editor, Gault Millau:* Deborah Patton; *Assistant Editors:* Taryn Bigelow, Colleen Dunn, Jan Stuebing; *Editorial Assistant:* Nancy D. Roberts; *Art Director:* Paula Schlosser; *Designers:* Robin Murawski, Nan Oshin; *Production Manager:* Larry Cooke; *Production Coordinator:* Joan Valentine; *Managing Director, Rosebud Books:* Robert Groag; *Financial Manager:* Joseph Goodman; *Financial Analyst:* Carlton Joseph; *Assistant Finance Manager:* Kerri Culbertson; *Fulfillment Services Manager:* Virginia Parry; *Director of Public Relations:* Jan B. Fox; *Promotions Manager:* Jeanie Gould; *Promotions Coordinator:* Joanne Denison; *Marketing Assistant:* Dolores Briqueleur; *Special Sales:* Lynn Blocker; *Department Secretaries:* Amy Hershman, Randy Levin

Book and jacket design by Paula Schlosser. Page layout by Robin Murawski.

The text of this book is set in Sabon, a face designed by Jan Teischold and based on early fonts created by Garamond and Granjon. Composition was performed by Publisher's Typography on the Penta/Merganthaler Linotron 202 system.

Color engraving by NEC, Inc.

Printing and binding by Kingsport Press on Mead Northcote, basis 80, furnished by WWF Paper Corporation-West.